Kabbalah

Kabbalah

THREE THOUSAND YEARS OF MYSTIC TRADITION

KENNETH HANSON, PH.D.

COUNCIL OAK BOOKS

TULSA AND SAN FRANCISCO

Council Oak Books, Tulsa, Oklahoma

Library of Congress Cataloging-in-Publication Data

Hanson, Kenneth, 1953-
  Kabbalah : three thousand years of mystic tradition / Kenneth Hanson.
      p.   cm.
  Includes bibliographical references.
   ISBN 1-57178-072-6 (pbk. : alk. paper)
   1. Mysticism--Judaism--History.   2. Cabala--History.   I. Title.
BM723.H33   1998
296.1'6--dc21

Designed by Carol Haralson

Contents

INTRODUCTION   7

The Chariot-throne   11

The Mystics of Qumran   28

Early Sages, Early Christians   50

The Opti-Mystic Sages of the Talmud   74

Creation "By the Book"   88

Mystic Europe   107

The Book of Splendor   130

Magical Mystical Tour   149

The "Frankenstein" of Kabbalah   161

It Happened in Smyrna   171

Christian Kabbalah   184

The Master of a Good Name   192

A Very Narrow Bridge   205

The Rebbe of Brooklyn   211

The Angel of History   219

Cosmic Kabbalah   224

Contemporary Kabbalah   243

REFERENCES   254

NOTES   258

INDEX   264

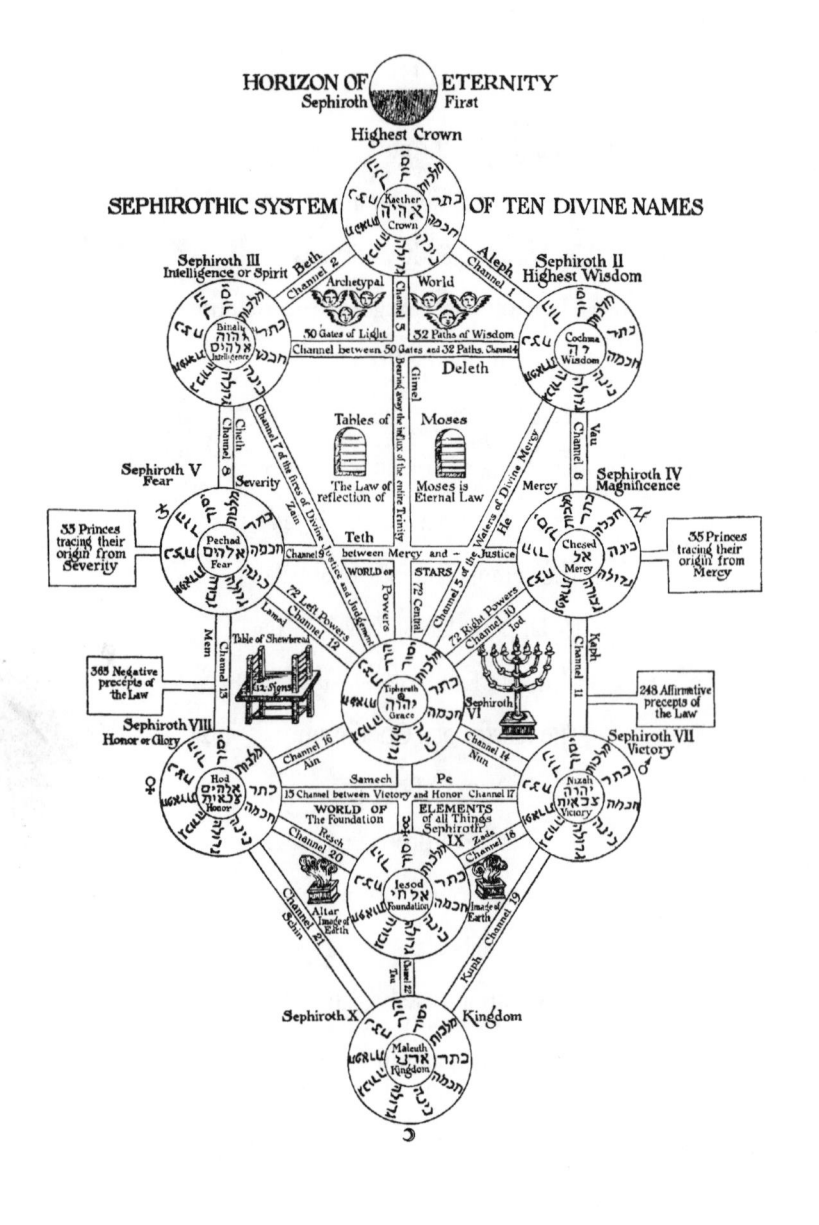

HORIZON OF ETERNITY
Sephiroth First

Highest Crown

SEPHIROTHIC SYSTEM OF TEN DIVINE NAMES

Sephiroth III
Intelligence or Spirit

Sephiroth II
Highest Wisdom

Archetypal World
50 Gates of Light   32 Paths of Wisdom
Channel between 50 Gates & 32 Paths.

Deleth

Tables of   Moses
The Law of   Moses is
reflection of   Eternal Law

Sephiroth V
Fear

Sephiroth IV
Magnificence

Teth
between Mercy and
WORLD or   STARS   Justice
72 Right Powers

33 Princes
tracing their
origin from
Severity

33 Princes
tracing their
origin from
Mercy

72 Left Powers

Table of Shewbread

365 Negative
precepts of
the Law

248 Affirmative
precepts of
the Law

Sephiroth VIII
Honor or Glory

Sephiroth VII
Victory

15 Channel between Victory and Honor Channel 17
Samech   Pe
WORLD OF   ELEMENTS
The Foundation   of all Things
Sephiroth
IX

Altar
Image of
Earth

Image of
Earth

Sephiroth X   Kingdom

Introduction

"Four rabbis ascended into the Orchard, Ben Azzai, Ben Zoma, Acher, and Rabbi Akiva. . . . Ben Azzai gazed and died; Ben Zoma gazed and became demented; Acher became apostate; Rabbi Akiva departed in peace." [1]

TALMUD, *CHICAGAH* 14B

"Whoever reflects on four things, it were a mercy if he had never come into the world, namely, what is above, what is beneath, what is before and what is after."

MISHNAH, *CHAGIGAH* 2:1

"Seek not out the things that are too hard for thee, and into the things that are hidden from thee inquire thou not. In what is permitted to thee instruct thyself; thou hast no business with secret things."

TALMUD, *CHAGIGAH* 13A; *BEN SIRA* 3:21FF

Why does the story of creation begin with the letter bet (ב)? "In the same manner that the letter bet is closed on all sides and only open in front, similarly you are not permitted to inquire into what is before or what was behind, but only from the actual time of Creation."

TALMUD, *CHAGIGAH* 77C

Jerusalem is hardly a city where a young American, of Scandinavian heritage, might expect to find himself, immersed in the study of the Hebrew language and the Dead Sea Scrolls. But such was my passion for knowledge that I never gave a second thought to why I was living at the American Institute for Holy Land Studies, inconspicuously nestled among the maze of structures occupying Mount Zion. I had come as a student of world history, and I wanted to understand the roots of western thought and culture. The sights and smells of this land on the cusp of three continents are strange and foreign to western sensibilities. Nevertheless, Jerusalem seemed a fitting place to study western origins, and the Dead Sea Scrolls, two-thousand-year-old parchments produced by a sect of pious Jews who lived during the days of Jesus and John the Baptist, seemed a perfect point of reference for my search.

I was a good student, dedicated and disciplined, and it took me only about a year to learn Hebrew well enough to navigate in modern Israeli culture, order food, and fight my way onto crowded municipal buses. But my acquisition of Hebrew also enabled me to read with fluency the texts of the ancient past, including the Hebrew Bible, the Mishnah and Talmud, and the Dead Sea Scrolls. My work with this library of ancient literature opened up new vistas of thought and understanding, which I researched and evaluated in the most rational way I knew how, given my training as a historian. The body of literature comprising the Dead Sea Scrolls consists of poetry, psalms, rule books and manuals, apocalyptic epics, and eschatological visions of the future, in addition to the oldest copies of the Bible in the world. There is certainly ample material to study.

One of the scrolls, however, arrested my attention immediately. Found in a desolate cave, in a chalky marl ridge, across from a lake of salty brine shimmering in the distance, this particular document is devoted to an entire genre of Jewish literature called Kabbalah. This unique discipline is considered the font of Jewish mysticism, and this example of Kabbalah is among the oldest in existence. On a personal level, I was loathe to enter the field of mysticism. I was too rational, and Kabbalah was too "slippery." Whenever, during the course of my studies, I opened any of the mystical texts, I was baffled and bewildered. I could find no objective yardstick by which to measure a literature devoted to theosophical speculations about the throne of the Almighty and a host of "emanations" from the "Eternal" into the created universe.

I could not, however, escape the lonely voice of the Dead Sea Scroll called *The Song of Sabbath Sacrifices*, which spoke to me from across the eons. My focus was further sharpened when I realized that a single copy of the same scroll was found at another location in the Judean desert, far to the south, along the shore of the Dead Sea, on top of a rocky promontory called Masada. It was here that a group of radical freedom-fighting Zealots made a last stand against the legions of Rome. It was here that 960 souls committed suicide rather than surrender to the Roman general in one of the most pathetic if not heroic episodes in history. It was here, in the synagogue atop Masada, that the enraged legionnaires mutilated scrolls of the Torah — the Hebrew Bible — and the strange mystical document called *The Song of Sabbath Sacrifices*, prior to abandoning the rock to the ravages of time. And it was here, in a massive excavation effort in the 1960s, that the crumbled synagogue yielded its secret cache of parchments.

As a scholar of the Dead Sea Scrolls, my drive to know out-weighed my natural hesitation to probe the realm of Kabbalah, and I began, slowly and carefully, to enter "the Orchard."

The Chariot-throne

Merkavah is a Hebrew word with many connotations. In its simplest form it means "chariot," a horse-drawn vehicle of war, vital to the success of military campaigns. In today's Hebrew, *Merkavah* is the name of the Israeli-manufactured battle tank that has proven to be the winning ingredient in scores of battles during the Arab-Israeli conflict. However, *Merkavah* is also the descriptive term for the earliest layers of Jewish mysticism, dating from the days of Jesus of Nazareth and before. It consists of meditative reflections and ruminations on the throne of God, described by the prophet Ezekiel as a kind of heavenly chariot.

An entire literature of *Merkavah* mysticism has been preserved in Jewish tradition, in documents dating from early medieval times. To be sure, the contents of this literature are far older, and were certainly passed down by word of mouth, long before being recorded in the medieval sources. Now, thanks to a single Dead Sea Scroll, we have a clear reference to the chariot-throne of God. In *The Song of Sabbath Sacrifices* we read:

> His chariot-throne's glorious wheels appear something like an utterly holy spiritual fire. All around are what appear to be streams of fire, resembling electrum, and shining handiwork comprising wondrous colors embroidered together, pure and glorious.[2]

The passage clearly hearkens back to the prophet Ezekiel, whose visions and revelations are the stuff of legend. To understand the Dead Sea Scrolls and the mystic writer whose work I found myself reading, I had to understand Ezekiel, as I had never understood him before. Who indeed was Ezekiel, and what were the great questions with which he wrestled?

Prophet of Exiles

Long before the Christian era, the ancient Israelite kingdom of David and Solomon fell on hard times. The once mighty realm came to an ignominious end, after centuries of decline and decay, being swallowed up in the sixth century B.C. by the mighty empire of Nebuchadnezzar, king of Babylon. King Nebuchadnezzar decided that the best way to emasculate what was left of little Judea was to deport thousands of its leaders and their families to faraway Babylon in what became known as the great Babylonian captivity. Among these captives was a young boy who was later to be heralded as the prophet of the exiles. His name was Ezekiel — "God is mighty." His warnings were to ring out across the land, as his letters were carried from his home in exile back to the hapless inhabitants of Zion. There were messages of doom and disaster, of torment and woe, as well as encouragement and hope for a people who had not quite learned all the lessons their historical circumstances were teaching them.

But Ezekiel is mostly remembered not for his prophetic admonitions but for his mystical insights, his union with the spirit of the Most High, his ecstatic visions in which he sees the very throne of God. In one of the most profoundly enigmatic accounts in world literature the prophet writes:

As I was among the exiles by the river Chebar, the heavens were opened, and I saw visions of God. . . . As I looked, behold, a stormy wind came out of the north, and a great cloud, with brightness round about it, and fire flashing forth continually, and in the midst of the fire, as it were gleaming bronze. And from the midst of it came the likeness of four living creatures. . . . Now as I looked at the living creatures, I saw a wheel upon the earth beside the living creatures, one for each of the four of them. As for the appearance of the wheels and their construction: their appearance was like the gleaming of a chrysolite; and the four had the same likeness, their construction being as it were a wheel within a wheel. When they went, they went in any of their four directions without turning as they went. The four wheels had rims and they had spokes; and their rims were full of eyes round about. And when the living creatures went, the wheels went beside them; and when the living creatures rose from the earth, the wheels rose. Wherever the spirit would go, they went, and the wheels rose along with them; for the spirit of the living creatures was in the wheels. . . . Over the heads of the living creatures there was the likeness of a firmament, shining like crystal, spread out above their heads. . . . And above the firmament over their heads there was the likeness of a throne, in appearance like sapphire; and seated above the likeness of a throne was a likeness as it were of a human form. And upward from what had the appearance of his loins I saw as it were gleaming bronze, like the appearance of fire enclosed round about; and downward from what had the appearance of his loins I saw as it were the appearance of fire, and there was brightness round about him. Like the appearance of the bow that is in the cloud on the day of rain, so was the appearance of the brightness round about. Such was the appearance of the likeness of the glory of the Lord (Ezek. 1:1,4,5,15-20,22,26-28).[3]

Some have speculated that Ezekiel was recording nothing less than an encounter with a UFO, bearing extra-terrestrial life. But for generations of pious Jews, Ezekiel's visions became the seed-bed of the entire genre of mysticism called *Merkavah*.

What was the fundamental message of Ezekiel's vision? In truth, the prophet was, by virtue of his divine revelations, making a powerful, even revolutionary statement. For long centuries during the reigns of Israel's kings it was thought that God had a single House, a dwelling place that was the domain of Deity, located in a city of the Deity's choosing. The book of Deuteronomy declares: "But you shall seek the place which the Lord your God will choose out of all your tribes to put his name and make his habitation there" (Ezek. 12:5). That House was the great Temple of Solomon, and that city was Jerusalem, called in Scripture "the city of the great King." This is why the so-called Wailing Wall (more properly the Western Wall) is still venerated by Jews today; there is still the belief that the divine presence may be found among the stones of the Wall.

Ezekiel, however, was saying something new. He was announcing that the presence of God, called in Hebrew the *Shechinah*, might now be found in a new place entirely. The divine presence might be found apart from the Temple, apart from the city of Jerusalem, apart from the land of Israel itself. Even in exile, even in the house of bondage, in Babylonia, which seemed like half a world away, the Almighty could be seen, felt, and approached by those who possessed knowledge, wisdom, and insight. This was Ezekiel's greatest contribution — the revolutionary concept that God, ultimately, can be experienced anywhere — and everywhere. Ezekiel's visions did more than simply to provide the prophet with an authoritative platform from which to speak. They framed the fundamental question, persisting until this day, of how a spiritual resonance may be attained. It is a question posed universally, by all peoples of all cultures.

The Great Question

At the heart of Kabbalah is this essential, universal question: How can Infinite, Eternal Deity, whose essence is beyond the grasp of mere mortals, be known intimately by those very mortals? A kindred question is a logical extension of the first, on a cosmic level: How can the Eternal, who is beyond space and time, be intimately involved with the cosmos, in the midst of space and time?

There is hardly a human being alive on this planet who does not have a sense of the eternal and who does not want to come to grips with the infinite "scheme of things." Most people, whatever their religious or cultural heritage, have a sense of a Creator, an Infinite Being, whose presence energizes the universe, and us with it. The problem is how to establish a link, or perhaps even experience a oneness or unity, with this Infinite Being. Can mere flesh and blood know the mind of God?

On the one hand, we have an inherent sense that the Eternal One is beyond knowing, and, therefore, ought to be extolled and magnified as such. In fact, from earliest human history, we know that people spent endless hours praising the virtues and character of omnipotent Deity. In ancient Egypt, for example, a movement arose (called Atenism) in which the pharaoh and his subjects became lost in the worship of the pure disk of the sun (the Aten), arguably the earliest archetype of genuine monotheism. The sun's disk, however, could not be intimately known or apprehended.

On the other hand, the mystic, from ancient times to the present, has always been looking for a way to "break in" to the realm of Deity. The mystic has sought a point of contact, or, in terms of modern astrophysics, a "singularity," through which the infinite and the finite may meet. Ezekiel found such a point, in which the heavens opened before him. So did the writer of *The Song of Sabbath Sacrifices*.

Three Stages of Faith

Gershom Scholem, the great modern scholar of the world of Kabbalah, conceived the idea that biblical religion has itself evolved through various stages.[4] First there was the "primitive" stage, in which God, or "the gods," as the case may be, was perceived as being one with the cosmos — the sun, moon, stars, and essential elements that energize the planet. Primitive societies worshipped the forces of nature, seeing deity in every aspect of nature. However, they most often felt helpless before those very forces, which were as fickle as they were rhythmical. When the rains fell, the harvest was plentiful; when the rains were withheld, the crops failed and people died.

Next came the "creative" stage, Israel's unique contribution to the evolution of religion, in which God was separated from His own created universe. This is the essence of the experience at Mount Sinai, when the Ten Commandments were given to Moses. More than just a jumble of laws, the overarching message of Sinai is that God is above and beyond the cosmos. God is not only all-powerful, but all-just. Human beings, as God's creations, are no longer at the whim of the elements or at the mercy of a compassionless universe. In this view, God is above and beyond flood and drought, famine and pestilence. God is good and just. But being omnipotent, God is also well beyond the reach of humans to grasp or to comprehend. God becomes distant — a benevolent Father, though far removed from His lowly subjects.

The third stage, the "mystical" stage, comes full circle to the first. In mysticism, God's subjects can find their way back to a deep and intimate relationship with the Creator. God, who had been called *El Melekk Ram* — "the Mighty King" — now becomes *Yedidi* — "My Dear Friend." Kabbalah, then, is no tangential entity; it serves an essential purpose, making possible a personal relationship between God and humans.

Hidden Things

Perhaps knowingly, perhaps unknowingly, the prophet Ezekiel had opened a door to an entirely new world, rarely glimpsed in the Hebrew Bible, rarely experienced in the days of the Israelite kings. It was a world of special revelations and divine encounters, experienced in mystical states of semi-trance. It was a world of dreams and visions, of heightened awareness of the supernatural universe. Subsequent generations would explore Ezekiel's link with the world of spirit, fostering a whole genre of literature called Apocrypha. The word *apocrypha* is the plural form of the Greek *apocryphon*, meaning "hidden." This is literature which expounds "hidden things," secrets heretofore untold. Apocrypha consists of a mini-library of books, composed in the first two centuries B.C., most of which never made it into the accepted "canon" of Holy Writ. Taking their cue from Ezekiel, the Jewish writers of these two centuries tell of many deeply mystical experiences. The beginnings of the formal mystical trend in Judaism, later called Kabbalah, may be traced to this period. The authors of this literature are unknown but they are propelled by the idea that God is knowable, deeply and intimately, in spite of hardship and suffering.

Who were the faithful Sages of those days who turned to mysticism to find solutions to the perils of their age? They were and will always remain anonymous, but to discover more about them, we can at least consider the tenor of the times.

A Tale of Woe

It was an age of persecution and terror. By the middle of the second century B.C., little Judea had for decades been under the occupation of cruel foreign overlords. They were the Syrians. At their helm was King Antiochus IV, called Epiphanes, which meant "manifestation of God." Everyone hated him — all the Jews, that is. Even the children laughed behind his back, twisting his name and calling him "Epimanes" — "madman."

One day, an intoxicating rumor spread along the narrow streets of Jerusalem: "He's dead! Antiochus Epiphanes is dead!" A general revolt broke out among the Jews. The Syrian garrison found itself in full retreat. The figurehead High Priest, installed by the Syrian overlords, was abruptly ousted, and another, more faithful Jew, given the holy vestments. It was a scene of utter jubilation. There was only one problem. Antiochus IV was very much alive, and in short order he appeared in Jerusalem at the head of an army. Unfortunately for the inhabitants of Jerusalem, despotic tyrants don't take kindly to being thought dead, and Antiochus responded with full fury. He reinstalled his High Priest and vented his full fury on his wayward subjects. Worst of all, he declared open war on the Jewish faith. His goal was the extermination, the extinction, of an entire religion. All who resisted would be summarily executed.

The atrocities began. Syrian troops made periodic "sweeps" through the city, seizing and burning scrolls of the holy Torah — the Bible — hauling the religious leaders, the "rabbis," off to prison, even grabbing newly circumcised infants from the arms of screaming women and dashing them onto the stone pavement. The penalty for defying the ban on the study of Jewish religious books — crucifixion — sent shock waves through the whole city.

All the while, the "Abomination of Desolation" hovered over the Sanctuary like a shadowy menace, and the wrath of the Almighty hung over the people. These were the days of what the traitorous High Priest, Menelaus, might well have called the "new paganism." In the spirit of the eastern mystery religions, monuments of the cult of Antiochus Epiphanes went up all over the city — in the marketplace, before the doors of houses, even in front of abandoned *Betei Midrash* — "houses of study." A great slab of marble was hauled up to the Temple Mount, and slowly, by the work of numerous sculptors, it took the form of the Olympian Zeus, save for the head, which bore the visage of Antiochus himself. In due time, the "graven image" was brought within the Temple compound, and set up proudly before the Most Holy Place. No longer was the blood of sacrificial animals sprinkled to the God of Israel within the dark recesses of the Holy Sanctuary. Instead, there were sacrifices to *Baal-Shemin*, the so-called Lord of the Heavens, offered beneath the open sky, in an enclosure, according to the Greek ideal and the practice of the cults of Syria. Upon the altars that now adorned the city, multiple pagan sacrifices were daily offered, in demonstrative expression of zeal for the "new paganism." There was particular insistence that sacrifices be offered every month on the date corresponding to Antiochus' birthday.

The martyrs were many. But, incredibly, a goodly number of the city's inhabitants sheepishly submitted to Antiochus and his High Priest-henchman, Menelaus. A troupe of temple prostitutes, whom Menelaus had personally recruited from the eastern provinces of the Seleucid empire, were soon being kept busy by a steady stream of curious males, young and old alike, who had never before seen the like in the Holy City. Many others were wooed to participate in the bacchanalian festival of Dionysus, the celebration of the Greek god of wine. The intoxicated participants adorned themselves with ivy, like the Greeks in their formal processions, opened barrels of wine by the score, and proceeded to utter wild cries of ecstasy in honor of Bacchus. Furthermore, Menelaus continued to order his emissaries into every village and town in Judea, to compel the inhabitants to join in pagan sacrifice, in a kind of "litmus test" of who continued to hold fast to the Torah, even clandestinely. Of course, those who refused the sacrifice and, thereby, the "new paganism," were dealt with appropriately, generally facing crucifixion or other grievous tortures. Thus, the shadow of one dark wing descended over all the land. Never before, in the collective memory of Jewry, had the very existence of the people of Israel — spiritually — been so gravely imperiled.

In this climate, the faithful of the city found themselves in clandestine gatherings, in their courtyards and confined to the inner chambers of their homes, chanting their prayers in liturgical unison, their muffled hum inaudible from the streets without. Their scrolls and loose parchments having been systematically seized, their liturgy consisted entirely of what they had committed to memory. Underground "societies" of *Haver-im* — "friends" — cropped up. They were Jewish pietists, also known as "Hasidics," who met together to undertake the study of the sacred scrolls. These scrolls included not only the books of the Hebrew Bible, but also the assorted interpretations and legal rulings of generations of Israel's Sages. The members of these societies met under cover of darkness, breaking bread and dining together on an almost daily basis, changing their location from house to house so as to avoid detection by the Syrian overseers. Often they would listen to the teaching of a wise and seasoned elder, who would lecture well into the night. It was a form of resistance to the abominable edicts of Antiochus IV, and it represented an escape to a world of spirit and camaraderie. Persecution tends to heighten spiritual devotion, and so it was with the writers of the apocryphal literature. They saw these days as prophesied from long ago, and they believed that their suffering served a higher purpose.

Writings and "False Writings"

Many researchers today believe that the book of the prophet Daniel may be dated to these terrible times. Daniel is devoted to visions and dreams, to persecution and perseverance, to the end of the world, and to the growing trend of mysticism. The mystical Sages of those days simply ascribed their own writings to Daniel (who presumably had lived long before, in the sixth century B.C.) to lend them more weight, more credence. The writings they produced may be given the general title Pseudepigrapha or "false writings," and include a veritable library of ancient books, most of which never became a part of the standard biblical "canon."

One of the most important texts of this library is the book of Enoch, which purports to have been written by the biblical patriarch Enoch, in antediluvian times. Of course, the real writer is an anonymous mystic who simply ascribes his work to the early Patriarch to lend it authority. The book of Enoch is a composite text, which recounts a trip through the heavenly spheres to the Throne of Glory.

Throughout the book of Enoch there is a particular emphasis on the Watchers, a group of disobedient priests from the heavenly Temple (the counterpart of the earthly structure, which stood on Mount Zion). These angelic beings, writes the author-mystic, are the very ones described in the passage in the book of Genesis dealing with fallen angels: "The sons of God saw that the daughters of men were beautiful; and they took wives for themselves, whomever they chose" (Gen. 6:2 NAS). The result was a race of half-breeds — half-human, half-angel, described by the book of Genesis as "Nephilim" — "fallen ones." This terrible crime, insists the author, accounts for the explosion of sin upon the earth, which culminated in the great flood of Noah. The whole earth became corrupt; and just as corruption reigned supreme in those days, so it has become corrupt once more. Such ideas helped explain the suffering and persecution of the era in which the mystics lived. The only answer is to find God in a new, intimate way. Such is the lesson of Kabbalah.

A dominant idea, expressed by the author of Enoch as well as other ancient mystics, was that this infinitely powerful Deity, while He could be experienced anywhere, could not be approached easily and directly. He required a host of intermediaries to bridge the gap between the perfection of the heavenly realm and the corruption of the physical universe. The mystics called them *mal'akhim*, literally "workers" of the divine will. Today, we call them "angels." Returning to the "great question" — How can the perfect and most holy God of the cosmos have any form of contact with the corrupt and defiled physical world? — the postulation of a multitude of angels seemed to solve the problem. The Holy One does get involved with the affairs of this world, an involvement accomplished through the angelic host. Even if the Eternal One seemed distant during times of persecution and torment, mystical Jews found intimate contact with the invisible world through the unseen presence of the angels. The medieval mystic Moshe Chaim Luzzatto wrote, "These transcendental beings . . . exist on different levels, each having an inherent nature, depending on its level and place in the general scheme."[5]

The mystic who wrote the book of Enoch recounts: "I saw a hundred thousand times a hundred thousand, ten million times ten million, an innumerable and uncountable multitude who stand before the glory of the Lord of the Spirits." In time angels, along with the theme of the chariot-throne, become central to the developing world of Kabbalah. Enoch lists four by name: Michael (Who is like God?), Raphael (God heals), Gabriel (God is mighty), and Uriel (God is my light).

Another important angel, mentioned by the author of Enoch, would become a central figure in the centuries to come, as the ideas of Kabbalah were set down in the encyclopedic volume called the *Zohar*. He is called Metatron. According to the folklore, the patriarch Enoch did not live out his natural life. The Bible itself simply states that "he was not, for God took him" (Gen. 5:24). The book of Enoch fills in the details, recounting how the patriarch was not just spirited away, but he was transformed into a pure flame, literally becoming the angel Metatron. Now in the heavenly realm, Metatron is a chieftain of the angelic host. He ministers before the Throne of Glory, he becomes high priest of the heavenly Temple (the perfect holy sanctuary, of which the earthly Temple is merely a copy), and, as "minister of wisdom," he guards the keys to the mysteries and secrets of the supernatural world.

What's in the Name?

Another idea, central to early mysticism and subsequently to the whole realm of Kabbalah, has to do with the divine name of God. Somewhere along the line, perhaps as far back as Babylonian captivity (following the conquest of ancient Judah by King Nebuchadnezzar in 586 B.C.), the early mystics elevated the character and the very name of God. Since God is so great, almost unknowable, the sacred name is not to be taken lightly.

A mystical tradition about the earliest days of the biblical Patriarchs recounts: "Seth also had a son, and he named him Enosh. At that time men began to call on the name of the Lord" (Gen. 4:26 NIV). This brief account gives us no details. It simply leaves the sacred name in the realm of mystery.

There is a good deal of popular folklore that the biblical name of God means "I AM" (which is, at least in English, what the Almighty said when he first appeared to Moses), but this is not exactly true. The actual name of the biblical Deity is composed of four distinct Hebrew letters: יהוה the English equivalent of which is Y-H-W-H.[6] We transliterate these letters as *yud – hey – vav – hey*, which may best be understood as a combination of the tenses of the Hebrew verb "to be." Specifically, if we take the letters of the word "He was" (היה), the word "He is" (הווה), and the word "He will be" (יהיה), and combine them, searching for a common denominator, we arrive at יהוה, the four-letter name, known as the Tetragrammaton. If indeed the name is a combination of the tenses of "to be," then what we have is a statement of eternal "being," who was, is, and is to come.

Of course, if a name exists, one inevitably wants to pronounce it. This is where Kabbalah gets sticky. A name which connotes the very essence of the universe obviously carries great power, and one is not to pronounce it. Indeed, to pronounce the ineffable Tetragrammaton would be to lessen it, to cheapen it, to take the name in vain. "Thou shalt not take the name of the Lord thy God in vain," says the Ten Commandments, and to put the Tetragrammaton upon human lips therefore amounts to nothing less than the "desecration of the name."

As centuries passed, the sacred name (which seems to have been pronounced with regularity by the earliest Israelites) was made the domain of the priests who served in the Temple only. Eventually, only the High Priest was allowed to pronounce the name at all, and then only on a single day of the year — Yom Kippur, the Day of Atonement. An awesome responsibility thus lay on the shoulders of the High Priest, who, should he bring offense to the Deity in his priestly duties, might be struck dead and have to be dragged out of the most holy place by a cord attached to his ankle. The Temple and the entire sacrificial system, however, was not to remain forever. After the Temple was razed to the ground, there was no longer a High Priest to utter the ineffable Tetragrammaton. With the passing of more centuries, the precise pronunciation of the holy name was lost, and to this day, we may only speculate on how it was vocalized on the lips of the High Priests of old. The more intricate speculation lies in the realm of Kabbalah.

An attempt to articulate the Tetragrammaton was made in the early Middle Ages by the great Christian cleric Jerome. It was Jerome who translated the original text of the Bible into Latin, in what is called the Vulgate version. Jerome rendered Y-H-W-H as J-H-V-H, supplying vowels from the Hebrew word for *Lord* (*Adonai*). The resultant error has persisted into the current century — *Jehovah*. Bear in mind, the word *Jehovah* is not the subject of kabbalistic speculation, though the Tetragrammaton itself certainly is.

Four or Forty-Two?

Moreover, the idea developed over the centuries that the four-letter divine name is in reality a shortened form of a much longer name for God, consisting, not of four, but of forty-two letters. The information regarding this name brought to its possessor so much power that even its study carried with it the requirement that the individual be at least middle-aged, and known as a person who "shuns revenge." This latter prerequisite suggests that the power of the forty-two letter name of God was so awesome that, if used to exact vengeance, the results might be terrifying.

Jubilees

Another anonymous mystic of the period produced a classic work of Pseudepigrapha called Jubilees. It is presented as a direct revelation from God via the Angel of the Presence, who relates it to the presumed author of the book, who in turn tells it to Moses, who writes it down. Jubilees retells the biblical stories of creation through the giving of the Ten Commandments at Mount Sinai, dividing history into fifty periods of forty-nine years each, hence the term Jubilees. The Hebrew word for *jubilee* (יובל), actually signifies a trumpet or a ram's horn, which was used to declare the beginning of the fiftieth year — the year of jubilee. The book seems to teach that history is not haphazard. There is a plan and purpose in everything. Consequently, nothing happens by accident. Everything that happens is designed to lead into some higher plane of existence. Though the Almighty may seem at times unknowable and beyond reach, his angel communicates the divinely predestined meaning of things. Weaving through it all is a complex numerology, which will become increasingly central in the unfolding tradition of Kabbalah.

Embraced by the Light

Other authors of these days begin to develop increasingly visionary experiences. Many recount an "assumption" into the heavenly realm — what might be referred to as an "out-of-body-experience." There are accounts called *The Assumption of Moses*, *The Assumption of Isaiah*, and *The Apocalypse of Baruch*, all of which expound the supposed out-of-body-experiences of biblical characters. The mystics of this literature always describe entering or ascending into Paradise, followed by an overpowering spiritual experience. *The Assumption of Isaiah*, for example, depicts a total of seven heavens. As the prophet ascends in the company of a guardian angel the heavens become increasingly glorious and sublime. While in the sixth heaven, Isaiah's angelic guide explains, "If you rejoice over this light, how much more will you rejoice in the seventh heaven when you see the light where the Lord is and his beloved." One cannot help but be reminded of modern near-death experiences, in which people relate an ascent through a narrow, darkened tunnel, to encounter a very bright light at the other end. The tradition of *Merkavah*, it would seem, is still alive and well.

Then there is the *Life of Adam and Eve*, which we can link directly with Ezekiel's chariot:

While we were praying, Michael the archangel and messenger of God came to me. And I saw a chariot like the wind and its wheels were fiery. I was carried off into the Paradise of Righteousness, and I saw the Lord sitting, and his appearance was unbearable flaming fire. And many thousands of angels were at the right and at the left of the chariot.

No one is certain exactly when the *Life of Adam and Eve* was first composed, but it does represent one of the earliest clear examples of *Merkavah* mysticism — ruminations on the chariot-throne.

The Mystics of Qumran

The thread of *Merkavah* mysticism weaves delicately through the fabric of the first two centuries B.C. Sometimes the thread gets lost against the complex tapestry of ancient Judea, immersed in an ongoing struggle for independence from foreign oppressors — the Syrians, and later the Romans. But this struggle all the more accentuates the mystical threads of Jewish history, for only in mysticism can meaning be found in a troubled and perplexing age.

One of the most fascinating of those threads emerged from obscurity in a settlement of religious zealots adjacent to a series of caves along the shore of the lowest spot on the face of the earth — the Dead Sea. The history of this Dead Sea sect is largely conjecture, but here is what we can piece together.

They fled the cities of Judea, Jerusalem in particular, during the darkest days of the Syrian tyranny. They devoted themselves to maintaining the highest levels of ritual purity, forging a community of shared possessions and complete submission to the will of God, in this most inhospitable territory on earth — a place that would be known by the Bedouin Arabs of the twentieth century A.D. as Qumran.

The dedication of the Dead Sea sect was astounding. They would rise every morning an hour before dawn and begin a process of meditation, to "incline the heart" toward the Deity. Their hearts had to be pure and undefiled before they would even begin their prayers, which were described as "spontaneous effusions of the heart." On their foreheads and forearms they wore *tefillin* — tiny boxes containing minuscule parchments on which were written the central declaration of the Jewish faith: "Hear, O Israel! The Lord our God is One!"

It was a meditative life, which focused on copying and recopying the books of the Hebrew Bible, as well as a veritable library of additional texts, their own compositions highlighting their prophecies and supernatural revelations.

At their helm was a shadowy figure, an enigmatic character of charismatic power who founded the group. Known only as the "Teacher of Righteousness," he was the prototype and quintessence of the Hasidic masters who would later lead and guide the mystical movement down through the ages. He taught his followers to elevate their senses, to be in touch with the universe and to hear the voice of the Holy One. He propounded many mysteries to them. Some of them revolved around the Messiah to come and the end of all things. Some had to do with special revelations surrounding the chariot-throne of Ezekiel.

Divine Polarities

The members of the Dead Sea sect had a keen awareness of supernatural powers of good and evil manifest in the physical world. They were convinced that the universe, far from being an impersonal mechanism, is energized by unseen powers beyond flesh and blood. These powers, they believed, course through human beings like fire and possess the ability either to heal or destroy. Life itself is part of a great cosmic conflict waged on the battlefield of the heavenly spheres and fought equally by human beings and angels.

Over the whole host of nefarious evil spirits mentioned in the scrolls, we find the supernatural arch-orchestrator of evil, called "Belial" (a name which would appear in a later writing in the New Testament). Chief among Belial's troupe of demonic powers is the "Angel of Darkness." According to the scrolls, he "leads all the children of righteousness astray, and until his end all their sin, iniquities, wickedness, and all their unlawful deeds are caused by his dominion in accordance with the mysteries of God" (*Manual of Discipline*, col. 3).[7] Apparently, the members of the Dead Sea sect believed that even the power of the Evil One is ultimately subject to the will of God — to the "mysteries of God." They were grappling with the ages-old problem of evil — why evil exists and why human beings suffer so much. Their answer was that supernatural power — demonic agency — leads people astray, but that even this evil dominion is somehow in accordance with the "mysteries of God," and therefore redeemable. Such concepts are at the heart of Kabbalah. Is it possible that even what is perceived as evil is somehow a part of the greater good? The people of the scrolls thought so. They held an unshakable conviction that nothing is accidental. Their writings maintain:

> From the knowledge of God comes all that is and shall be.
> Before they ever existed, He established their whole design, and
> when, as ordained for them, they come into being, it is in
> accord with His glorious design that they accomplish their task
> without change (*Manual of Discipline*, col. 3).[8]

To Govern the World . . .

The Dead Sea sect also held that one must "gird up the loins" for battle and enter a great combat, waged within one's soul, but expressed as part of a greater spiritual struggle in the physical world. The end of it all, they believed, is nothing less than complete dominion over the created universe — to be "governors," to be "stewards" as it were, of the whole earth. The scrolls themselves put it like this:

> He has created man to govern the world, and has appointed for him two spirits in which to walk until the time of His visitation: the spirits of truth and falsehood. Those born of truth spring from a fountain of light, but those born of falsehood spring from a source of darkness (*Manual of Discipline,* col. 3).[9]

Typically, these words are full of mysteries and are meant only for those with understanding. But the message is clear. The Almighty has made His children rulers by proxy, in His place. They are given a stewardship over everything that is — over the earth, sea, and sky, and even over the governments of the world. They are appointed to lead; their destiny is conquest. They are to be victors, not the vanquished.

As *Merkavah* becomes full-fledged Kabbalah, the nature of what it means to be spiritual is redefined. There is an ever increasing awareness of the concept of a "calling," to be stewards, protectors of the material world. There is the concept that if the world is ever to be a place fit for God, for "His visitation," it must first be made fit for human beings. And that job is left to those with insight. But how is dominion taken? How is nature rescued? How is human government to be redeemed? According to the scrolls, the task starts in each of the "Sons of Light" individually. The battle between the spirits of truth and falsehood is to be joined and the "Sons of Darkness" defeated.

For the ancient Dead Sea sect, as for the Kabbalists who followed, everything was a process of developing a seasoned spiritual maturity. Moreover, the process continued over the course of years. As an aspiring member of the sect, one did not wake up one day and discover an intimate connection with spiritual power. It took time — a long time — to learn the so-called *razei El*, "the secrets of God." Consider the strict regimen to which the aspiring member of the ancient brotherhood had to subject himself:

> Whoever approaches the Council of the Community shall enter the Covenant of God in the presence of all who have freely pledged themselves. He shall undertake by a binding oath to return with all his heart and soul to every commandment of the Law of Moses, in accordance with all that has been revealed to the Keepers of the Covenant and Seekers of His will (*Manual of Discipline*, col. 5).[10]

Elsewhere, the scrolls require the following of new initiates:

> They shall seek God with a whole heart and soul, and do what is good and right before Him as He commanded by the hand of Moses and all His servants the Prophets; that they may love all that He has chosen and hate all that he has rejected; that they may abstain from all evil and hold fast to all good; that they may practice truth, righteousness, and justice upon earth and no longer stubbornly follow a sinful heart and lustful eyes, committing all manner of evil (*Manual of Discipline*, col. 1).[11]

There was much to live up to. Nor did it end with a few oaths and monumental proclamations. Each initiate had to go through an extensive three-year period of probation, during which time his every action was closely scrutinized by the head of the congregation — the so-called Overseer. As spiritual leader of the community, the Overseer was to provide guidance in the daily affairs of the community, to stand in the place of the departed Teacher of Righteousness, to shepherd the little desert flock:

The Overseer shall instruct all the Sons of Light and shall teach them the nature of all the children of men according to the kind of spirit which they possess, the signs identifying their works during their lifetime, their visitation for chastisement, and the time of their reward (*Manual of Discipline,* col. 3).[12]

Sons of Darkness, Sons of Light

"Sons of Light." This is how the scrolls refer to members of the brotherhood. Those who don't belong to the community — the outsiders — are called "Sons of Darkness." But for all those ruled by the "spirit of truth," there is a "fountain of light." A "fountain of light" suggests a never-ending, constantly self-renewing source of God's eternal essence. Such is the foundation for those foreordained to walk in the way of truth.

To be sure, the members of the sect believed that they were the possessors of light. However, being a Son of Light did not necessarily mean that one knew how to rule the light within. One had to learn to master the inner well of spiritual power. The scrolls state:

It is through the spirit of true counsel concerning the ways of man that all his sins shall be expiated . . . that he may contemplate the light of life. He shall be cleansed from all his sins by the spirit of holiness uniting him to His truth, and his iniquity shall be expiated by the spirit of uprightness and humility. And when his flesh is sprinkled with purifying water and sanctified by cleansing water, it shall be made clean by the humble submission of his soul to all the precepts of God. Let him then order his steps to walk perfectly in all the ways commanded by God concerning the times appointed for him, straying neither to the right nor to the left and transgressing none of His words (*Manual of Discipline,* col. 3).[13]

Again, everything comes back to light — the "light of life." Attaining the spirit of holiness — of uprightness and humility — is, according to the scrolls, an inward work, a transformation of heart and soul, a renewal of life. There are many aspects of spiritual discipline that can be learned, as if by rote — prayer, study of the Scripture, honor of the Sabbath. But holiness, uprightness, humility . . . these cannot be learned. They are inbred. They are either present, or they are not.

In the Company of Angels

Bear in mind, the Sons of Light are not about to be left alone in the work of personal transformation that they are to undertake. The desert congregation believes there is a whole host of helpers — supernatural beings, ever present, but unseen. They are messengers of God; emissaries and divine ambassadors. They are angels. Literally, the very word *angel* — the Hebrew word *mal'akh* — means "worker." Angels are transcendent entities, potent and vigorous, who do the works of God. They are not, however, sovereigns. They are servants, and they exist for no other purpose than to bring about God's presence in the created universe. This means that they are also servants of human beings; they are attendants to the Sons of Light. The Dead Sea Scrolls declare the following:

> But the God of Israel and His Angel of Truth will help all the Sons of Light. For it is He who created the spirits of Light and Darkness and founded every action upon them and established every deed upon their ways. And He loves the one everlastingly and delights in its works forever; but the counsel of the other He loathes and forever hates its ways (*Manual of Discipline*, cols. 3-4).[14]

"His Angel of Truth will help all the Sons of Light"? We wonder how the Angel of Truth and the host of other angels aid their human lords and masters? The scroll continues:

These are their ways in the world for the enlightenment of the heart of man, that all the paths of true righteousness may be made straight before him, and that the fear of the laws of God may be instilled in his heart:

- a spirit of humility,
- patience,
- abundant charity,
- unending goodness,
- understanding, and intelligence;
- a spirit of mighty wisdom which trusts in all the deeds of God;
- a spirit of discernment in every purpose,
- of zeal for just laws,
- of holy intent with steadfastness of heart,
- of great charity towards all the sons of truth,
- of admirable purity which detests all unclean idols,
- of humble conduct sprung from an understanding of all things, and
- of faithful concealment of the mysteries of truth
(*Manual of Discipline*, col. 4).[15]

Incredible, that the most basic purpose and function of the angels, according to the scrolls, is not the working of wonders, nor the parting of the sea, nor the crumbling of walls, but instruction in the "mysteries of truth," the fountainhead of *Merkavah* mysticism and Kabbalah to follow. If angels do anything, they whisper by a still, small voice, building character through communicating hidden wisdom.

There are evil angels as well, say the scrolls, who inspire a spirit of wickedness in the sons of men. What is the lot of those who manifest this spirit? They are to be consumed by a different angelic host, the "destroying angels":

> And the visitation of all who walk in this spirit shall be a multitude of plagues by the hand of all the destroying angels, everlasting damnation by the avenging wrath of the fury of God, eternal torment and endless disgrace together with shameful extinction in the fire of the dark regions (*Manual of Discipline,* col. 4).[16]

The problem of evil in the world is the deepest question with which human beings have ever wrestled. Evil, say the scrolls along with the entire realm of early mysticism, is not an autonomous, independent agency. The Almighty created evil, to serve His divine purposes. Therefore, evil angels are servants of God, just as good angels. These angels are to serve as executors of divine wrath.

Life on Another Level

The admonition is clear. Let these traits be laid as the foundation of the person's life by the ministering angels. Only then, say the scrolls, do the angels bestow another level of blessing:

> And as for the visitation of all who walk in this spirit, it shall be healing, great peace in a long life, and fruitfulness, together with every everlasting blessing and eternal joy in life without end, a crown of glory and a garment of majesty in unending light (*Manual of Discipline,* col. 4).[17]

Again, we come back to light, pictured here as a garment. As the level of faithfulness among the Sons of Light increases, so do the lengths to which the angels will go to intervene from the realm of the supernatural into the realm of the physical world. We are told in ancient sources that the members of the Essene community invited, kabbalistically, the "invasion" of the world that is seen by the world that is unseen. The result, say the ancient sources, was the working of miracles by Essene hands. They were regarded, by Josephus and other historians, as the divine healers of the ancient world. They were "doers" of the will of God, which, say the sources, was becoming increasingly manifest among their number.

Consider the fact that the old Aramaic word for *doers*— that is, of God's will — is *osin* (pronounced "o-seen"). It doesn't take a great leap of imagination to understand how this word could have been corrupted over the generations to a kindred word — *Essene* — which is, today, the dominant theory for the identity of the Dead Sea sect. They were the "doers" of the will of the Almighty. And, if this theory is correct, this means that we have, in the Dead Sea Scrolls, an entire library of the Jewish sect called Essenes. Recall in the New Testament the apostle James' admonition: "Be doers of the word, and not hearers only" (James 1:22) I suggest that James was not talking merely about obeying the commandments, but about doing the works of Israel's God, including the affecting of wonders and healings, standing in proxy for God Himself, in the physical world. Perhaps James, as another early "Kabbalist," acknowledged something that the Essenes of the desert also recognized — that "inclining the heart" toward heaven (called *kavanah*) does more than produce a perfected character, it actually begs the intervention of the heavenly host for the sake of humanity, to effectuate physical healing, mental healing, and a corporate healing for the House of Israel.

In Jewish teaching, *kavanah* signifies intention, purpose, and devotion. It involves directing one's soul outward and is the perfect corollary of Kabbalah, which involves the inward process of receiving. It is related that a *Tzadik* (a righteous person) once said: "Note well that the word Kabbalah stems from *kabbel*, to receive, and the word *kavanah* from *kaven*, to direct outward. For the ultimate meaning of all the wisdom is to take upon oneself the yoke of God's kingdom, and the ultimate meaning of all the art of *kavanah* is to direct one's heart to God."[18]

Angels Angels Everywhere

With the focus of *Merkavah* mysticism on the chariot-throne, it is little wonder that angels should occupy the minds and writings of the people of those times. We know the angels of the Essenes by precise classification, as listed by the Dead Sea Scrolls. They include:

• *Ministering Angels*, whose purpose is simply to attend to the Almighty and to meet human need. Be it physical health, clothing and shelter, or peace of mind, they exist to offer aid and succor to the Sons of Light:

Angels of wondrous strength minister unto Thee, and they walk at the side of the meek and of them that are eager for right-doing, and of all the lost and lorn that stand in need of mercy, lifting them out of the pit, when their feet are mired (*Psalms* Scroll, col. 5).[19]

• *Angels of Sanctification*, who stand as "witnesses" in the affirmation of divine covenants and ordinances, and who serve to set apart those human beings called to holy service, especially the priestly class:

The Lord bless you from His holy abode and crown you in majesty in the midst of the Holy Beings, and renew for you the covenant of everlasting priesthood, and give you a place in the holy habitation (*Blessings*, col. 3)[20]

• *Angels of the Presence,* who manifest the supernatural emanations of the Almighty to the Sons of Light. Literally, they are called Angels of the Face, for they stand before the face of God:

> For Thou will bring Thy glorious salvation to all the people of Thy Council, to those who share a common lot with the Angels of the presence. Among them shall be no mediator to invoke Thy Name and no messenger to make reply; for they shall reply according to Thy glorious word and shall be Thy princes in the company of the Angels (*Psalms Scroll,* col. 6).[21]

• *Cherubim,* the only angels said to have wings, whose only stated purpose is to mark the place of the chariot-throne — designating its precise location, and . . .
• a hierarchy of seven archangels, who oversee the work of all the other angels.

These angels were the subject of the author of the scroll called *The Song of Sabbath Sacrifices.*

An Angelic Liturgy

We do not know precisely who was the author of *The Song of Sabbath Sacrifices* or when he lived, but the document he composed, discovered both at the caves of Qumran and the rocky plateau called Masada, is perhaps the great "missing link" in understanding the evolution of Kabbalah. Here we have a transitional text, which stands between the early mysticism of the apocryphal literature and the later flowering of the mystical tradition in medieval times. The author of *The Song of Sabbath Sacrifices* gives us a series of liturgical hymns, in the mouths of the angels on high, which accompany the weekly burnt offering in the Jerusalem Temple on the Sabbath. Each Sabbath sacrifice had its own special significance and its own name, transmitting the teachings of the Qumran sect.[22]

Kabbalah teaches that everything below has a counterpart above. The earthly reality is really just a reflection of the heavenly reality. It is the Hebraic equivalent of the ancient Greek concept, expounded by Plato, called *mimesis*. Things on the earth are but a copy of things in the realm of the ideal. The craftsman, wrote Plato, fashions a copy of the ideal object, located somewhere in the realm of the eternal. The earthly copy is always at least "one remove" from the perfect image, in the ideal realm.

It is an incredible phenomenon that Greek and Hebrew philosophies, which appear on so many levels to be at odds with each other, come together in the realm of Kabbalah. The angelic host in *The Song of Sabbath Sacrifices* serves in a spiritual Temple, of which the earthly shrine is merely a copy. Scripture itself queries, through the words of King Solomon: "But will God indeed dwell on the earth? Behold, heaven and the highest heaven cannot contain thee; how much less this house which I have built!" (1 Kings 8:27). *Merkavah* mysticism, even at this early stage, solves the dilemma by positing a heavenly Temple in the realm of perfection, at which minister the angels — supernatural counterparts of the Jerusalemite priests of flesh and blood. It is they whose songs are recorded in the *The Song of Sabbath Sacrifices*.

The document goes on to describe the actual utterance of the angels, their "song":

> While they are soaring aloft, a murmur of angel voices is heard, and the lifting of their wings is accompanied by a clamor of joyous song. It is the murmur of angels blessing the Chariot-like Throne above the firmament of the cherubim, while they themselves, from below the place where the Glory dwells, go acclaiming in joyous song the splendor of that radiant expanse.[23]

It is a vivid picture of the unseen realm of the divine presence. It is nearly the same vision seen by the prophet Ezekiel, centuries earlier, describing a heavenly chariot, carrying the exalted throne of God. Ezekiel describes four angelic beings; yet, his focus is on God and His throne. But the Dead Sea text fills in the blanks about the angels:

> Whenever the wheels of that Chariot are in motion, angels of sanctification dart to and fro all around it, between its glorious wheels. Like fiery apparitions, they are most holy spirits, looking like streams of fire, in the likeness of burnished metal or of lustrous ware; clothed in luminous garments, an array of wondrous colors, diffuse with brightness; live angelic spirits, constantly coming and going beside the glorious wonderful Chariot.[24]

The emphasis here is on the visual senses — on light and fire, designating the presence of living spirits. Moreover, the writer of this scroll appears to be describing something that he has actually witnessed — a purely supernatural apparition. Next, the writer describes in detail what he hears, audibly:

> Amid all the noise of their progress, a murmured intonation of blessings is heard, and whenever they come round, they shout their holy hallelujahs. When the angels soar aloft, they soar in wondrous unison; and when they alight, they stay standing. Then the sound of the paean is hushed, and the murmur of angelic benedictions pervades all the camps of those godly beings. From the midst of their contingent, they utter praise, as in holy worship, each of their ranks breaks forth into joyous song, one after another.[25]

Their very words have power, and seem to fall in groups of seven, each set emphasizing a central theme: nobility, sublime truth, and mystical prowess. We read: "Finally, with seven words of His mystical holiness, the seventh archangel blesses, in the name of His holiness, all the saintly beings among those who have laid foundations for true knowledge."[26]

In the end, everything comes back to "true knowledge," and a foundation of truth, uprightness, and exemplary character.

Who's an Angel?

Beyond their appointments in the heavenly hierarchy, the Dead Sea Scrolls go on to spell out the precise names of particular angels. We have for example:

- *The Prince of Light,* who rules the spirit of the righteous and guides them in the right paths: "All the children of righteousness are ruled by the Prince of Light and walk in the ways of light" (*Manual of Discipline,* col. 3).[27]
- *The Angel of Truth,* who aids the Sons of Light in discerning good and evil;
- *Gabriel,* meaning "God is mighty," interpreter of dreams and visions, and harbinger of glad tidings;
- *Michael,* meaning "Who is like God?," the great prince who protects the House of Israel;
- *Raphael,* meaning "God heals," who carries angelic treatments for the sick; and
- *Sariel,* meaning "God is my Prince," another defender of the holy flock.

Several of these angels are mentioned in one striking passage from the *War Scroll:*

They shall write on the shields of their towers: on the first, Michael, on the second, Gabriel, on the third, Sariel, and on the fourth, Raphael. Michael and Gabriel shall stand on the right, and Sariel and Raphael on the left (*War Scroll,* col. 9).[28]

Clearly, the protection of the angels in time of battle was greatly sought after by the desert community of Qumran. The revelation of these angels, their names and their very existence, was an integral part of ancient mysticism, Essene-style.

War in Heaven, War on Earth

Another important aspect of mysticism has always been a near obsession with apocalypticism — the "end of the world" — and the tumultuous warfare prophesied during the final generation. Consider the single Dead Sea scroll devoted entirely to battle, called the *War Between the Sons of Light and the Sons of Darkness,* or simply, the *War Scroll.* Essentially, it is an account of seven great battles at the end of the days between the powers of good and evil. The foes are formidable, and are spearheaded by the wicked Kittim, a mysterious and warlike tribe who come up against the Holy Land:

> The king of the Kittim shall enter into Egypt, and in his time he shall set out in great wrath to wage war against the kings of the north, that his fury may destroy and cut off the horn of Israel (*War Scroll,* col. 1).[29]

Another Armageddon

In short, we have here another version of the Battle of Armageddon, set on the physical plane of future history. It is all to be part of the dreaded "pangs of the Messiah," the time of testing and tribulation for the holy flock prior to final judgment. The entire cosmic contest is to last for some forty years, which could be a symbolic number signifying a long and torturous period. Furthermore, the combat is to be waged by both humans and angels. The first stage of the war lasts six years. It is a time when all of the Sons of Light engage the Kittim in mortal combat. The *War Scroll* declares:

> The sons of Levi, Judah, and Benjamin, the exiles in the desert, shall battle against them when the exiled sons of light return from the Desert of the Peoples to camp in the Desert of Jerusalem (*War Scroll,* col. 1).[30]

What is the "Desert of the Peoples" but the many cities in Judea and beyond where small Essene communities were scattered? And what is the "Desert of Jerusalem" but the barren wasteland of Qumran itself — the headquarters of the sect, from which come all instruction and enlightenment (the "marching orders"). In other words, a small multitude of Essenes will gather together at Qumran, from all the places of their dispersion, to take their stand against the powers of darkness, and their earthly agents, the Kittim.

Spiritual Warfare

The warfare depicted in the *War Scroll* is more spiritual than physical, another way of saying that every type of conflict on earth has its counterpart on the supernatural plane. According to the scrolls, outcomes are determined in equal measure by uprightness, holy conduct, and action, the end of which is not, as in most wars, carnage, but dominion and authority to rule the world. In mystical language, the scroll states: "This shall be a time of salvation for the people of God, an age of dominion for all the members of His company, and of everlasting destruction for all the company of Satan" (*War Scroll,* col. 1).[31]

The members of the sect, the Essenes, believed that up until that moment, the world had been under the dominion of forces of great evil. But all wickedness is to be vanquished, in the coming Armageddon-like conflict between good and evil. Again, the conflict is waged on two coequal plains, in the physical dimension and in the spiritual dimension. The dominion of the Sons of Light is to be established on both of these plains, and rule of the Sons of Darkness, expressed through the mysterious Kittim, is to be obliterated: "The dominion of the Kittim shall come to an end and iniquity shall be vanquished, leaving no remnant; for the sons of darkness there shall be no escape" (*War Scroll*, col. 1).[32]

For the righteous — the Sons of Light — the physical victory culminates in a new age, a new dimension, a new world:

> The sons of righteousness shall shine over all the ends of the earth; they shall go on shining until all the seasons of darkness are consumed and, at the season appointed by God, His exalted greatness shall shine eternally to the peace, blessing, glory, joy, and long life of all the sons of light (*War Scroll,* col. 1).[33]

Clothed in Light

Kabbalah, it seems, always comes back to light. Light brings joy and long life. The Sons of Light are clothed in light, and they themselves emanate light. They shine with radiance, and their light is enveloped in God's. The description sounds a great deal like the New Testament description of the New Jerusalem, in the book of Revelation (which we can also place loosely in the category of *Merkavah* mysticism):

> The city does not need the sun or the moon to shine on it, for the glory of God gives it light, and the Lamb is its lamp. . . . There will be no more night. They will not need the light of a lamp or the light of the sun, for the Lord God will give them light (Rev. 21:23; 22:5 NIV).

Light is the domain of angels. It is weightless; it has no dimensions, no physical properties. Light itself is colorless, though it brings illumination — and life — to every physical thing on which it shines. So it is, kabbalistically, when the spiritual world invades the physical. That which is without dimension casts its luminous, redemptive properties on the things of the material world. Light itself cannot be seen, but its effects are breathtaking. So it is with Deity and with angels. The New Testament sums it up: "We write this to make our joy complete . . . . God is light; in him there is no darkness at all "(1 John 1:4-5 NIV).

According to the scrolls, spiritual light will bring physical retreat to the enemies of God, during the "Armageddon" that is forecast, as the Sons of Light take dominion over a renewed world: "The trumpets of alarm shall sound for massacre, and for ambush, and for pursuit when the enemy shall be smitten" (*War Scroll,* col. 3).[34]

The Character of the Righteous

At the heart of the *War Scroll* is not the combat itself, but a series of symbolic words written on ceremonial trumpets. They tell the story of the triumph of the community of the righteous, their character and their deeds:

• On the trumpets calling the congregation they shall write, *The Called of God* [each "Son of Light" must recognize and evaluate his own calling]
• On the trumpets calling the chiefs they shall write, *The Princes of God* [the success of the community shall be determined by the quality of its leaders, its "Princes"]
• On the trumpets of the Levites they shall write, *The army of God* [the community is more than a spiritual company; it is a physical army, doing battle in the material world]

• On the trumpets of the men of renown and of the heads of family of the congregation gathered in the house of Assembly they shall write, *Summoned by God to the Council of Holiness* [the congregation is only as effective as its commitment to fellowship in the holy assembly]

• On the trumpets of the camps they shall write, *The Peace of God in the camps of His saints* [the congregation shall experience the fullness of God's peace only when assembled together]

• On the trumpets for breaking camp they shall write, *The mighty deeds of God shall crush the enemy* [to see evil vanquished, the righteous must let God do His part]

• On the trumpets for battle formations they shall write, *Formations of the divisions of God for the vengeance of His wrath* [spiritual victory requires physical battle]

• On the trumpets summoning the foot-soldiers to advance . . . when the gates of war are opened they shall write, *Reminder of vengeance in God's appointed time* [do not engage prematurely; before the battle is joined, the congregation must first wait for the "gates of war" to be opened]

• On the trumpets of massacre they shall write, *The mighty hand of God in war shall cause all the ungodly slain to fall* [even though the righteous must do battle, the victory is God's alone]

• On the trumpets of ambush they shall write, *The mysteries of God shall undo wickedness* [spiritual insight is just as important as physical strength and courage]

• On the trumpets of pursuit they shall write, *God has smitten all the Sons of Darkness* [God's fury will not be satisfied until the victory is complete]

• On the trumpets of retreat, when they retreat from battle . . . they shall write, *God has reassembled* [when the victory is complete, the congregation must assemble together again]

and . . .

• On the trumpets of return from battle . . . when they journey to the congregation in Jerusalem they shall write, *Rejoicings of God in the peaceful return* [the congregation must return to a restored and rededicated Jerusalem] (*War Scroll*, col. 3).[35]

In the end, the Dead Sea Scrolls insist that "Armageddon" is not a future cataclysm, to be feared and dreaded. For even the heat of battle is a glorious opportunity to share with a company of angels in creating a purified world. Let the rest of humanity quiver in fear and dread of the coming holocaust that threatens to engulf the planet. Let them panic and quake and look for shelter. The Sons of Light are to be quietly confident in the spiritual dynamic they have trained in. They are to trust in the force of their own righteousness, and know that the battle, ultimately, is God's to wage — they are only instrumentalities.

Fighting from Heaven

The scrolls set out the course of the conflict. Three battles are to be won by the Sons of Darkness; three are to be won by the Sons of Light. But the final, seventh battle is to be won by God Himself, along with His angels, who intervene on behalf of the members of the community:

> For Thou wilt fight with them from heaven. For the multitude
> of the Holy Ones is with Thee in heaven, and the host of the
> Angels is in Thy holy abode, praising Thy Name. . . . Thou
> shalt muster the hosts of Thine elect, in their Thousands and
> Myriads, with Thy Holy Ones and with all Thine Angels, that
> they may be mighty in battle, and that they may triumph
> together with the elect of heaven (*War Scroll*, col. 12).[36]

It is a kabbalistic testimony which presages the spirit of the New Testament, and acts as a literary bridge between the world of the Hebrew Scriptures of old and the developing world of Christianity. Therefore, says Paul:

> Be strong in the Lord and in his mighty power. Put on the full armor of God so that you can take your stand against the devil's schemes. For our struggle is not against flesh and blood, but against the rulers, against the authorities, against the powers of this dark world and against the spiritual forces of evil in the heavenly realms. Therefore put on the full armor of God, so that when the day of evil comes, you may be able to stand your ground, and after you have done everything, to stand (Eph. 6: 10-13 NIV).

Such was the burden of the apostle, and such was the burden of the little Essene community, which occupied the lowest (1,200 feet below sea level) and most desolate tract on the surface of the globe. Here, in the geographic center of the world, and at the point where heaven above is at its highest from the earth beneath, they brought forth what we may definitively call *Merkavah* mysticism. Living two full centuries before the coming of Jesus of Nazareth, their vision and goal was astoundingly similar to what the early Church would later declare as its own — to glimpse the throne of God.

Early Sages, Early Christians

The Circle-Drawer

Miracle workers had been many in the land of Judea. In the first century B.C. an ancient Hasidic master came out of nowhere to mesmerize the population. They called him Khoni the Circle-Drawer because, during a long drought, he audaciously drew a circle in the sand, stood in the center, and declared that he would not move until the Almighty sent rain. One does not make such demands upon the Deity, decreed the contemporary Sages. But Khoni the Circle-Drawer was a folk hero, and folk heroes are not easily excommunicated.

The Talmud recounts the event:

It once happened that the people turned to Khoni the Circle-Drawer and asked him to pray for rain. He prayed, but no rain fell. What did he do? He drew a circle and stood within it and exclaimed, "Master of the Universe, Thy children have turned to me because they believe me to be as a member of Thy household. I swear by Thy great Name that I will not move from here until Thou hast mercy upon Thy children." Rain then began to fall. He said, "It is not for this that I have prayed but for rain to fill cisterns, ditches, and pools." The rain then began to come down with great force. He exclaimed, "It is not for this that I have prayed but for rain of benevolence, blessing and bounty." Rain then fell in the normal way.[37]

This kind of intimacy with the Almighty, coupled with a bold audacity, can be seen at the heart of Kabbalah. We might simply call it "chutzpah." The historian Josephus goes on to describe the ultimate demise of Khoni, at a time when two warring factions of the people — priests and lay folk — approached him to pray on their behalf. He responded with typical chutzpah: "Master of the Universe, these men are Thy people, and those who are besieged are Thy priests: I beseech Thee *not to do what they ask!*" Josephus records in melancholy tones what happened next: "He was thereupon stoned to death." Indeed, martyrdom has been the lot of many a kabbalistic master.

Jesus the Kabbalist

The prophet of Nazareth, known as *Iesus* in Greek and *Yeshua* in Hebrew can be seen not only as the Father of the Christian faith, but a Hasidic teacher in the true tradition of Khoni the Circle-Drawer. It is difficult if not impossible to sift through the mists of two millennia of Christian tradition to find the "historical Jesus," but those who embark on this journey can only imagine what the Great Galilean must have looked like and how he would have behaved . . . .

His piercing, dark brown eyes peered ahead, expressing the quiet confidence and stubborn faith of an Israelite. His weathered complexion, dark and ruddy from years under the Galilee sun, betrayed his Middle Eastern heritage, as did his pronounced features — his broad forehead, bushy eyebrows, and thickly sculpted lips. His dark brown hair was thick and matted and tightly curled, giving way to a full beard, neatly groomed and worn with pride. Almost hiding his ears were long and prominent side-curls, worn in fulfillment of an ancient commandment delivered to his ancestors, that the corners of the beard were not to be trimmed, as a perpetual sign of devotion to the Almighty. He was fairly short in stature, just over five feet, though his build was solid and muscular, almost stocky. He was called *Yeshua*, from the Hebrew root *Yasha*, meaning "salvation." In the Galilean dialect, however, he was often called *Yeshu*, without the final guttural letter, which Galileans found difficult to pronounce. In later generations his name would be given a Greek form, *Iesus*, and ultimately anglicized, to the name by which he is known today — Jesus.

Oxford scholar Geza Vermes writes, "Most people, whether they admit it or not, approach the Gospels with preconceived ideas. Christians read them in the light of their faith; Jews, primed with age-old suspicion; agnostics, ready to be scandalized; and professional New Testament experts, wearing the blinkers of their trade. Yet it should not be beyond the capabilities of an educated man to sit down and with a mind empty of prejudice read the accounts of Mark, Matthew, and Luke as though for the first time."[38]

Let's face it. Varying religious backgrounds notwithstanding, Jesus of Nazareth existed. He was a historical character, and the movement he created was not only Jewish in every respect, it was to some extent kabbalistic — another example of ancient mysticism. Furthermore, notwithstanding the Christian concept of the "uniqueness" of Christianity, there wasn't anything all that unique about it. Ninety percent or more of what Jesus taught lined up with Pharisaic Judaism, laced with a mystical messianic bent. Jesus was in fact another ancient Hasidic, in the line of the revered Khoni the Circle-Drawer.

The prominent scholar of comparative religion at the Hebrew University of Jerusalem, David Flusser, writes, "Jesus was close to the world of the Hasidim (the Pious), who were in their turn close to the world of the Sages. . . . One should mention, as an example, Khoni the Circle-Drawer, who was killed in 62 B.C. Khoni drew a circle and prayed for rain, and this brought about a clash between him and Simeon ben Shetakh, who at the time represented the Establishment Sages. One should also mention Rabbi Hanina ben Dosa, who lived [at the time of] the destruction of the Temple. . . . According to Rabbi Hanina, 'wisdom is not on a par with good deeds (*Avot* 3:12).'"[39] Compare this with the words of Jesus: "In the same way, let your light shine before men, that they may see your good deeds and praise your Father in heaven" (Matt. 5:16).

Flusser also notes, "The Pious were regarded as sons of God. When Khoni the Circle-Drawer had brought about rain, Simeon ben Shetakh said to him: 'Were you not Khoni, I would have had you excommunicated . . . but what can I do to you, who coax the Almighty to do your will, like a son coaxes his father to do his will?' (*Taan.* 23a)."

Flusser continues, "When the world was short of rain, the Sages used to send for a Pious man called Yohanan the Withdrawn. They would send children, who would grasp at the edge of his garment and implore him: 'Father, father, bring us rain.' The Pious man would say: 'Master of the Universe, do it for the sake of those who do not discern between a father who brings rain and a father who does not bring rain.' (*Taan.* 23b) Long ago scholars noticed the similarity between this story and Jesus' usual address 'Father!' They noted the parallel between the feeling of familiarity with God among the Pious and Jesus' special familiarity with his Father in Heaven. Jesus felt that he was a son of God. The Sages, too, recognized the special familiar relations of the Pious to God, a relation which originated in their extraordinary deeds."[40]

Such connectedness with God, however one conceives of Him, is what the world of the mystics is all about. It is with a certain audacity, not unlike that of Khoni the Circle-Drawer, that Jesus declares, "The knowledge of the secrets of the kingdom of God has been given to you, but to others I speak in parables, so that, 'though seeing, they may not see; though hearing, they may not understand'" (Luke 8:10 NIV). Else-where, we read: "At that time Jesus said, 'I praise you, Father, Lord of heaven and earth, because you have hidden these things from the wise and learned, and revealed them to little children'" (Matt. 11:25 NIV). Early Kabbalah takes pains to discuss both the "hidden things" and the "revealed things," and on that score Jesus fits very well within the domain of Jewish mysticism. Make no mistake, the essential teachings of Jesus are on the whole far more practical than they are mystical. Jesus should not be seen as utterly dominated by kabbalistic teach-ing and lore. But there is a place in his thought — in his world — for deep and powerful mystical experience.

We should consider also the Gospel account known as the book of John. From its first words it is the most mystical, and therefore the most kabbalistic, account of Jesus' life. It opens with the classic statement:

> In the beginning was the Word, and the Word was with God,
> and the Word was God. He was in the beginning with God; all
> things were made through him, and without him was not any-
> thing made that was made (John 1:1-3).

The idea that the figure of the Messiah was in fact preexis-tent, and present at the moment of creation is also found in the apocryphal book of Enoch. Furthermore, the book of Jubilees declares that God "has created everything by His Word." And the Wisdom of Solomon states, "By His knowledge everything came to be . . . and without Him nothing is done." When modern scholars examine the evidence, it seems increasingly clear that the notion of the Messiah as a supernatural being (equivalent with the Divine Word and with true knowledge), present in the beginning with God, is not a later addition of Christian theology, but reflects an early layer of Jewish thought, in the form of Kabbalah!

In another passage from John's Gospel, Jesus is quoted as saying, "If you had known me, you would have known my Father also; henceforth you know him and have seen him" (John 14:7). Jewish mystics imagined an "Archetypal Man" — a "son of man" — in whose image Adam was made. This Archetypal Man would act as the "Messiah Above." His counterpart was the "Messiah Below." Jesus, in kabbalistic fashion, seems to be identifying himself with the "Messiah Below," a true reflection of the "Archetypal Man," and therefore, the Father.[41]

Paul the Kabbalist

If Jesus, however, has a somewhat esoteric bent, then the apostle who established his church, Paul of Tarsus, is a well-defined early Kabbalist. Here is a man whose apostolic mission leads him on a quest for a higher truth and a greater revelation of spiritual reality. Describing his personal quest for a higher plane of truth, he writes: "When God, who set me apart from birth and called me by his grace, was pleased to reveal his Son in me so that I might preach him among the Gentiles, I did not consult any man, nor did I go up to Jerusalem to see those who were apostles before I was, but I went immediately into Arabia and later returned to Damascus. Then after three years, I went up to Jerusalem" (Gal. 1:15-18 NIV). Paul has much in common with other Jewish mystics, who invariably retire to some secretive locale to receive their special revelations. Whatever Paul learned during those years of isolation, he seems to have been motivated for the rest of his life by the esoteric secrets he acquired.

In one of the most striking passages in all of his letters, he writes:

I know a man in Christ who fourteen years ago was caught up to the third heaven. Whether it was in the body or out of the body I do not know — God knows. And I know that this man — whether in the body or apart from the body I do not know, but God knows — was caught up to paradise. He heard inexpressible things, things that man is not permitted to tell. I will boast about a man like that, but I will not boast about myself, except about my weaknesses (2 Cor. 12:2-5 NIV).

Interestingly, more than one commentator on this passage believes that the man of whom Paul writes is Paul himself. In any case, Paul's account is similar to one from the apocryphal book, *Ascension of Isaiah* (probably written by a Jewish Christian, expanding earlier Jewish texts): "Those who love the Most High and His Beloved will go up there through the angel of the Holy Spirit."

Consider also that the Talmud describes "seven heavens," the Garden of Eden being in the third:

There are seven heavens, named respectively: *Vilon, Rakia, Shechakim, Zebul, Maon, Machon,* and *Araboth. Vilon* performs no other function than that it retires in the morning and issues forth in the evening, and renews the work of Creation daily. . . . *Rakia* is that in which the sun, moon, stars, and planets are fixed. . . . *Shechakim* is that in which the millstones are located and grind manna for the righteous. . . . *Zebul* is that where the Celestial Jerusalem is and the Temple in which the altar is erected, and Michael, the great Prince, stands and offers a sacrifice upon it. . . . *Maon* is that in which are bands of ministering angels, who utter a song in the night but are silent during the day for the sake of the honor of Israel. . . . *Machon* is that in which are the treasuries of snow and the treasuries of hail, the loft containing harmful dews, the lofts of the round drops (which injure plants), the chamber of the whirlwind and storm, and the cavern of noxious smoke, the doors of which are made of fire. . . . *Araboth* is that in which are righteousness, judgment, and charity, the storehouses of life, of peace and of blessing, the souls of the righteous, the spirits and souls which are still to be created, and the dew with which the Holy One, blessed be He, will hereafter revive the dead (*Chagigah* 12a-b).[42]

We see from this that, as impressive as the spiritual ascent reported by Paul may have been, he never claims to have journeyed past the third heaven (presumably *Schechakim*). In spite of Paul's familiarity with mystical lore and with the Talmud, much of what the self-proclaimed apostle of Christianity writes involves a new approach to some very old commandments. The justification for this new approach is found in the realm of the supernatural — the purely spiritual plane. In the overall development of Kabbalah, Paul stands somewhere between the earliest layers of *Merkavah* mysticism (the *Heikhalot* tradition of the Throne of Glory) and the *Sefirot* tradition of subsequent rabbis. His kabbalistic inclination is evidenced when he writes:

We . . . speak a message of wisdom among the mature, but not the wisdom of this age or of the rulers of this age, who are coming to nothing. No, we speak of God's secret wisdom, a wisdom that has been hidden and that God destined for our glory before time began. None of the rulers of this age understood it. . . . We have not received the spirit of the world but the Spirit who is from God, that we may understand what God has freely given us. This is what we speak, not in words taught us by human wisdom but in words taught by the Spirit, expressing spiritual truths in spiritual words. The man without the Spirit does not accept the things that come from the Spirit of God, for they are foolishness to him, and he cannot understand them, because they are spiritually discerned (1Cor. 2:6-8,12-14).

Note that Paul's use of the word *received* echoes the precise terminology of Kabbalah — "that which is received."

The Pharisee mystics of Paul's day taught, in addition to the chariot visions of *Merkavah* mysticism, the "Lore of Creation," recounting the hidden truths of Genesis. Paul was clearly familiar with this tradition, which expounded the idea of a "Heavenly Man," in the image of the Almighty, who is the equivalent of the "Messiah Above." For everything on earth there is a heavenly counterpart; Jesus, in Paul's mind, is the earthly image of the Heavenly Messiah. He also writes: "The first man was of the dust of the earth, the second man from heaven. As was the earthly man, so are those who are of the earth; and as is the man from heaven, so also are those who are of heaven" (1 Cor. 15:47-48 NIV). Paul continues this theme in a later epistle:

> He is the image of the invisible God, the firstborn over all creation. For by him all things were created: things in heaven and on earth, visible and invisible, whether thrones or powers or rulers or authorities; all things were created by him and for him. He is before all things, and in him all things hold together (Col. 1:15-17 NIV).

Just as Jesus is the physical counterpart of the "Heavenly Man," so the city of Jerusalem, with its great Temple, is the earthly counterpart of a heavenly city: "But the Jerusalem that is above is free, and she is our mother" (Gal. 4:26 NIV). This Platonic concept, of perfection existing in the realm of the ideal, and earthly things being mere copies of that ideal, is expressed again and again in Paul's writings, as well as in those of the proponents of "standard" Jewish mysticism. There is, it was theorized, a hierarchy of heavenly realms, in ascending order, which may be approached only through the contemplative disciplines of kabbalistic practice. Paul writes, "That power is like the working of his mighty strength, which he exerted in Christ when he raised him from the dead and seated him at his right hand in the heavenly realms" (Eph. 1:19-20). Are the "heavenly realms" of which Paul writes the same as the *Sefirot* of early Jewish mysticism? The interplay of terms here is compelling evidence that Paul, as progenitor of early Christianity, must have been schooled in the ways of the Kabbalists of his day.

John the Kabbalist

The Kabbalah of the New Testament doesn't end with Paul. There is a continuing stream of mysticism coursing through the later writings of Christian canon. The apostle John is a case in point. In the epic work of apocalyptic visions, the book of Revelation, we find the following:

> I, John, your brother and companion in the suffering and king-dom and patient endurance that are ours in Jesus, was on the island of Patmos because of the word of God and the testimony of Jesus. On the Lord's Day I was in the Spirit, and I heard behind me a loud voice like a trumpet, which said: "Write on a scroll what you see and send it to the seven churches: . . . . " I turned around to see the voice that was speaking to me. And when I turned I saw seven golden lampstands, and among the lampstands was someone "like a son of man," dressed in a robe reaching down to his feet and with a golden sash around his chest. His head and hair were white like wool, as white as snow, and his eyes were like blazing fire. His feet were like bronze glowing in a furnace, and his voice was like the sound of rush-ing waters. In his right hand he held seven stars, and out of his mouth came a sharp double-edged sword. His face was like the sun shining in all its brilliance. When I saw him, I fell at his feet as though dead. Then he placed his right hand on me and

said: "Do not be afraid. . . .Write, therefore, what you have seen, what is now and what will take place later" (Rev. 1:9-17, 19 NIV).

Again, we have mystical secrets, revealed to a man who is secluded and sequestered, in language hauntingly reminiscent of the visions of Ezekiel and Daniel. Each element of the vision carries symbolic meaning, in a code of sorts, to be appreciated by those privy to the esoteric insights. Thus, the book of Revelation can be seen as the greatest mystical text of the New Testament. But it is only one more step in the development of kabbalistic thought, which continued in an ascending slope across the first several centuries of the common era.

The Miracle Worker

Just decades after the life of Jesus of Nazareth, another mystical teacher appeared on the scene. His name was Hanina ben Dosa, and he was renowned as a divine healer of ancient Judea. Like Jesus and numbers of other ancient rabbis of a kabbalistic bent, he had the idea that a truly pious person may, with an incredible audacity, mandate the decrees of God on earth. Ancient sources record that Rabbi Hanina would pray indefatigably over those sick with various maladies. The inevitable question was: Why are some healed and some not? Rabbi Hanina, speaking, as it were, as God's "surrogate," seemed to know. Even during his prayers, he took to saying, "This one will live; that one will die." "What kind of brazen impudence is this?" people wanted to know. "How can he presume to know who will live and who will die?" Rabbi Hanina responded, quite mystically, that it was all a matter of how easily the words of his prayer seemed to form upon his lips. This in turn told him whether his petition for the sick person was "accepted" in the eyes of the Almighty or not. He announced, "If my prayer is fluent in my mouth, I know that he is accepted; but if not, I know that he is rejected."

A famous story is told of how the son of the famous rabbi Gamaliel contracted a sickness. Gamaliel dispatched two of his disciples to Rabbi Hanina ben Dosa, asking the famed miracle worker for prayer, that his son might be healed. Rabbi Hanina, on seeing the pupils of Gamaliel approaching, climbed to an "upper room" and began to pray. Some time later, Rabbi Hanina came down, declaring, "Go, the fever has left him."

Gamaliel's disciples asked, incredulously, "Are you a prophet?"

But the miracle worker, with uncharacteristic humility, answered, "I am no prophet nor a prophet's son (Amos 7:14); but so is my tradition."

He went on to explain that if the prayer seemed to form effortlessly in his mouth, he knew that the sick person had been "accepted." The dumbfounded emissaries of Gamaliel sat down on the spot and made note of the time. Returning to their teacher they explained the odd behavior of the miracle worker and the curious response their plea had evoked. When they related the exact time at which Rabbi Hanina had spoken his "prophetic" remark, the great Gamaliel became stunned, in utter amazement.

"By the Temple-service!" he exclaimed. "You have neither understated nor overstated the time. But thus it happened; at that very hour the fever left him, and he asked us for water to drink."[43] Thus, it was through an expression of mystical power that the son of the greatest Jewish leader of the age, Gamaliel, was restored to health.

Miracle workers being similar to one another in *modus operandi*, one can hardly help thinking of a certain New Testament story, related as follows:

At Capernaum there was an official whose son was ill. When he heard that Jesus had come from Judea to Galilee, he went and begged him to come down and heal his son, for he was at the point of death. Jesus therefore said to him, "Unless you see signs and wonders you will not believe." The official said to him, "Sir, come down before my child dies." Jesus said to him, "Go; your son will live." The man believed the word that Jesus spoke to him and went his way. As he was going down, his servants met him and told him that his son was living. So he asked them the hour when he began to mend, and they said to him, "Yesterday at the seventh hour the fever left him." The father knew that was the hour when Jesus had said to him, "Your son will live"; and he himself believed, and all his household (John 4:46-53).

Rabbi Hanina summed up his theology in a manner similar to Jesus and his disciples: "See, my sons!" he railed. "It is not a serpent that kills, but rather it is sin that kills!"[44] In other words, not all sickness is the direct result of some sin the person has committed; but a life of sin certainly leads, more often than not, to one sickness or another. If sin were the operative factor in a person's life, Hanina discerned it through a kabbalistic "sixth sense," and his prayers for healing were ineffectual. But for those not dominated by sin — which the Sages called the "evil impulse" — prayer for healing was infinitely powerful. Perhaps that is why, from that day to this, traditional Hebrew bedtime prayers have included the petition, "May the evil impulse not rule over me." It is all part of the greater stream that Hebrew tradition calls "Practical Kabbalah."

The Great Revolt

The mystically ominous words of John's Revelation, as well as of the Dead Sea *War Scroll*, found a horrifying fulfillment in the events of 66 A.D. and the years which followed. The entire land was convulsed in cataclysm, a terrifying revolt fomented by a radical element of anti-Roman militants, the Zealots, and their cousins, the Sicarii, or "Dagger Men." They were undoubtedly imbued with a sense of messianic determination to bring about by the sword the deliverance of which the mystics spoke. They were poor in comparison with the riches of Rome, but their richness in spirit would carry the day. They were hopelessly outnumbered, but the angels would fight with them. They had no powerful allies, but they were allied with heaven.

The revolt began in the city of Caesarea, on the Mediterranean coast, where anti-Jewish civic strife provided the spark that would ignite a war. From there it spread to the great rocky plateau jutting out of the Judean wilderness, near the Dead Sea, Masada, where the Roman garrison was forcibly ejected. In short order the whole land was in open rebellion, from Jerusalem to the highlands of northern Galilee. It took more than mere swordsmanship to drive the revolt. It took messianic fervor, even in the absence of a Messiah; it took the mystical impulse, wedded to the most violent militancy.

The Romans for their part were unwilling to let Judea go its own way. The crack general, Vespasian, was dispatched, along with his son, Titus, to retake this eastern flank of the empire. The legions wasted no time in their forward march into the land of Israel. First they turned on the north, spreading blood and fire across the whole of Galilee. A horrific battle on the Sea of Galilee produced a carnage of floating corpses and splinters of rafts and little boats which carried the rebels and their dreams. The siege of two Galilean settlements, Gamla and Yodfat, produced a series of Jewish suicides in the face of capitulation — a practice unheard of in Jewish life and experience. Next, the legions descended on little Qumran, on the Dead Sea shore, where the frantic Essenes hid their precious scrolls in caves prior to their ultimate capture and slaughter, save for the few who fled south to Masada.

General Vespasian returned to Rome, the tyrant Nero having been assassinated, to assume the title of emperor. His son Titus remained in Judea, laying siege to the city of Jerusalem and trapping her desperate inhabitants in a vice-grip of hunger and internal strife. The brazen order to torch the great Temple left the once-proud structure a mass of crumbling stone, the gold ornamentation melting into the cracks. Jerusalem was leveled to the ground, resulting in more than a million casualties. But the gruesome task of the legionnaires was not yet complete. The final subjugation of rebellious Judea came more than seven months later, with the taking of Masada, whose defenders committed suicide rather than submit to the conquering Romans. So ended the Great Revolt. Judea was laid waste, her Temple in ruins, her people savaged. The process of rebuilding would take decades, but the people would rebuild — their hopes and dreams if not their Temple. Amid the smoldering embers, mystical hope was badly injured, though by no means extinguished.

Akiva, the Mystical Master

He was a towering giant among those of his own generation, and he was revered in ages to come, honored in his death, even as he ruled Israel in his life. His name was Akiva, and he passed along the mystical impulse from his generation to the next. Like so many mystics, his origins were humble. He was but an uneducated shepherd until the age of forty, whereupon he began a life of study and contemplation. His saintly wife, Rachel, urged him on, though he had to sit in class with small children, learning the alphabet for the first time. After fifteen long years of study, he made an incredible ascent to the throne of authority, as adjudicator and leader of his people.

Akiva became one of a select group of leaders who rose to prominence in the wake of the Temple's destruction. When others despaired of national pride and even of life itself, now that the seat of Israel's pride lay in ruins, the disciples of Rabbi Yohanan ben Zakkai, having ensconced themselves in a town not far from the Mediterranean coast called Yavne, held forth an intoxicating optimism. When the great rabbinical court, the Sanhedrin, moved north from Yavne, to a town in Galilee called Usha, Rabbi Akiva ascended to its helm. It was he who would receive and confirm ordinances and commandments established by prior Sages. It was he who would submit each new and distinctive formulation of laws to the entire assembly.

Akiva was convinced that a Supreme Intelligence had communicated the Holy Scriptures to Israel and that this same Supreme Intelligence had inspired every word of the sacred text. Not only is every word inspired, but every letter of every word has a definitive meaning and value. Even the decorative spurs and assorted "crownlets" adorning the letters have precise significance. The importance of this concept was not lost on subsequent generations of mystics, down to the present day. The story is told that when Moses ascended on high, he found the Holy One Himself bent over the scroll of the Torah, adding "crowns" to the letters. Moses asked, "Master of the Universe, who has given You this extra labor?" God responded, "After some generations a certain individual will rise up. He shall be called Rabbi Akiva ben Yosef. From the crowns of these letters he will derive heaps and heaps of laws." Moses entreated, "Lord of the Universe, show this man to me!" God promptly complied, transporting him — by miracle — to the rabbinical academy of Akiva. There sat Moses, perched on a chair, eight rows back, in Akiva's study hall, not understanding a word! Not comprehending the laws being propounded by the great master, Akiva, Moses felt faint with anguish.

A Sage must prove his mettle before entering "the Orchard"

of the mystics, and for this reason, requirements for entering the sphere of hidden wisdom were trifold. First, the aspiring mystic must be over forty years of age, since (at least presumably) wisdom advances with seniority. In other words, all mystics must be "over the hill." Secondly, one must be married, matrimony being another emblem of maturity (notwithstanding that some moderns consider it an emblem of insanity). Of course, much of the symbolism of Kabbalah, even in its early stages, is overtly sexual, and the unmarried might not be able to comprehend its significance. Thirdly, the initiate must have, in Talmudic terminology, "a full stomach." This has nothing to do with having a rotund midriff, or with participation in the gluttony of Roman banquets. It simply refers to being sated with Jewish Law, the Torah, as with fine food. Rabbi Akiva, hardly a glutton, was precisely such a Sage.

The story is told that when he journeyed to Rome on a political mission, he was entertained by a certain prefect, who threw a lavish banquet in Akiva's honor. The long table was set with every imaginable delicacy, from roast duck to wild boar with an apple in the mouth. In the presence of this assortment of non-kosher food, Akiva only nibbled on a pear and a few other pieces of fruit. The bewildered Roman host then offered the rabbi two of his prettiest servant girls for a night of pleasure; but Akiva in his guest quarters chose to lay perfectly still, sandwiched between the two, without touching either of them. The following morning, the mortified Roman, outraged at the rabbi's ingratitude, demanded an explanation for this odd behavior. Akiva explained that just as he barely touched the banquet the night before, he did not touch the servant girls. They, like the impressive array of food, were considered *trefe* (non-kosher) and, as he put it, "God forbade me." The Roman considered the episode a serious breach of decorum, but it gained Akiva a reputation of unimpeachable rectitude, prerequisite to expounding his own brand of mysticism.

Indeed, there must have been a strong mystical trend in those days, a contagious optimism which, even in the reality of a destroyed Temple and a land laid waste by the Roman Tenth Legion, led its adherents to new heights of ecstasy.

It was in such a milieu that a piece of folklore arose, depicting four of the towering Sages of the day — one of whom was Rabbi Akiva — and their attempts to acquire the esoteric secrets of mysticism. Akiva's stature as a scholar enabled him to counsel his fellows how to approach the Almighty. The throne of God, the mystics held, was composed of "stones of pure marble," and this was the end toward which they all reached. One must take care, Akiva admonished, not to appropriate any of the theories of the pagan Greeks, who held that water was the source of the universe — that the universe was formed from this element. We read in the Talmud this classic passage:

> Four rabbis ascended into the Orchard, Ben Azzai, Ben Zoma, Acher, and Rabbi Akiva. Rabbi Akiva said to them, "When you arrive at the stones of pure marble do not exclaim, 'Water, water!'" Ben Azzai gazed and died; Ben Zoma gazed and became demented; Acher became apostate; Rabbi Akiva departed in peace.[45]

We know very little about this unusual experience or the other Sages involved, who appear as a foil to Akiva. Clearly, Akiva was the leader of this group of initiates into mysticism. The story serves to teach us that Akiva the scholar, Akiva the leader, became, in the course of time, Akiva the mystic. It also serves to show that there are no "intermediaries" (such as water) in the creation, as the Greeks imagined. God alone is the source of all — in terms of later philosophers, the "First Cause" — from whom everything in the universe emanates. This fundamental principle must be the starting point of every mystical journey.

We know equally little about what these journeys entailed, the precise nature of the discipline involved, whether in meditation or trance or frenzied ecstasy. Such details were suppressed and never found their way into the sacred records of the rabbinic age. However, an entire book of early mysticism, called *The Smaller Book of Celestial Palaces (Heikhalot Zutartey)*, takes up the story of Rabbi Akiva's ascension into the heavenly orchard. We can certainly imagine that mysticism must have formed an integral part of Akiva's daily life and experience. More than studying the Scriptures, he and his disciples entered into the text in a personal way, finding a oneness with the Almighty *via* the Hebrew letters on scrolls of parchment.

Son of the Star

Akiva ruled unchallenged, his authority so universally acknowledged that he did not hesitate to enter the forbidden realm of estotericism, the mystical crown of knowledge. In poring over the ancient scrolls of the Bible, Akiva tuned his soul so as to discover the deeper, hidden meanings. In the book of Deuteronomy Moses had declared in a "farewell address" of sorts to his assembled people, "The Lord your God will raise up for you a prophet like me from among you, from your brethren — him you shall heed" (Deut. 18:15). Who was the mysterious person? Who would this "second Moses" be? Surely this was a prefiguring of the Messiah to come. But when would he arrive and in what guise? As Akiva pondered such questions, his eyes fell upon another verse from the biblical text, one of the most mystical and mysterious in the entire sacred canon. In it the prophet called Balaam declares: "I see him, but not now; I behold him, but not nigh: a star shall come forth out of Jacob, and a scepter shall rise out of Israel; it shall crush the forehead of Moab, and break down all the sons of Sheth" (Num. 24:17). Whom does the prophet behold? What, or who, is this "star" who shall come forth from Jacob, the ancient Patriarch of Israel's twelve tribes? Surely, this is another reference to the Messiah, the anointed King, who shall someday appear and bring the people into a glorious redemption.

One day Akiva met his Messiah. He came not from Jerusalem, or from any of the Israelite towns of hallowed memory, Bethlehem or Hebron, Ashkelon or Sepphoris, but from a diminutive, out-of-the-way village called Coseba. He was called Simon, son of Coseba — in Hebrew Shimon ben Coseba. He was a rebel, an anti-Roman agitator, of charismatic personality and a fanatic's determination. The details are sparse; the sources are few from that distant era. But this we know, that when the paths of these two — the illustrious rabbi and the fanatical freedom fighter — crossed, Akiva knew he had found his man. He became convinced, by a glimmer of supernatural insight, that this Simon, from the town of Coseba, was the one of whom the Scriptures had prophesied. He was the Anointed One, the Messiah, and he was destined to sit as king upon the throne of David.

Just as Akiva believed that even the decorative crownlets on the letters of the Torah had a mystical significance, he also believed that such meaning was to be found in people's names. He began to play with the name of his newly found Messiah and decided that the town of Coseba sounds hauntingly like another word — *kochba* — the Aramaic rendering of the Hebrew *kochav* — meaning "star." Akiva then made a fateful link, recalling that "a star (*kochav*) shall come forth out of Jacob." Could this Simon bar Coseba be the embodiment of the messianic "star" from the passage in Genesis? The great rabbi decreed that his Messiah should no longer be called Simon son of Coseba, but Simon bar Kochba — "son of the star."

What happened next was little short of astounding. Simon bar Kochba was a gruff and rugged commander of a Jewish militia. He was hardly a mystic, but in his own way he stole the heart and soul of the nation. He became a militaristic prima donna, a peerless leader who commanded the unquestioned obedience of the whole of Judea. Not only was he the supreme chieftain of a revived Judean army, but a religious firebrand as well. With Rabbi Akiva's blessing, bar Kochba ascended the Temple Mount in Jerusalem, in rich messianic splendor. There, on the most sacred turf in all the world, the new Messiah did the unthinkable. He commanded that a sacrifice be offered, a live animal, in accordance with the commandments of the Torah — only without a Temple. Yes, this was the Temple Mount, but the edifice itself had lain in ruin ever since the fiery destruction of the city, a full generation earlier in the year 70 A.D. The Temple may not have been resurrected, but the hopes and dreams represented by the sacred stones were very much alive in the soul of the people. The mystical tradition declared that only the Messiah was fit to rebuild the Temple. But this man was indeed the Anointed One, chosen by the Eternal for this moment. Surely, one greater than the Temple was here. Under his direction, it would not be the Temple that would precede the sacrifice, but the sacrifice that would precede the Temple! Bar Kochba ordered a special coin struck to commemorate the occasion. It depicted the Temple standing once again on Zion's hill.

On the political horizon things had changed. The Roman emperor, Hadrian, eager to consolidate his realm in a uniformity of peace, issued an edict destined only to rob peace from the empire. He issued a total ban on the Jewish practice of circumcision. It amounted to an open declaration of war against the Jews of Rome, and Hadrian's Jewish subjects would fight it to the hilt. Who better to raise the standard of revolt than the prophesied "star" from Jacob? What better ideal to redeem them than Akiva's mystical messianic vision?

The "Second Wind" of Revolt

There is something about the hidden world of the spirit that cares little about the realities of the corporeal world. Political exigencies and the hard facts of foreign occupation, backed by overwhelming military might, matter hardly at all to those who see a higher plane, who have laid hold of a higher reality still. The time was ripe for a "second wind" of rebellion in the face of ultimate tyranny. The year was 132 A.D. when the Land of Israel exploded in a second great revolt against the masters of the world. As in those earlier days of 66 A.D., when the Essenes and their ecstatic prophecies spurred on the cause of the anti-Roman Zealot party, the revolt of bar Kochba was doomed to failure before it began. The rebels were ill-equipped to take on the might of empire. Judea was still only a buffer zone bordering Parthia, a backwater province on the edge of the desert. If the Judeans had any hope of success, they needed the full support of the Jews of Galilee, to the north. But Galilee had no desire to suffer the wrath of Rome again, so Judea would have to go it alone.

The rebels scored some early victories, to be sure. The Roman Twenty-second Legion poured into the land from Egypt, only to be utterly wiped out. But the desperate rebels were no match for the well trained, well-armored, red-plumed legionnaires who filled the Roman ranks. Within three years it would all be over. Swooping down on little Judea, the legions gave no quarter to the beleaguered bar Kochba. The Jewish general deposited his frantic correspondences in a cave along the western shore of the Dead Sea, where they would be discovered nineteen centuries later, along with the remains of the ancient Essene library, known collectively as the Dead Sea Scrolls. The last stand of the freedom fighters took place at a town in central Judea called Beitar. The rebels fought bravely to the end, only to be overwhelmed in a sea of blood. Among the dead was Simon, son of Coseba — Simon bar Kochba. The Roman victory was purchased at horrific cost. Sometimes what is recounted in the historical record is not as important as what is not recounted. In this case, the carnage was so awful that the emperor Hadrian, in reporting back to the Senate, deleted the usual salutation, "I trust you and your children are well; I and my legions are well." Clearly, though victorious, the troops were not well. So ended the final hope for messianic deliverance from Rome, intensely fueled by the earliest layers of Kabbalah.

Beyond the fate of bar Kochba, the enduring memory from this sad era relates to the fate of his chief adherent, Rabbi Akiva. The venerable Sage survived the din of battle, only to be captured by his Roman enemies. Determined to make an example of this spiritual icon, the Romans stretched out his body on the rack and proceeded to tear off his flesh with metal tongs. In his final agony, Akiva did not flinch with pain, nor succumb to the temptation to curse his torturers. With all courage, he began chanting the words of the supreme declaration of his faith, the *Sh'ma*: "Hear, O Israel, the Lord our God is One!" The executioner, astounded at such composure, queried, "Are you a sorcerer?" But Akiva was only a mystic, gratified at the opportunity to display his love for the Almighty by his glorious martyrdom. With "Hear, O Israel" on his lips, Akiva gave up his spirit, entered "the Orchard" once gain, to return to this world no more. A mystical legend relates that at the moment of his death a voice issued forth from the heavens, in the hearing of all, announcing, "Happy are you, Rabbi Akiva, that your soul went out with that word *'One!'* "[46]

A generation of Judea's finest scholars perished in the conflict. Among the Sages of that generation, some of whom endeavored to scale the mystical heights to the throne of God, few survived the war's fury and its dreadful aftermath. The Romans wrapped one scholar in the very scrolls from which he had studied and taught, then set him on fire, as a human torch. They pierced another through, like a sieve. They decapitated yet another. But Akiva's martyrdom was the profoundest of all. With his passing, life in Judea would never be the same. The standard of independence would never more be raised aloft. Never again would the mystical impulse so captivate Judea's population as to prompt a drive toward liberation from their Roman overlords. But the impulse itself would not die; it would only seek incarnation in other ways.

What of the Romans?

Sages came and went, living out their lives under the yoke of foreign oppressors. Two centuries of Roman rule had left a horrific legacy. The province of Judea, now called Palestine, had become little more than a desolate wasteland. The Jewish subjects along the eastern stretches of the Mediterranean had launched not one, but two unsuccessful revolts against the Roman overlords. The response of the metropolis on the Tiber had been swift and furious. The city of Jerusalem was razed to the ground, the great Temple of Solomon, fabulously enlarged by King Herod the Great, reduced to a blackened ruin. Groups of forlorn ascetics, called "Mourners of Zion," wandered through the land, despairing of life itself.

Attempts were made to keep the flame of learning alive. Academies of study had cropped up over the decades, in Yavne, near the coast, in Tiberias, along the shore of the Sea of Galilee, and in Sepphoris to the north. But in time it became increasingly clear that if any hope were left at all, it lay elsewhere. For many the road to a new life led east, to Babylonia and the great academies along the Euphrates River, Sura and Pumbeditha. For those who remained in the land of Israel, life became almost unbearable. In this crucible the next layer of Kabbalah was born.

The Opti-Mystic Sages
of the Talmud

F aith is an extraordinary commodity. It pays no homage to
cruel reality; it does not flinch in the face of hardship,
misfortune, and suffering. Mysticism, as a fleshly incarnation of faith itself, is ultimately optimistic. It looks forward,
upward, and beyond, to a better, brighter realm. As the second
century advanced to the third, and as the Jews of Palestine
began their endlessly steady trek eastward to Babylonia, it was
this optimism that charged and energized them. Never mind
that the Temple was destroyed, that no spiritual house stood on
the Temple Mount. A new age was dawning. It conceived of an
idealized kingdom, where the Temple stood and where the
mystical presence of God — the *Shechinah* — dwelled richly
among the people. The Sages of a new generation declared,
"When Israel went into exile, the *Shechinah* went with them."

It is difficult to say exactly when the "Talmudic age," as the
ensuing era came to be known, actually began, because the rabbis quoted in this literature lived as far back as the first few centuries B.C. Moreover, the sayings of the rabbis, such as the universally revered Hillel the Elder, were, by official decree, not to
be written down but committed to memory. In a "reversal" of
sorts of the modern science fiction tale, *Farenheit 451*, in which
the books of the world are committed to memory by a devoted band of disciples, lest they be forgotten, the rabbis of old

finally wrote down the teachings of the Sages, for fear they would be forgotten.

It fell to the early rabbinic academies, at Yavne near the Mediterranean coast, Tiberias on the Sea of Galilee, and Sura and Pumbeditha in faraway Babylonia, to collect and edit the assorted maxims of the Sages. It was a process that went on for generations, through the fifth century A.D., in the great halls of study extending from Palestine eastward, to the Tigris and Euphrates Rivers. A student of the sacred text would stand and recite a passage from an earlier Sage by memory. Another would expand and elaborate on the saying quoted, adding more detail, which in turn would be elaborated on, in what evolved into a spirited debate over each and every point of Law. The work they began to assemble was a compendium of wisdom and lore unlike any other. It was rambling and chaotic, but it embodied a veritable sea of folklore, in addition to innumerable ordinances and regulations — many relating directly to the Temple that was no longer standing. It was encyclopedic in nature, consisting of sixty-three separate tractates, together known as the Talmud.[47]

The editors of this rabbinical sea of commentary were officially anti-mystical, possessed as they were by a strong rationalism. By the time the Talmud was officially set down in print, around 500 A.D., its compilers frowned on the ecstatic flights of fancy of many of their forefathers. Consequently, the mystical tones of the Talmudic age were suppressed, the lore of early Kabbalah de-emphasized. But the thread of mysticism, while it is sometimes lost in the greater tapestry of Jewish life, never totally disappears. In fact many of the teachings of early Kabbalah did find their way into the Talmud, surviving in some of its more obscure and esoteric passages. Especially notable are two distinct branches of study, known as "The Works of Creation" (*Ma-aseh Beresheet*) and "The Works of the Chariot" (*Ma-aseh Merkavah*). The particulars of these inquiries were only revealed in the confines of private study sessions. Only the most elite of scholars and disciples were allowed to partake of these secrets, and they were only to be communicated on a one-on-one basis. The collected body of Talmudic Kabbalah was thus passed from Sage to Sage.

Many of the Sages of the Talmudic age, from the second through the sixth centuries, were in fact "opti-mystic" leaders of their wandering people, and a close look at the pages of the Talmud will reveal — despite later editing — the subtle splendor of their lives.

Twelve Years in a Cave . . .

Early in the second century A.D., at the very beginnings of the great migration eastward, another miracle-working rabbi appeared on the scene, treading as it were in the footsteps of Rabbi Akiva. His name was Simeon ben Yokhai. The most famous story about Rabbi Simeon is recorded in the Talmud. We are told that Rabbi Judah and his compatriots were sitting together, when Rabbi Simeon shamed the ruling Roman authorities:

> Whatever they have done was only for their own benefit! They made streets in order to set harlots in them; baths in order to enjoy themselves in them; bridges in order to collect tolls from those who cross them.

The Romans, upon hearing these remarks, decreed death for Simeon. The faithful rabbi and his son hid in the synagogue for safety, while his wife brought them bread and water. But Simeon declared, "It may be that the Romans will torture her and she will expose us." At this, they hid themselves in a cave. The Talmud recounts:

A miracle occurred, and a carob tree and a well of water were created for them. . . . Thus they dwelt twelve years in the cave. Then Elijah the Prophet came and stood at the entrance to the cave and exclaimed, "Who will inform ben Yokhai that the emperor is dead and his decree annulled?" Then they left the cave.[48]

The story of Rabbi Simeon's death adds to his authority all the more. We are told that between the feasts of Passover and Shavuot (Pentecost in Greek), the disciples of the illustrious Rabbi Akiva — 24,000 in number — were killed by a devastating plague, because they did not sufficiently honor one another. Suddenly, however, the plague ceased, on the very day that Simeon ben Yokhai died. To this day in Israel, those of kabbalistic bent commemorate the death of Rabbi Simeon, making procession to his burial place in the town of Meron (near the mystical city of Safed). Amid songs, dances, and the lighting of bonfires, an ancient liturgical hymn is chanted: Bar Yokhai Ashreikha . . . "Blessed are you, ben Yokhai . . ." Kabbalah, it seems, is still alive and well in Israel.

Rabbi Eliezer and the Study House Walls

The Talmudic age well illustrates how Kabbalah became a focal point of debate among the rabbinic Sages. What indeed is the role of mysticism in developing a healthy spiritual life? What is the ground of truth? What is the basis for knowledge . . . for law. . . for human conduct? Is supernatural revelation sufficient? Or are reason and logic alone the foundation of ethics and morality?

The story is told of Rabbi Eliezer, who entered into a fierce debate over a legal issue.[49] He propounded all manner of proofs before his compatriots, who nonetheless remained adamantly opposed to his reasoning. What does a rabbinic Sage do when reason fails? In this case Rabbi Eliezer turned to the secrets of

Kabbalah. He thundered, "If the law is according to my view, let this carob tree prove it." Amazingly, so the story goes, the carob tree uprooted itself and moved itself a distance of a hundred cubits. But for Rabbi Eliezer's rational friends, no such miracle was sufficient to establish a matter of law. Rabbi Eliezer then declared, "If the law is according to my view, may this water channel prove it." By another miracle, the flow of water in the nearby aqueduct reversed itself, flowing backward. This event, however, left the rabbi's friends equally unsympathetic. Next, Rabbi Eliezer announced, "If the law is according to my view, let the walls of this House of Study prove it." Suddenly, the Study House began to quake and tremble, the walls themselves tottering inward, to the point of collapse. Rabbi Joshua, standing nearby, spoke directly to the unstable walls, rebuking them for heeding the argument of bickering rabbis: "If students of the Torah contend with one another on a point of law, what has it to do with you?" The imperiled walls did not cave in, as if heeding Rabbi Joshua's rebuke. They did not, however, straighten themselves, due to Rabbi Eliezer's command. For this reason, Talmudic mythology explains, the walls of the Study House are still precariously slanted.

The Talmud goes on to explain that a divine voice finally issued from on high, saying, "What do you have against Rabbi Eliezer? The legal decision is *always* according to his view." God Himself, it seems, took sides, favoring one rabbi over another.

Rabbi Joshua, undaunted even by a voice from heaven, still remained unconvinced. Another compatriot, Rabbi Jeremiah, then chimed in, "We pay no attention to a divine voice!"[50] The editors of the Talmud were insisting, via the rabbinical friends of Rabbi Eliezer, that reason, not mysticism, is the final arbiter of the meaning of Scripture.

Did the miraculous events described actually happen? Did the walls of the Study House really start to lean? The point of the story may well be applicable to all mystical experience, summarized in the old adage: For those who disbelieve, no proof is sufficient; for those who believe, no proof is necessary.

The Eyes of Satan

Not all Kabbalists of the Talmudic age were eminent rabbis. There are records of ordinary individuals who "entered the Orchard," trafficking in the supernatural realm. And this experience frequently involved "spiritual warfare" with the forces of wickedness. The story is told of a man named Pelimo who was accustomed to doing battle with Satan. He would be heard, on a daily basis, to be shouting, "An arrow in the eyes of Satan," which clearly perturbed the spirits of wickedness.

On one occasion, on the Day of Atonement, Satan took on the form of a beggar and came knocking at his front door. Pelimo, moved with compassion, gave the stranger a loaf of bread. But the beggar (who was really Satan), asked, "On such a day as this, when all people are in their homes, am I to remain outside?" Pelimo then invited him in, only to be asked why, on this of all days, he should be alone. Pelimo then bade him sit down with his family. When Pelimo told the man, who was covered with boils and ulcers, to sit down properly, his devilish guest demanded a cup. When the cup was offered, the man spat phlegm into it, to be rebuked sternly by Pelimo for his lack of decorum. At this point, the stranger fell down, feigning death.

Suddenly, a series of demonic voices were heard to cry out from somewhere in the room, "Pelimo has killed a man! Pelimo has killed a man!" In blind terror, Pelimo, the spiritual warrior, bolted to the closet, where he hid himself behind the door. The stranger, realizing how shaken his host was, picked himself up from his pretense of death, rushed over to Pelimo's hiding place, and revealed his satanic identity as well as the purpose of his visit. "Why do you use that expression, 'An arrow in the eyes of Satan'?" the stranger demanded. The still-cowering Pelimo answered the question with another question.

"What, then, should I say?"

"Say this," replied the stranger. "May the All-Merciful rebuke Satan."[51] At this we are reminded of the words of the ancient prophet Zechariah, "The Lord rebuke you, O Satan! The Lord who has chosen Jerusalem rebuke you!" (Zech. 3:2). There is also "kabbalistic" advice of the New Testament book of Jude, "But when the archangel Michael, contending with the devil, disputed about the body of Moses, he did not presume to pronounce a reviling judgment upon him, but said, 'The Lord rebuke you'" (Jude 1:9). In other words one should not become overly arrogant in asserting one's spiritual prowess, nor one's kabbalistic authority over the powers of darkness.

Bear in mind, the general teaching of the Talmud is that "Satan, the Evil Inclination, and the Angel of Death are all one."[52] The word *satan* means in Hebrew simply "adversary," and can be applied to any contrary force which battles against humankind, be it angelic, animal, or human. The source of evil is perceived as a force operating within every human being, rather than a distinct, separate power from without. But who, in reality, is the mysterious stranger in the story of Pelimo? Is he really "Satan," Dark Lord of the underworld? Or is he merely the personification of the evil characteristics (the "evil inclination") that lurk in everyone — over which no one should arrogantly presume to hold dominion? Pelimo, it seems, had come face to face with himself. The world of Kabbalah is a world full of demons and mysterious supernatural forces. One should be careful, therefore, in every sentence uttered in doing spiritual battle. As Pelimo found out the hard way, there is no room for pride.

The Exorcists and "Practical Kabbalah"

The age of the Talmud had relatively little to say about Satan. The Sages believed, after all, that God is King, and they did not want to ascribe too much power to any entity aside from God. Demons, however, were another matter, and the mystical folklore of the age was replete with them. Demons, far from being "anti-Gods," were perceived as nuisances, who needed to be brushed aside and occasionally swatted like flies. These evil spirits occasionally pounce upon human beings as well as beasts, inducing manias and madnesses. How did demons come about? Talmudic folklore, unlike the earlier *Merkavah* mysticism of the Apocrypha, makes no reference to the idea of fallen angels. One account in the Talmud depicts the demons as having been created by God, like all other human souls. Before He could create their bodies, however, the Sabbath came, and God ceased His creative work. As a result, they never achieved corporeal reality, but became disembodied souls, making their way across the universe.

Heading up the hierarchy of evil spirits, according to Talmudic lore, is "the wicked angel Samael, the chief of all the Satans."[53] As chief among female demons, the Talmud names a certain Lilith, demon of the night, whose name is related to the Hebrew word for night, *lailah*. The Talmud forbids a man to sleep alone at home, inasmuch as he might be apprehended by the long-haired Lilith.[54] Much later in kabbalistic lore, this same female demon came to be regarded as a child-snatcher, who needed to be warded off by incantations and amulets. The use of such magic, from charms to nullify the evil eye, to pictures on walls, to special formulations of blessings, is what came to be called "Practical Kabbalah," and it grew over the centuries into a mystical science.

The Talmud relates a story of a certain scholar who sets off to relieve himself by a group of caper trees. He is met by a female demon, whereupon he flees. The demon chases after him, only to become entangled in a palm tree. In the end the palm withers and the female demon bursts.

In another incident the watchman of a certain town happens to stand not far from a sorb bush — a plant species, each plant of which was known to be the habitat of sixty demons. Without warning, he is attacked by all sixty demonic spirits of that particular sorb bush. The watchman quickly finds a rabbi, to write him an amulet against the demons. However, the uninformed rabbi is unaware that a sorb bush is inhabited by sixty demons, and he writes an amulet against only one demon. At this point the demons begin audibly mocking the rabbi, singing, "This person's turban is like that of a rabbinic scholar, but we have proved that he does not know how to pronounce a benediction!" Finally, a rabbi comes along who realizes that indeed sixty demonic spirits inhabit a sorb bush. This rabbi writes an amulet against all sixty demons, whereupon they are heard to say audibly, "Clear out from here!"[55]

The Talmud also depicts evil spirits as especially active in locales where water is present. One Talmudic rabbi tells of a certain Abba Jose of Tzaytor, who chose to sit by a village well while studying. Suddenly, a demonic spirit who lived there materialized in front of him.

The spirit said, "You know how many years I have resided here, and yet you come out and your wives in the evening and at the new moon, but you have not been harmed. You should be informed, however, that a certain evil spirit which will do injury to human beings desires to take up its abode here."

"What shall we do?" Abba Jose inquired.

The spirit responded, "Go and warn the inhabitants of the place and say to them, 'Whoever has a hoe or spade or shovel should come here tomorrow at dawn and watch the surface of the water.' When they notice a ripple on the water, they should beat it with their iron implements and exclaim, 'The victory is ours!' They must not depart until they see a clot of blood on the water's surface."

Abba Jose did as the spirit warned him. He went out and raised an alarm about the impending danger and about what the townsfolk needed to do in response. At dawn the next day they were out in force, hauling their iron implements with them. At once they began beating them on the first ripples they observed, shouting, "The victory is ours! The victory is ours!" Indeed, the Talmud reports, a clot of blood was observed on the surface of the water, and they knew the demon had been killed.[56] In this and many other examples of Practical Kabbalah, Talmudic folklore emphasized the working of supernatural forces in the physical world. On the other hand, however, it demystified those very forces, depicting them as unspectacular nuisances which could be driven away by a word, an amulet, or the ultimate power of the Torah itself.

Somewhere along the line, an entire book of Practical Kabbalah was composed. Called the *Book of Secrets* (*Sefer ha-Razim*), it is a basic handbook and manual for how effectively to use potions, prayers, spells, and conjurations. Though rationally oriented rabbis have, through the centuries, felt somewhat embarrassed by its very existence, it nonetheless represents an increasingly serious trend in mystical thought and practice.

"This Too Is for Good"

Kabbalah in the Talmudic age was hardly just an exercise in esoteric trivia. On the contrary its practice deeply enhanced the quality of the Sages' lives, turning tragedy into triumph. Sometimes the "opti-mystical" impulse was responsible for incredible serenity and peace, even in the face of overwhelming adversity. A case in point is the life of a Sage named Nahum, from the town of Gimzo. He came to be called, however, "The

Man of Gamzo," which means in Hebrew "this too." This is because, whatever befell him in life, he had a habit of saying, "This too is for good." A story is told to explain further this particular designation. It seems that the rabbis came to a decision to placate the emperor by sending a gift. A discussion arose over who should be the one to send it. In the end they decided, "Let us send it through Nahum, the man of Gamzo, because he is used to miracles happening to him." Apparently the Man of Gamzo was well acquainted with the realm of Kabbalah.

And so, the leaders of the community purchased an exquisite gift, placing it in a leather bag. As Nahum traveled on his journey, he paused to spend an evening at an inn. While he slept, some of the occupants of the inn came upon his bag, pilfered from it the gift for the emperor, and filled it instead with dust. Unaware that he had been robbed, the Man of Gamzo traveled on, reaching his destination and presenting the bag to the emperor. Rather than the expected delight, the emperor scowled in anger when he peered into a bag filled with dust. "The Jews are making a laughing stock of me!" he sneered. Thereupon he ordered that Nahum the Man of Gamzo should be taken out and executed. But Nahum was a Sage of mystical faith, and, bearing out the name by which he was called, he declared, "This too is for good!"

This is when the miracle transpired. None other than the prophet Elijah materialized, in the guise of one of the emperor's attendants. He begged the emperor to reconsider, saying, "Perhaps this dust is part of the dust of their Patriarch Abraham. Whenever he threw some of it at his enemies, it turned into swords, and when he threw stubble it turned into arrows." Intrigued by such an explanation, the emperor ordered that this "mystery dust" be tried in battle against a certain province which had heretofore eluded conquest. To the amazement of all, the enemy army was defeated and the province subdued. In overwhelming gratitude, the emperor took his newly honored guest, Nahum, to the imperial treasury and filled his empty bag with all manner of jewels and pearls. Never before had a guest of the emperor been so richly honored and rewarded. Indeed, as Nahum had proclaimed, "This too is for good!"

Returning homeward, the Man of Gamzo stopped for the night at the same inn where he had lodged before, when his original gift was purloined. The occupants now queried, "What did you take to the emperor that such great respect has been shown to you?"

"I only took what I carried away from here," Nahum replied.

The astonished thieves thereupon decided to send some of the same dust to the emperor, imagining that they too would be honored in like manner. This time, however, the dust proved of no avail when hurled against the enemies of the emperor. Rather than receiving honor and riches, the dishonorable occupants of the inn were rounded up and executed. Miracles, it seems, happen only for those worthy of them. Moreover, when entering "the Orchard of Kabbalah," one's frame of mind is not the chief thing; it is the only thing. To be able to say "This too is for good" is the pinnacle of personal growth, and in this regard the Man of Gamzo was a true "optimystic."[57]

Rabbi Joshua and Heaven's Gate

One more mystic of the Talmudic age was Rabbi Joshua ben Levi, who was renowned also as a towering leader and teacher of the Law during the third century of the common era. The Talmud tells us that, aside from being a consummate politician, journeying to Rome itself on behalf of his people, he was especially revered for his mastery of *Aggadah*, the rich folklore of his people, full of tales of miracles and wonders. Confident of divine protection, he would make frequent visits to the sick, with little regard for his own health or fear of contracting infectious diseases. Many wondrous happenings are recorded with regard to Rabbi Joshua, so many that the scholar of folklore became part of the folklore himself. It was while in Rome that the venerated Sage encountered a statue shrouded in drapery to protect it from the cold, while a poor beggar sat nearby, dressed in tattered rags. It is to this city, the "capital of the world," declared Rabbi Joshua, that the Messiah shall come! Indeed, the Messiah must surely be here already, disguised as a lowly servant among the beggars and the cripples who wander the narrow lanes of the vast city. When the moment is right, he shall make himself known and bring about the redemption of all Israel. The teaching is clear. Do not expect the Messiah to be born of privilege, pomp, and status. The Messiah is to be revealed in humility, but will deliver in power and glory.

Such revelations could not be Rabbi Joshua's own invention. It was said that he held intimate and arcane conversations with the prophet Elijah, who revealed to him the secrets of the ages. It was said that even the powers of death had to surrender before the spiritual might of Rabbi Joshua. Once the rabbi wrestled personally with the Angel of Death, purloining his sword and ascending to heaven. He calibrated the length and breadth of the heavens. He measured the scope of Paradise and Gehenna as well. He passed his findings down to Rabbi Gamaliel, via the Angel of Destruction, whose comings and goings he personally commanded.

We know little more about the life of Rabbi Joshua, except he was said to be the author of a work which was not printed until the Middle Ages — *Yalkut Shimeoni* — a vivid description of heaven itself, presumably the product of his own supernatural experiences. What is Paradise like? According to Rabbi Joshua, there are two ruby gates, guarded by sixty hosts of ministering angels. Their faces shine like the firmament. Whenever a new righteous saint ascends to this place, the angels exchange the person's burial clothing for eight different robes, woven from the clouds of glory. Then they crown the new arrival with two glorious crowns, one crafted of pearls and assorted gemstones, the other of purest gold.

Each saint is escorted to a resplendent chamber, assigned according the degree of honor gained during that person's lifetime. Inside each chamber is a table bearing piles of pearls and gemstones, while a group of sixty angels serve each saint. For them there is no night, only the resplendent glory of endless day.

Four streams rush forth from this holy place, reminiscent of the Bible's description of the Garden of Eden. But in this mystical Paradise the streams do not run with water. One flows with milk, a second with wine, a third with balsam, and a forth with the sweetest honey. In the exact center of all is the Tree of Life, with branches overspreading the whole of Paradise. On its leafy boughs grow five hundred thousand different varieties of fruits. In this incredible vision, Paradise Lost becomes Paradise Regained.

However Rabbi Joshua described the visions of glory he beheld, his teaching about what people will be doing in the hereafter is striking, even for modern Kabbalists. Paradise is not a place for languid ease and eternal quietude, he declared. "The Holy One . . . will give each righteous person three hundred and ten worlds as an inheritance."[58] The more moderns learn about theories of parallel universes, the more we wonder if Rabbi Joshua might just be right.

Creation "By the Book"

Somewhere between the third and sixth centuries A.D., a curious text called the *Book of Creation* (the *Sefer Yetzirah*) surfaced. As with so many works of Kabbalah, the author is anonymous. However, the claim was made that none other than the biblical Patriarch Abraham wrote the *Book of Creation*. Of course this claim is ridiculous, since Abraham lived some two thousand years before the first copies of the *Book of Creation* appeared. But making such a claim certainly lent authority to the book, and all who believed the claim took its ideas much more seriously. We certainly know that the *Sefer Yetzirah* was an early work, since references to it appear scattered across other rabbinic literature of a very early date. A prominent biblical scholar concluded, "So ancient is this book that its origins are no longer accessible to historians."[59] Whoever the author was, he writes in polished Hebrew, in a style common to the 200s A.D. His theme centers on the "paths of wisdom," the "heavenly books," and the multiple names of Deity:

> With thirty-two wondrous paths of wisdom He engraved: Yah, YHWH, Hosts, God of Israel, Living God and Eternal King, El Shaddai, Merciful and Gracious, High and Exalted, Eternally Dwelling, of High and Holy Name, Who created His universe with thirty-two books, with number, and text [or "book"], and communication [or "story"].[60]

The wording is obscure, invariably raising more questions than it answers. What, precisely, are the thirty-two wondrous paths? What's so special about the number thirty-two? What is the significance and meaning of all the names of God? Why the thirty-two books? What do *number, book,* and *story* mean? Of course the nature of Kabbalah is that it leaves one wondering. It stretches the imagination and challenges the intellect. While the word *story* implies a narration, from storyteller to hearer, the word *communication* suggests a two-way relationship — between God and human beings. The Kabbalists believed that God has communicated with us through creation itself.[61]

When the *Book of Creation* says "wondrous" it means unknowable through the intellect alone. Reason and rationality cannot alone explain God or God's universe. Indeed, there has always existed a tension between "faith" and "reason," which goes all the way back to the ancient Greeks. Aristotle tried to evaluate the universe on the basis of what can be observed by the senses, and all of modern science is based on this principle. Yet, paradoxically, science in its cold calculation has in the last decades of the twentieth century come face to face with the unknowable; and it sounds increasingly like the science of Kabbalah.

Perhaps the greatest insight to be gleaned from the *Book of Creation* is that multiple paths are delineated, rather than only one. There is something eclectic about Kabbalah, resonant with a healthy pluralism. Ideas despised by "fundamentalists" are proclaimed by Kabbalah — there are many paths to truth. The paths are like threads in the great tapestry which Jews called the Torah. The Torah is God's communication, but more importantly, His "communion," with human beings.

Why thirty-two? Of course, a healthy pluralism demands more than a single explanation for any particular tradition, and the thirty-two paths of wisdom is a case in point. As it happens, the first letter in the Torah (the first letter of the book of Genesis) is the Hebrew letter *Bet* (ב), which carries the numerical value of 2. (Bear in mind that all Hebrew letters carry a numerical value.) The last letter in the Torah (at the end of the book of Deuteronomy) is the letter *Lamed* (ל), which carries a numerical value of 30. Added together, we have the number 32 — the number of paths of wisdom.

This, however, is only one explanation. Interestingly, the Hebrew name for God (*Elohim*) figures thirty-two times in the six-day creation account of Genesis 1. Another explanation involves the fact that there are twenty-two letters in the Hebrew alphabet. Add to that the number ten, for the ten distinct names of God listed in the passage, and we arrive at thirty-two paths.

Consider also that the numerical value of the Hebrew word for *path* (*netiv*) is 462. Then consider that when each of the twenty-two letters of the Hebrew alphabet is combined with all the other letters, the resultant possible combinations are 22 x 21 = 462. Such is the intricacy of the art of Kabbalah.

The Ten "Spheres"

Still another explanation involves the idea that there are ten "spheres" of the physical universe, to which the twenty-two letters of the alphabet are added.

Bear in mind that in early Kabbalah, two distinct "systems" of thought emerged, an early layer gradually yielding to a second, more intricate layer. The earliest system, the traces of which we find in ancient texts from Ezekiel to the Dead Sea Scrolls, is called the *Heikhalot* tradition, which means "palaces" and has to do with the abode of God — the palaces which surround the Throne of Glory. This is the heart of *Merkavah*, the chariot-throne on high. The subsequent system, which would ultimately evolve into full-blown Kabbalah, is called the *Sefirot* tradition, named for the "spheres" which emanate from the center of the universe and represent physical creation. The *Book of Creation* represents perhaps the earliest formulation of the system of *Sefirot*. Across these *Sefirot* — spheres — are "emanations" of the divine, which course through every aspect of the created world. In Kabbalah the *Sefirot* are often depicted pictorially, as circles within circles, with the boundless essence of God at the center. Like layers of an onion, the ten spheres symbolize not only God's work in creation, but the way God has interacted with the creation down to the present day. Significantly, the expression "God said" appears exactly ten times in the creation account, corresponding with the ten *Sefirot*.

The complex word plays in Hebrew are of course lost on modern westerners; but consider the fact that the root which lay behind the words *number*, *book*, and *story* is *sefer* — the very root of the word *Sefirot*. Thus, from its first sentence, the *Book of Creation* is teaching, in all of its intricacies, the concept of the heavenly spheres. In all of these enigmatic formulations, the advice of the Kabbalists was simple: There are many threads, many paths which weave through divine revelation. Do not be locked into one. Be eclectic; seek out all of them!

A corollary of the multiple paths are the multiple names of the Deity mentioned in the passage — a hallmark of kabbalistic thought. There is a deep sophistication here. God cannot be put in a box, nor can His paths be summarized in just a single thread. Each name represents another aspect of who God is and how He acts in the universe.

Bear in mind that the *Sefirot* tradition, outlined in the *Book of Creation*, was, when first set down, very much secondary to the main emphasis of *Merkavah* — the *Heikhalot* tradition of the palaces. But over time the heavenly *Sefirot* would come front and center, becoming the main focus of Kabbalah.

The second paragraph of the *Book of Creation* gets more specific about the *Sefirot* and the letters of creation: "Ten 'spheres' of nothing, and twenty-two letters of foundation, three mothers and seven doubles and twelve singles."[62]

What, precisely, are these spheres — the *Sefirot* — formulated by the *Book of Creation* — and how can they be "of nothing"? Bear in mind, the ten spheres detailed here are not related to the "seven heavens" described above, and to which the apostle Paul apparently alludes. The kabbalistic *Sefirot* are not the *abode* of God and the angels, but a metaphysical "schema" for understanding God's relationship with the material world. They are aspects of God; they are spiritual "emanations" into the physical universe.

Of course each of the *Sefirot* has a Hebrew name.[63] Arranged from highest to lowest, they are:

- "CROWN" — *KETER* — REPRESENTING GOD'S WILL (ALSO CALLED "ELEVATED HEIGHT" — *ROM MA'ALAH*).

At the center of the universe is God's unfathomable Will. The mind of God is by nature totally beyond human beings to comprehend. It is ultimate mystery and may never be grasped by finite creatures such as ourselves. An investigator may probe only so far into the origin of the universe and the mind of God. Beyond this boundary one may not go, for *Keter* is the real of ultimate divine power.

Within "Crown" there is found no individuality, no differentiation, no "thingness." "Crown" is therefore not only eternal; it is co-eternal with what Kabbalists called the *Ain Sof* — another euphemism for God's divine name, meaning "He who has no end."

Modern science refers to a point in the universe where the

laws of physics themselves break down and no longer apply. Such a point is called a "black hole." What we have in *Keter* seems an ancient depiction something similar to a concept on the cutting edge of modern astrophysics.

Furthermore, we seem to have a mystical model for the scientific principle that a degree of uncertainty is built into the very heart of the universe. On a spiritual level, there are those individuals who believe they have certain knowledge of everything, whose rigid opinions are based on this certainty. A failure to acknowledge the uncertainty in everything has led to insidious manifestations of hatred and bigotry throughout history. Kabbalah wisely recognizes a "sphere" at the center of everything, called "Crown," which we cannot fully know.

- "WISDOM" — *KHOKHMAH* — THE BEGINNING OF CONCEPTUALIZATION.

At this point the mind may begin to formulate basic notions, perceptions, ideas, and thoughts about God and His universe. Wisdom is beyond the intellectual process; it involves things that are "conceived," things that are "perceived," deeply in the soul. Wisdom is the domain of angelic power.

There is a point where intellectual process will take us only so far, and after which we must come to rely on something higher, something greater than ourselves. A popular modern prayer states it well: "God, grant me the serenity to accept the things I cannot change, the courage to change the things I can, and the *wisdom* to know the difference."

- "UNDERSTANDING" — *BINAH* — THE POINT AND BORDER TO WHICH THE WORLD OF INTELLIGENCE EXTENDS.

This is the realm of rational thought, directly connected with our cranial capacity, our gray matter. Before one can attain true "Wisdom," one must first acquire "Understanding" on a rational level. Understanding involves learning, and learning implies study, discipline, and dedication. This sphere is also the domain of prophetic power. In an age dominated by whatever feels good and a "quick fix" approach to life, the concept of understanding gained through the discipline of study and research is all but ignored. But the Kabbalists recognized that mystical experience without the anchor of intelligence could leave one adrift in a sea of confusion.

- "LOVINGKINDNESS" — *HESED* — FROM WHICH THE ANCIENT HASIDICS DERIVED THEIR NAME.

The psalmist declares of God: "Thy lovingkindness [*hesed*] is better than life" (Ps. 63:3 NAS). This is the level on which divine goodness penetrates into the present world order. It is the translation of knowledge and understanding to the realm of human need. It is also the domain of compassionate power.

It is, of course, one thing to learn about a world in need, all around us — of starving children, famine, pestilence, and disease. It is quite another to respond to the suffering we witness, with our gifts of charity and in man-hours donated. "Lovingkindness" is the translation of knowledge to action, to make a concrete difference for our planet.

- "JUDGMENT"— *DIN*, "FEAR"— *PAKHAD*, OR "POWER"— *GEVURAH* ... AS IN THE ADMONITION, "THE FEAR OF THE LORD IS THE BEGINNING OF WISDOM" (PROV. 9:10).

Kabbalistically, we have the idea that the awe of God is prerequisite to gaining true insight into spiritual things. There has always been a tension between human intellect, striving under its own motivation, and "enlightened" intellect, submitted to the great revelation at Sinai. Autonomous intellect leads to self-realization; the awe of God leads to the higher levels of revealed wisdom. This is the realm of judgmental power — passing judgment with the fear of His strength.

The Kabbalists had the idea that there might arise a situation of imbalance, in which too much "Lovingkindness" (*Hesed*) might emanate into the universe. This would result in criminals going free or tyrants unchallenged. On the other hand, if too much "Judgment" (*Din*) were to emanate, the innocent might be punished or people suffer inordinately.

- "BEAUTY" — *TIFERET* — THE POINT AND BORDER TO WHICH THE WORLD OF THE SOUL EXTENDS.

From that which is invisible and subjective we move to that which is visibly seen and objectively evidenced in the world. It is the realm of the aesthetic, things which adorn the physical creation. In this realm there is "Compassion" (*Hesed*), in "Fear" (*Pakhad*), upon the lower worlds.

God, it seems, has two faces, one of judgment, the other of compassion. While these characteristics appear as mutually contradictory, they are in fact meant to be in balance, in a divine coexistence. When the opposing forces in the universe are maintained in perfect balance, all inequities and injustices are avoided. There is true "Beauty" in the world.

- "VICTORY" — *NETZAKH* — ALSO CALLED "ETERNITY."

The expression of beauty in the material world must be accompanied by action among those who labor together with God in continuing the works of creation. Creation did not cease after six days. There was merely a rest, a Sabbath, after which God formed a partnership with humanity to continue creation, eternally. In this realm there is a nurturing power, which strengthens the vegetative soul.

Whenever a person performs a positive commandment, whenever an individual does something truly "good," that person has entered the realm of "Victory." There is power for goodness here, redemptive power to change the world.

- "SPLENDOR" — *HOD* — ALSO CALLED "MAJESTY."

Divine magnificence has a way of unsettling those who are complacent. Thus, God works in the world not only to display His might and His wonders, but in so doing to shake complacent souls to their foundation. Often it is weakness that most stirs those enmeshed in spiritual slumber. This is the domain of power which weakens and enfeebles the vegetative soul.

Even in weakness, when an individual feels most vulnerable, most fragile, even subject to collapse, this is precisely the point when God's majesty is most often evidenced. Our pain is therefore not the problem we make it out to be. It is a hammer blow, to shake us from the very complacency which robs from us the ability to grow and to become better human beings.

- "RIGHTEOUS ONE," or "FOUNDATION OF THE WORLD," — *TZADIK, YESOD OLAM.*

The idea that the world has a "foundation" isn't new; but that "goodness" rather than capricious acts of petty deities govern that foundation is a unique element of ancient Israelite monotheism. God, the "Righteous One," is separated from the cosmos He created; yet He is still at one with it, imbuing all with justice and truth. This realm draws together all powers in the universe, to bring about specific purposes in accordance with the divine Will.

The universe is not to be seen as fragmented or the sum of capricious forces which are impersonal and purposeless. Every force, every power in the created world works together to bring about God's purposes. We may not understand God's Will, but we see its manifestation in a thousand different ways, as the creation unfolds around us.

- "KINGDOM" — *MALKHUT, OR SHECHINAH* —
THE POINT TO WHICH THE WORLD OF THE
BODY EXTENDS.

This is the lowest of the spheres — the one closest to human beings and human concerns. "Kingdom" contains the lower attribute of "severity." In order to experience the *Shechinah* (which may also be thought of as the Holy Spirit), one must be prepared to accept God's discipline in every aspect of life. The measure of God's goodness is God's severity.

The rabbis of old had much to say about the "Kingdom of Heaven," which consists of the reign of God on the earth in justice. It was said, "Whoever says, 'Hear O Israel, the Lord our God is One' takes on the yoke of the Kingdom of Heaven." This "yoke" is the severity with which God judges human character and behavior. It is the domain of the power of all the other powers, in order to judge the "lower worlds."

Of Stones and Stories...

These are the "spheres" to which the *Book of Creation* refers. On a mystical level, however, there are any number of additional meanings to which the term *Sefirot* may refer. The Hebrew word *Sapir* means "sapphire" or "gemstone," suggesting a verse in Exodus: "And they saw the God of Israel; and there was under his feet as it were a pavement of *sapphire* stone, like the very heaven for clearness" (Ex. 24:10). The verbal root *Sipper* means "to tell," as suggested by a verse in Psalms: "The heavens are telling the glory of God; and the firmament proclaims his handiwork" (Ps. 19:1). There is a mystical story to recount, and the *Sefirot* are intent on telling it. Additionally, the Hebrew word *Sefor* means "number," which is of huge importance to the realm of Kabbalah. The very idea signifies the vast and complex web of mathematical relationships which course through the universe. The science of *gematria* (the study of the numerical value of letters) thus came to occupy a central place in kabbalistic speculation. The mystics knew, long before modern physicists, that everything in the created world is governed by precise mathematical laws. Modern scientists query why the universe should go to all the bother of existing, simply to satisfy a set of immutable laws and equations. The Kabbalists, however, believed that the *Sefirot* energize the laws, which in turn bring the universe into being. Letters, like mathematical equations, have no weight or mass or substance in themselves. Yet, from the likes of $E = MC^2$ the universe is. Truly, letters are "of nothing," existing entirely in the realm of the Idea. In Platonic terms, the Idea has greater reality than what we call "physical reality." It is toward this higher plane, boundless, yet bounded in God, that the *Sefer Yetzirah* aspires.

Numbers, Numbers Everywhere . . .

In the realm of *gematria*, there is indeed something special about the number ten, as the designated number of the *Sefirot*. The medieval rabbi, Nachmanides, was later to write about the *Book of Creation* as delineating an enclosure of ten, noting that just as there are ten *Sefirot*, there are Ten Commandments. There are also only two single-digit integers, seven and three, which happen to add up to ten. Seven is a mystical number by nature, reserved for godly things associated with the end of creation (which took six days). Three represents a Jewish "trinity" of God, Israel, and the Torah.

This helps us understand the interesting statement at the end of the passage in question: "three mothers and seven doubles and twelve singles." In the Hebrew alphabet, there are three letters considered "mother letters": *Aleph* (א), *Mem* (מ), and *Shin* (ש). They stand for *Avir* (air), *Mayim* (water), and *Esh* (fire). As the *Sefirot* are laid out in schematic form, the spheres on the left side (*Binah*, *Gevurah*, and *Hod*) symbolize severity and harshness — "fire." The spheres on the right side (*Khokhmah*, *Hesed*, and *Netzakh*) symbolize mercy and compassion — "water." Those in the middle (*Keter*, *Tiferet*, *Yesod*, and *Malkhut*) — "air" — are the mediators between strictness and kindness. The "three mothers" are identified with the uppermost of the *Sefirot*, *Binah*, *Keter*, and *Khokhmah*, which "give birth" to the seven lower *Sefirot*—the seven double letters.

The "double letters" of the Hebrew alphabet are those which have two different pronunciations, hard or soft, and are as follows: *Bet* (ב), *Gimmel* (ג), *Dalet* (ד), *Kaf* (כ), *Peh* (פ), *Resh* (ר), and *Tav* (ת) — a total of seven. Just as letters may be pronounced in a hard or soft fashion, so aspects of the creation may express themselves in terms of kindness or severity. This is why we see the world around us in terms of cruelty on the one hand, mitigated by cords of mercy on the other. It is all an expression of a cosmic, kabbalistic tug-of-war between attributes inherent in the universe. As God Himself declares: "See now that I, even I, am he, and there is no god beside me; I kill and I make alive; I wound and I heal" (Deut. 32:39).

The twelve "single letters" which remain are those which can only be pronounced one way. These letters symbolize various aspects of the sphere of *Tiferet*. Bear in mind that the Kabbalists attached various letters of the Tetragrammaton (יהוה) to the *Sefirot*. The letter attached to *Tiferet* was *vav* (ו), which, when spelled out as a word, has a numerical value of twelve! Furthermore, just as Jacob had twelve sons, who sired the twelve tribes of Israel, so these twelve letters tell us of the life of the patriarch who wrestled with an angel (the attribute of severity) — and prevailed.

The "Spheres" and the Body

The *Book of Creation* continues: "Ten *Sefirot* of nothing, the number of the ten fingers, five opposite five, and the single covenant is in between, as in the circumcision of the tongue and the circumcision of the penis."[64]

Everything has its parallel and counterpart, the physical and the spiritual, the world above and the world below, the natural and the supernatural. Just as human beings have a body of flesh and blood and bone, so God has a supernatural "body," consisting of the *Sefirot* themselves. One is a mirror-image of the other. The ten fingers of the human body correspond with the ten *Sefirot*. And the *Sefirot* are in their own right like the hands of God and the fingers of God. This helps explain the anthropomorphic reference in Scripture to God's hands and fingers. We find, for example: "And [God] gave to Moses, when he had made an end of speaking with him upon Mount Sinai, the two tables of the testimony, tables of stone, written with the *finger of God* " (Ex. 31:18). The tables of the Law of course contain the terms of the "covenant," which mediate between the right hand and the left, between severity and compassion.

But how is this mediation accomplished? The *Book of Creation* next speaks of "the circumcision of the tongue and the circumcision of the penis." Just as the foreskin is removed in the traditional ceremony of circumcision, the prophets of old had spoken of a spiritual circumcision, in which impurity is cut away from the heart: "Circumcise yourselves to the Lord, remove the foreskin of your hearts, O men of Judah and inhabitants of Jerusalem" (Jer. 4:4). Likewise, impurity is to be cut away from the tongue, a sentiment reflected, kabbalistically, in Hebrew prayer books to this day: "May God guard my tongue from evil and my lips from speaking deceitfully. To those who curse me let my soul be silent; and let my soul be like dust to everyone."[65] This prayer, composed by a fourth-century rabbinic Sage named Mar, is very much a part of the liturgy of modern Judaism. We are told in commentaries on the prayer book that another Sage of old, Rabbi Simeon ben Gamaliel, once directed his servant to purchase "good food." The servant came back, having bought tongue. Rabbi Simeon next told his servant to purchase "bad food," whereupon the servant again brought back tongue. The servant reportedly said, "When a tongue speaks good there is nothing better, but when a tongue speaks ill there is nothing worse."

Infinity

Another passage from the *Book of Creation* states: "Ten *Sefirot* of nothing, their measure is ten that have no end."

> The depth of the beginning,
> The depth of the end,
> The depth of good,
> The depth of bad,
> The depth of the heights,
> The depth of the bottom,
> The depth of the east,
> The depth of the west,
> The depth of the north,
> The depth of the south,
> and one master, God faithful King, rules them all, from His
> holy place till forever and ever.[66]

The *Book of Creation* is at this point trying to come to grips with eternity — with infinity. This infinity is in turn reflected in another mystical Hebrew term — *Ain Sof* — "He who has no end." After all, who can know God? Who can express God? Even the word *God* is weak and feeble and limited. *Ain Sof* therefore becomes the term of choice to describe One who cannot be described.

There are of course ten "depths" all together, though no one is quite sure which "depth" corresponds to which *Sefirah*. The *Sefirot* are, in any case, like vessels, which contain a measure of the light of God. God's light is certainly far too great to be contained in any one vessel. God's light, like God Himself, is infinite. Only a portion of God's light has come to reside in the vessels, but even this light, declares the *Sefer Yetzirah*, is infinite. The ten *Sefirot*, described in the passage as having a "measure" and therefore a "limit," have thus been called "limited infinities."

It is an apt term, incredibly akin to modern mathematical concepts. A simple example involves the set of all positive integers (positive numbers). It is a bounded set; yet its numbers constitute an infinity. Another bounded set of equal size consists of all negative integers. A bounded set of half the size consists of all even numbers, though this set is also of infinite size.

The *Sefirot* are limited, whereas the *Ain Sof* is limit*less*. Nonetheless, each *Sefirah* represents an attribute of God and is an infinity unto itself. The *Sefer Yetzirah*, in speaking of "heights" and "depths" and directions (east, west, north, south) also implies that the *Sefirot* are the source of dimensions in the universe. Whereas modern astrophysics addresses the "space-time continuum," the *Book of Creation* adds a dimension of morality in speaking of "the depth of good" and "the depth of bad." It is most significant that Kabbalah goes a step beyond astrophysics and conceives of a moral dimension to the universe. Again and again, the burden of mysticism is not merely to ponder the mysteries of the stellar night, but to combine their understanding with a positive obligation upon all human beings, in the dimension of morality. We are given tasks to perform; we are admonished to act!

The Power of Silence

Another passage from the *Book of Creation* deals with the positive value of quietude — the power of meditative silence:

Ten *Sefirot* of nothing, shut your mouth from talking and your heart from thinking. But if your heart runs, return to the place (*ha-Makom*), for that is the reason it is said, "And the angels run and return" [Ezek. 1:14], and on this matter a covenant was cut.[67]

Meditation has always been a substantial component of mysticism. And meditation involves not so much doing as refraining from doing. It involves closing the mouth and making a decision not to speak. But it also involves something deeply internal, in the heart. It is important to slow down, as it were, the beat of one's heart. The perennial problem of the student of meditation is how to prevent the mind from wandering, how to focus down and inward, how to become one with the universe beyond oneself. Whoever meditates must learn to bring one's focus back to "ground zero" — to return to a specific place. For this reason, mystics throughout the ages have recommended finding a focal point, in a word or phrase, to be repeated over and over, all the while slowing one's breathing and even one's pulse.

But the passage also contains a warning. One is not to use meditation or mystical practice to probe subjects beyond one's ability to grasp. Just as the disciples of Rabbi Akivah fell into trial and torment in delving into mysticism, every new student of Kabbalah must exercise due caution before entering "the Orchard." There are areas of esoteric speculation which are so far afield from human experience that they contain no value even for the heartiest of kabbalistic souls. Sometimes the aspiring mystic needs to return all thoughts to God, who is also referred to by the euphemistic term "the Place" (*ha-Makom*). Indeed, the determination not to delve into areas of speculation beyond our abilities to comprehend is nothing less than a "covenant" with God.

The Holy Spirit

Having registered this admonition, the *Book of Creation* proceeds to delineate the *Sefirot* themselves. Of the sphere of "Wisdom" (*Khokhmah*), we are told: "Ten *Sefirot* of nothing .... One is the spirit of the living God; blessed and blessed is the Name of He who lives eternally. Sound and wind and speech, this is the 'Holy Spirit.' "[68]

While "Wisdom" is the second of the ten *Sefirot*, it is identified with the beginning of creation, and it is therefore called "One." The highest sphere, called "Crown" (*Keter*) is unknowable, while the sphere of "Wisdom" represents the "being" which came from "non-being." It is the "something" that came from "nothing," and it is a non-technical means of describing what modern scientists call "creation from nothing." The term "Holy Spirit" in Hebrew may also be translated "holy wind," since it was God's breath — His "wind" — which gave, articulated, and energized the divine letters, from which creation came into being. The wind originates in the *Sefirah* of *Keter* (Crown), and "Wisdom" receives it. Creation is born.

The *Book of Creation* continues this theme in the next mysterious passage: "Two. Spirit from Spirit [or 'Wind from Wind']. He engraved and chiseled in her twenty-two letters of foundation, three mothers and seven doubles and twelve singles, and Spirit ['Wind'] is one of them."[69]

This seems to describe the *Sefirah* of "Understanding" (*Binah*), which is just below "Wisdom." The Kabbalists spoke of "Understanding" becoming pregnant from "Wisdom." The body of the lower *Sefirot* represent the flowering of the material or "lower worlds" composed of the primordial letters. We are reminded of the second verse in the Bible: "And the Spirit [or Wind] of God was moving over the face of the waters" (Gen.1:2). As a child's organs are formed within the womb, so the breath of God forms the letters within "Understanding."

The *Book of Creation* goes on to say: "Three. Water from Spirit [or Wind]. . . ." This seems to describe the sphere of "Lovingkindness" (*Hesed*), especially since moisture is a kabbalistic symbol of kindness and mercy. The next passage declares:

> Four. Fire from water. He engraved and chiseled in her the throne of honor, the Seraphim, the Ofanim, the Holy Animals [angels] and the ministering angels, and from the three of them He established His abode, as it is said, "He makes his angels the winds, His ministers flaming fire" [Ps. 104:4].[70]

The text apparently describes the *Sefirah* of "Power" (*Gevurah*). We ask, however, how can fire come from water? Even the ancients understood that the sun's rays, when refracted through water, can produce heat, and even fire, just as telescope lenses, when trained on the sun, can burn holes through paper. We are told that God engraves in holy fire the following:

- the throne of honor (from which the Almighty reigns)
- Seraphim (angelic beings, whose very name suggests "burning")
- Ofanim (which appear to refer to the wheels of the divine chariot)
- Holy Animals (referring to the angels of Ezekiel's ancient vision)
- ministering angels (who tend to the needs of human beings).

There is, however, a problem with the passage. Why does the passage say that God "established His abode" from three of them, when in fact it lists five? The likely reference is to the "trinity" of Spirit (or Wind), Water, and Fire, which the *Book of Creation* has taken pains to discuss.

But throughout all its speculations, Kabbalah never strays far from the angels who wend their way across the universe, translating God's unknowable Will (*Keter*) into the affairs of human beings. The angels, as the quoted psalm declares, *are* the winds; they *are* the flames of fire. As Milton would later write, "Thousands at his bidding speed and post o'er land and ocean without rest; they also serve who only stand and wait."

The Structure of Space-Time

The remainder of the *Book of Creation* examines all manner of esoteric subjects, including subjects probed by modern astrophysicists. What is the nature of space and time? We are told: "He sealed High . . . with the letters *Yud, Hey, Vav* [י, ה, ו — three of the four letters of the Tetragrammaton]. . . . He sealed Bottom. . . . He sealed East. . . . He sealed West. . . ."[71]

What are the nature of the emanations of the Almighty into the universe? What is the essence of divine justice, and the mediation between kindness and severity?

> The heavens were first created from Fire, the land was created
> from Water, and the Air mediates between Fire and Water.[72]

What is the nature of the heavenly realm? How many gates does heaven have? What was the primordial chaos — "formless and void" — from which the earth was formed? What is the meaning of the Zodiac? Why the distinction between the sexes? What are the male and female characteristics of space, time, and the soul?

> He engraved them and chiseled them, combined them and
> sealed with them the three mothers in the world, the three
> mothers in the year, and the three mothers in the soul, male
> and female.[73]

It is a work of wonder, which raises as many questions as it answers. But that is the nature of Kabbalah.

Mystic Europe

The continent of Europe can be a cold and forbidding place. The vast North European Plain stretches across Holland, Germany, and Poland, and eastward to the borders of Russia. The land is generally flat, though pocked here and there by interlocking hills left behind by ancient glaciers. There are the Baltic Heights, over four hundred feet in elevation, and framed by flatland, coursing along the coast of the Baltic Sea.

In the early Middle Ages, nearly a quarter of the region was home to dense forests of pine and spruce, beech and oak, an impenetrable thicket about which legends abounded. Diffuse meadowlands graced the hillsides. Farmland and grazing areas skirted the scattered towns and villages, much of it reclaimed from the native forest cover. The soil quality lacked uniformity from one locale to the next. Many areas in the north were sandy, mingled in places with clay. The land in general was not very fertile, save for former marshland from which the water had been drained. Rainfall was never terribly abundant, except in the more hilly regions.

Even the sky, most often a patchwork of gray and intermittent subdued blues, provided little relief or comfort for those who labored on the soil below. The warmth of summer with its long and listless days was all too short-lived, and the winter months seemed like a quilt of darkness, penetrated by only a few hours of light. January's wrath was universally dreaded. The farther east one would travel, the more one would surely suffer from the bone-chilling cold.

Northern Europe was home to many Jews, who had drifted into these parts long ago, when the Romans first imprinted their culture on the face of the continent. The culture of Rome was driven by reason and by cold and calculating judgments. The Romans were Stoics, chosen by fate to bear the burden of civilizing the world. But when the high civilization of Rome disintegrated, it was replaced by a different culture, a medieval world, diffuse and decentralized, where local folk, driven by fear, consumed themselves with spooky phantasms and with "things that go bump in the night." This was the world of a different stream of Jewish mysticism, spilling out of the land called *Ashkenaz* in Hebrew, what we today call Germany.

An Uncommon Breed of Piety

The *Hasidei Ashkenaz* (Pious of Germany) were never numerically large, but during the second half of the twelfth century they began to exert an influence far beyond their numbers. At their helm was Rabbi Samuel he-Hasid (Samuel the Pious) and his son Rabbi Judah he-Hasid (Judah the Pious). They were virtual rabbinic aristocrats, who headed up a very elite society. Together with Rabbi Eleazar ben Judah of Worms, they disseminated their collected discourses, which, as in the days of the prophet Ezekiel, involved visions of the Throne of Glory, divine beings, heavenly palaces, and of course the *Merkavah* — "the Chariots of God." God is awesome, magnificent, and beyond human beings to fathom. Yet, paradoxically, He is near; He is intimately approachable. He is, in the words of Hebrew Scripture, *Yedidi* — "My Dear Friend." Their esoteric doctrines were not, they claimed, of their own invention; they were faithfully received in a direct line of transmission from the early sages of ancient times.[74]

The ideas of the *Hasidei Ashkenaz* developed in feverish counterpoint with the teachings of Jewish philosophy, even with the greatest Jewish philosopher in history, Moses Maimonides. The approach of Maimonides was to blend the world of Aristotle with the world of faith; the mystics of old Germany instead reveled in the experience of God. Never mind the long, bleak months of winter. Fret not about the ever-present gloom of medieval life, the relentlessly cloudy skies, the back-breaking labor on the inhospitable land, the cramped and narrow alleys of the towns, the tumbledown shacks they were obliged to call home. They lived in simplicity but in joy.

They were in love with God, and they expressed that love in deep humility, in self-denial, in relinquishing worldly possessions for a higher calling. Their motivation was the fear of sin; their *modus operandi* was twofold — to be rigorous and demanding toward their own circles, but moderate toward the Jewish people as a whole. Their goal was not to condemn, but to educate humanity in how to live a moral life, a good life, a truly happy and contented life.

Those who wrote the most important work of this movement, the *Sefer Hasidim* (Book of the Hasidim), were driven by a major preoccupation — the manifestation of God in the physical universe. It was one more expression of the "Great Question": How can infinite Deity be experienced by finite mortals? If God is as holy as His divine name suggests, can He have anything to do with the corrupt material world? An unbroken mystical thread from antiquity, which played with the letters of the ineffable Tetragrammaton, had woven itself through the course of the centuries, sometimes almost disappearing in the tapestry of Jewish thought, only to surface again and again. The mystics of Ashkenaz linked the reasonable elements of faith with an other-worldly outlook, seeking to balance the two. They gloried in the power of words to heal and deliver, and to confound the forces of evil, sickness, and death.

Long ago Jesus of Nazareth had spoken of the "keys of the kingdom of heaven" (Matt. 16:19), metaphorically granting them to his disciple Peter. Now, the Hasidim of Europe resurrected this expression, counting and numbering each letter of the sacred Torah, looking for the keys that would unlock its mysteries. Since each letter of the Hebrew alphabet carries a numerical value, they looked for hidden mathematical codes, weaving throughout the holy text. They elevated numerology to a science, called *gematria*, which continues to fascinate people down to the present day.

And what of the sages, the leaders of the movement, who truly understood this power and knew how to invoke the divine name of God? A cult of personality crystallized around them. A rabbi who rose to such stature was called a *Baal Shem*, a "Master of the Name."

A Mystical Manner of Living: Meeting Ground of Jews and Christians

The teachings of each Baal Shem had certain common focal points, spinning out a more or less complete system, a "way of life." Don't allow the hardships of life, the pain of trafficking in the world, to steal your zest for living. Whether you are rich or poor, your inner self should be unaffected and therefore undisturbed by the suffering you experience. Seek to live in the higher spheres of being. Do not fear death, for those who pass to the world beyond never really leave our presence. Indeed, the souls of the departed are among us, praying with us every Sabbath in our synagogues. For the House of Israel is one indivisible body, which consists of the dead as well as the living. Those who have gone to the grave are as much a part of Israel as those who linger in this present world, in this vale of tears.

This new crop of European Kabbalists sometimes sounded like the apostle Paul, who waged war "against the principalities, against the powers, against the world rulers of this present darkness, against the spiritual hosts of wickedness in the heavenly places" (Eph. 6:12), and on that score, the messages of Jewish and Christian mystics dovetailed. In fact, history indicates that Kabbalah was a meeting ground for Christians and Jews, who, in the realm of mysticism, put aside their centuries-old disagreements and came together in the search for a higher spiritual reality. At this time, there seems to have been a growing cultural interplay between the Hasidim of Ashkenaz and the Christians of northern Europe, especially Germany. Christians had long held to the idea that self-denial (asceticism) is the key to a life of faith and devotion. Jesus had said, "Take up [your] cross daily and follow me" (Luke 9:23). In medieval Europe daily life generally involved a liberal dose of suffering, and taking up one's cross seemed like a realistic admonition. Monasteries cropped up, where clerics could devote themselves to seeking a higher level of reality.

Christian mystics became increasingly fascinated by Jewish mysticism. A common bond of suffering drew these Christians to their spiritual kinsmen, the Jews. Both ancient Jews and early Christians represented a counterculture in stark contrast to the pagan world in which they lived. The concept of martyrdom was one of the common elements. For just as the early Christian Church had been born in blood, in the crucible of persecution, so had the Jewish people suffered from the wrath of conquering empires, from the Romans to the armies of Islam to the marauding Crusaders. The Scriptures had called them the "Chosen People," but chosen for what? For dispersion and anguish, wandering across the face of continents in search of a hospitable habitat, only to find themselves treated as society's lepers. There was good reason for the Hasidim of Europe to develop an asceticism of their own, not unlike that of the monastic movement in Christianity. True joy would be found in simplicity, in a basic and uncluttered lifestyle. Behind the walls of their ghettoized communities they would find solidarity and warmth and a camaraderie of suffering.

There was a major difference, however. Unlike the celibate Christian monastics, some of whom (the "Flagellants") so despised their own flesh as to beat and flagellate themselves, the Hasidim took their asceticism only so far. Celibacy was unthinkable, no matter what their ancient counterparts the Essenes might have practiced. Their doctrine taught them that people are born good, not evil, that humanity is commanded to "be fruitful and multiply" (Gen. 1:28), and that family life must take precedence over the denial of self. Hasidic thought made much of sexual imagery, deriving some of its mystical power from the sex drive itself. Though replete with warnings about this aspect of one's "evil inclination," heterosexual love was highly praised in the Hasidic tradition. The Hasidim made much of a passage in the Talmud which declares that in the final judgment, each person will be asked to give an account of every good thing that he might have done, but did not.

Sanctifying the Name

Nonetheless, in Hasidic circles a certain theology of martyrdom developed. It was not a surprising development, given the events of those days; for terrible forces had unleashed themselves across Europe. While some Christians plunged into the study of Kabbalah, the great bulk of Christendom unleashed during the Middle Ages what can only be described as an anti-Jewish rampage. Again and again, Jews were targets for conversion to Christianity, if not by persuasion, by force. During the Crusades, armies of marauding Christian soldiers vented their wrath on Jewish communities across Europe, as they made their bloody way to the Holy Land. Many thousands of Jews who refused to be converted were murdered. During the Bubonic Plague, the "Black Death," which obliterated fully a quarter of Europe's population, the ignorant masses blamed the Jews, whom they accused of poisoning the water wells. In revenge, thousands more were murdered. Later, another villainous accusation surfaced — that Jews systematically kidnapped Christian children, killed them, and used their blood in the manufacture of matza crackers for Passover. Called "Blood Libel," it was used as an excuse for the murder of yet more Jews. Then, there was the charge of "Desecration of the Host," in which it was alleged that Jews stole into cathedrals, pilfered the consecrated wafers of the Eucharist, and mutilated them, as a way of crucifying, once again, the body of Christ. In rage, mobs of Christians demanded of their Jewish neighbors, "Choose Christ or die!" In such a climate, Kabbalah and its Hasidic adherents thrived all the more.

Some Jews did indeed convert to Christianity — at least outwardly — while continuing to practice Judaism in secret. But many chose death rather than submission to the insanity around them. Many more, encouraged by the Hasidic doctrine of martyrdom, chose to take their own lives. The Hasidim called it *Kiddush ha-Shem* (Sanctification of the Name). It was not to be thought of as suicide, not a morbid act of desperation, but as a sacrificial offering, sanctifying the name of God. A legend arose, expressed by a medieval poem, that when the time came for Abraham to "sacrifice" his son Isaac, the angel who stayed his hand spoke too late, and Isaac was actually killed. But the cherished son was transported to the Garden of Eden for three days, after which he was restored to Abraham in miraculous resurrection. The story circulated to comfort those who had lost loved ones by acts of *Kiddush ha-Shem*. Fret not; those who have taken their lives will not be judged for having committed suicide. They have done a noble thing, an honorable thing, making holy the very name of God. Like Isaac, they have died as a sacrificial offering. And like Isaac, they have gone on to Eden. They will live again, in resurrection! Such was the contribution of Kabbalah during some of the darkest days in history.

The Book of Brightness

The creative genius of the mystics was to transform medieval darkness into a supernatural light. They did this through yet another book, called the *Sefer ha-Bahir*, which means, literally, "*Book of Brightness*" or "*Book of Brilliance*." As with most works of Kabbalah, it abounds with mysteries. Who wrote the *Book of Brightness* and when exactly it was written are matters of conjecture. It first surfaced during the Middle Ages in southeastern France on the Mediterranean and the river Rhone in the rabbinic academies of Provence. Most scholars therefore assume that its origin is medieval.[75] But the language is Hebrew, intertwined with traces of Aramaic, and its style resembles ancient texts of Hebrew commentary, called Midrash. A prominent Sage of old, such as the venerable Rabbi Akivah, introduces each section of the book, although its structure as a whole is chaotic at best. Some literary critics even posit that the leaves of the original manuscript were somehow scattered in the wind and rudely patched together again!

Sources for the *Bahir, Book of Brightness*, appear to be multiple, including the *Book of Creation* (*Sefer Yetzirah*), the *Merkavah* (chariot-throne) and *Heikhalot* (heavenly palaces) literature, as well as the writings of the medieval German mystics, the Hasidei Ashkenaz. Another book of hoary antiquity, *The Great Secret* (*Raza' Rabbah*), also seems to have inspired the book called *Bahir*.

But whatever its sources, the *Bahir, Book of Brightness*, represents a quantum leap in mystical teaching. The goal of the book is the concept of "fullness" or "completeness," a theme emphasized in its commentary on the Hebrew prophet, Isaiah:

And what is "The whole earth is full of His glory" [Is. 6:3]? It is all that land which was created in the first day, which is above, corresponding to the Land of Israel, full of the Glory. And what is it? Wisdom, as it is written: "The wise will inherit glory" [Prov. 3:35].[76]

As the Land of Israel is "full" of glory, so are individual lives to be filled with wisdom. In a technique similar to that utilized by the Dead Sea Scrolls, the *Book of Brightness* seizes on a particular Biblical verse and comments on it by means of citing other verses, out of context, yet linked through mystical insight.

A Royal Family

Another technique used by ancient rabbis (as well as Jesus of Nazareth) involves the use of imaginative stories — parables — to convey a message. The parables involve classic images. . . of an earthly king "of flesh and blood," his royal palace, his courtly family, and his many subjects, both loyal and disloyal.

And what is this divine "Glory"? This can be explained by a parable. A king had a great lady [a matronita] in his room. She was loved by all his knights, and she had sons. They all came every day to see the face of the king, and they blessed him. They asked him: "Our mother, where is she?" He said to them: "You cannot see her now." They said: "Blessed is she, wherever she is."[77]

Bear in mind, in considering this passage, that there is a great deal of sexual imagery in Kabbalah, and that God is frequently depicted in feminine terms. Characters include, in addition to the "Queen," the "Bride," the "Wife," the "Sister," and the "Daughter." There is even a "Daughter of Light," who came from "a far away country." But who is the "great lady," the *matronita*, in the parable? She is the Glory, the Matron, who stands at the side of the king — who in turn represents the male aspect of the divine nature. She is also equivalent to the *Shechinah*, the female aspect of Deity. The "knights" in the parable are symbols of the angels on high, who, in the same passage of Isaiah's vision, chant in unison, "Holy, holy, holy is the Lord of hosts" (Is. 6:3). The "sons" symbolize the praying Israelites, who join the angels on high in the divine liturgy. In kabbalistic imagery, there is Israel above and Israel below, the heavenly Jerusalem and the earthly Jerusalem, the angels above and the Israelite congregants below. Neither the angels above nor the people below can say exactly where divine Glory resides. Yet, they praise and bless her, wherever she is.

The Unseen World, "The Force," and "The Dark Side"

In the world of the *Book of Brightness*, the unseen realm is depicted much like a great, growing tree. The part of the tree that is unseen — its large and complex system of intermingled roots — supports the part of the tree that is visible — its trunk, branches, leaves, and sprouts:

> And what are "Holy, holy, holy . . ." and then "the Lord of hosts whose Glory fills the earth"[Is. 6:3]? They are "Holy" — the Supreme Crown, "Holy" — the root of the tree, "Holy" — united and special in all of them.[78]

There is to be harmony between the physical and supernatural worlds, the visible universe and the unseen universe. There is also to be harmony between masculine and feminine attributes in the divine world.

Like the *Book of Creation* (*Sefer Yetzirah*) before it, the *Book of Brightness* presents a series of ten "spheres" or "emanations" of divine power (*Sefirot*), arranged, in descending order, from

"Crown" (*Keter*) to "Kingdom" (*Malkhut*). The *Book of Brightness* asks, "What are these ten utterances with which the world was created?" It also queries:

> And what is the reason for the raising of the hands and blessing
> them with a benediction? This is because there are ten fingers
> on the hands, a hint to the ten *Sefirot* by which the sky and the
> earth were sealed. And those ten correspond to the Ten Com-
> mandments.[79]

Through understanding the delicate interrelationships between the *Sefirot*, one can also get a sense of two distinct realms, one completely good and the other completely evil. One can think, in science-fiction terms, of a "Force" energizing the universe with goodness. There is, however, a "Dark Side," which perverts and distorts goodness, turning it to evil. But the evil inhabiting both the "upper world" and the "lower world" is hardly an autonomous power, over which God has no con-trol. The elements of evil are merely agents of the divine will, acting out the orders of the Almighty. Nor are these agents evil in their core and essence. For what human beings call "evil" ultimately serves the unseen purposes of God. "Evil" is there-fore redeemable. The "Dark Side" has a silver lining. Good and evil really are two sides of the same coin. And the coin belongs to God.

Mystic Spain

The verdant hills of central Spain bask in dazzling sunlight. It is a region called Castille, meaning "castle." By its very nature Spain is a castle, a fortress of grandiose proportions, washed on three sides by the Atlantic and the Mediterranean. There are tall mountains, comparable to the Swiss Alps, and narrow valleys which make their way inexorably to the coasts. The land is full of splendor, an enchanted realm of mystic wonder. It is the birthplace and home of countless dreamers and visionaries, nurtured by the brilliance of the turf itself. There was Saint John of the Cross, whose mystical poetry has inspired Christians down to the present day. There was Saint Teresa of Avila, the famed Spanish mystic of the sixteenth century. There was also, in the realm of Jewish mysticism, Isaac the Blind.

"Father of Kabbalah"

At the close of the twelfth and beginning of the thirteenth century lived a Franco-Spanish scholar named Isaac. Born the son of a great medieval teacher of Jewish Law, Rabbi Abraham ben David of Posquieres (who had written several important commentaries on the Talmud) Isaac had an enormous legacy to live up to. His Aramaic name was Saggi-Nehor, meaning "Full of Light." Living up to his name, if not his father's legalism, he devoted his energy and inspiration to the study of Kabbalah. Widely regarded as one of the earliest mystics in Spain and Provence, he passed along most of his maxims by word of mouth. But he wrote a major commentary on the *Book of Creation* (the *Sefer Yetzirah*) called *The Mystical Torah — Kabbalistic Creation*. In it he presented a mystical understanding of the creation event and of divine providence over the universe. He wrote in a style that was as cryptic as it was concise, which made it the subject of many later interpretations. It was Isaac the Blind who gave clear kabbalistic exposition to the idea of "cleaving" to God — *D'vikut*.

While he was said to have been blind from birth, his work is brimming with images of color. It was also said that, although he could not see, he perceived things that the eye could not behold, including the true nature of each soul with whom he came in contact. Isaac's legacy was such that he came to be called the "Father of Kabbalah."[80]

Rabbi Isaac's "light" fanned out like a solar corona to a new generation of mystics. They were headquartered in a small town in Catalonia, near Barcelona, called Gerona. Two prominent writers came forth from this circle, Rabbi Ezra ben Solomon and Rabbi Azriel. It was they who formulated many of the concepts which were to prevail in mysticism during the centuries to come. It was they and their disciples who transformed what had been an isolated and marginal element in Jewish thought into a dominant theme in medieval Jewish life.

So popular and widely read did the works of the "Gerona Circle" become that Rabbi Isaac once wrote an epistle to the two rabbis, Ezra and Azriel, insisting that the precepts of Kabbalah not be distributed to the public, and scolded that "a book which is written cannot be hidden in a cupboard."[81] In wake of Isaac the Blind's angry letter, the Kabbalists of Gerona appear to have made a sincere alteration in their *modus operandi*. No longer did they write down their mystical revelations, and they even went so far as to conceal some works which they had already composed.

While works of Kabbalah lessened in output, they by no means ceased. In the province of Castille, two brothers, Rabbis Jacob and Isaac Kohen, created their own circle of thirteenth-century mystics. Their writings focused on the characteristics of evil, which they wove together with the symbols of Kabbalah. They expounded a veritable hierarchy of demons, who rule in the invisible realm, including such notable names as Asmodeus, Satan, and Lilith. These demons emanate from the left side of the system of *Sefirot*, and they personify the all-too-human traits of lust, dominance, greed, and envy. It is their activities which are transmitted to unsuspecting individuals in the realm of flesh and blood. Moreover, the cosmic struggle between the forces of good and evil will find expression in the final battle, at the end of days, between Satan and the Messiah.[82] The Messiah, of course, will triumph in the end. In Kabbalah, it seems, nice guys finish first.

The Nomad, the Pope, and Yoga Instruction

One of the most fascinating figures to emerge from Spain's mythic splendor was born in Sargossa in the year 1240. His name was Abraham ben Samuel Abulafia, and he became known as a young man whose mystical ambition was perfectly matched by his inherent wanderlust. He was eighteen years old when his father died and he commenced his wanderings. He was looking for the mythical river of Sambatyon, where, legend had it, the ten lost tribes of Israel might be found. His search brought him, in the year 1260, to the Land of Israel. However, he came face to face with frustration, finding the Holy Land engulfed in the bloody Crusades and himself unable to venture beyond the coastal city of Acco. He never found his mystical river, but he never gave up his life of wandering.

He settled for a time in Greece, taking a wife, but purposing to continue his nomadic ways. He journeyed to Capua, in Italy, and finally to Barcelona, in his native Spain, where he devoured the *Sefer Yetzirah* for an entire year. He gathered a circle of disciples around him and began to proclaim to them the secrets of his prophetic inspiration. Wandering through Italy and Sicily, he returned to Greece, writing kabbalistic tractates and disseminating his ideas among more rational souls. In time he found himself back in Capua, where his speculations enticed a sizable following.

Surprisingly, some of his ideas bore striking similarity to certain Christian concepts, to the extent that a number of his disciples were baptized as Christians! To be sure, an interplay between Kabbalah and Christianity has long been evident (some kabbalistic notions sounding surprisingly like the concept of the "Holy Trinity), and Abulafia may simply have been giving expression to pre-existing trends in mystical thought. Conversion to Christianity was not, however, what Abulafia had in mind for his followers. Instead, he embarked on a personal pilgrimage to Rome, following his "inner voice," to confront the pope himself about the sufferings his people had experienced at the hands of Christians. Pope Nicholas III was not impressed. On the contrary, he decreed the death penalty for Abulafia, which, happily, was never carried out, due to the pope's timely death.

Following Abulafia's release from prison, he settled in Sicily, composing his tractates, *The Light of Wisdom* and *Treasury of the Hidden Eden*. He heralded the onset of the Messianic Age, and even hinted at his own messiahship. Many of his devotees began preparing for the journey to the Holy Land, which is to accompany messianic redemption. Opposition, however, was destined to arise. A clamor was heard, denouncing Abulafia as a demented fraud and a deliberate hoaxter. When the tide of criticism grew too strong, he fled to a barren island near Malta called Comino, where, in splendid isolation, he produced the greatest of his works during the years to come.[39]

Abulafia's mysticism, while based on the ten *Sefirot*, was unique in focusing on the combinations of letters of the Hebrew alphabet — called *tziruf* — as well as the numerical value of those letters — called *gematria*.[83] He further contemplated the mysteries of the divine name of God, the Tetragrammaton, as well as the legendary seventy-two letter name of God, which had never been revealed to flesh and blood. But ecstasy, he declared, is to be based on reason, and in this point similarities also exist with the doctrines of Islam. He even produced an engaging system of meditation, which, down to the present day, continues to fascinate practitioners of yoga and modern psychologists alike.

His meditative principles included the following points:

• The soul is circumscribed by knots and seals, by which it operates in the material universe, bound by time and space.

• It is these knots and seals which keep the stream of the divine light — which is far too great for human vessels to handle — from inundating and blinding the soul.

• The meditative task is to loosen the knots, withdrawing from the universe of multiplicity and complexity into the universe of unity.

• All images from the senses are to be dissolved.

• One must concentrate deeply, to organize, weigh, and modulate the letters of the alphabet, as a composer orchestrates individual notes.[84]

• Only then may one experience true communion with God, called by the important term: *D'vikut.*

Abulafia's legacy, in spite of the ardent opposition, was to dovetail with the broad stream of Spanish mystical esotericism, culminating in the next layer of kabbalistic expression . . .

"Man of León": A Jewish Don Quixote

Of all the great Sages down through history, none played such a key role in the development and transmission of Jewish mysticism as one Spanish Kabbalist of the thirteenth and early fourteenth centuries. Born around the year 1240 in León, in the province of Castille, he was known as Moses Shem Tov of León. The designation "Shem Tov" (Good Name) simply indicates his overwhelming popularity with the common folk, who became enamored with his writings. As might be expected of an individual of mystical bent, little is known about his early life, his tutors, or the nature of his education. But he seems to have been enticed by the study of philosophy and religion.

The printing press had yet to be invented, and books had to be copied laboriously by hand. He therefore counted himself fortunate to procure, in the year 1264, a copy of the greatest work of Jewish philosophy since the Bible, the *Guide for the Perplexed*, by the preeminent figure of medieval Judaism, Moses Maimonides. However, the *Guide for the Perplexed*, with its practical, down-to-earth approach to daily living, was too rational a methodology for him. He possessed an inner fire and a contagious enthusiasm. He began a life of wandering through the lush hills and fertile valleys of rustic Spain. Was he a Jewish version of Don Quixote, chasing imaginary windmills in search of the impossible dream? Or was he far more calculating in his desire to create an enduring legacy that would long outlive him?

Whatever his intentions, we know that during the seventh and eighth decades of the thirteenth century, he became friendly with the Spanish and Genoese Kabbalists of his day, living for a time in picturesque Guadalajara. Among his acquaintances and teachers were certain Gnostics, such as the spiritual leader of the Jewish community in Castille, Rabbi Don Todros Abulafia. Also called the "head of the Spanish exile," this Abulafia proclaimed that God may be found only through personal experiences of great ecstasy. During the course of his wanderings, Moses de León turned to writing, producing the first of his works around 1285. He would produce many books during his long and illustrious career; however, his writing yielded little fame and even less income. He ran into the perennial problem for writers from ancient times to the present: How does an aspiring author get noticed? His answer was simple: Pretend to be somebody else! Like many authors, he resorted to a pen name; but in his case the *nom de plume* was that of a famous figure of antiquity. His claim for the voluminous work he set to writing was that he hadn't written it. Rather, it was the work of none other than

Simeon ben Yokhai, the famous mystical Sage of the second century A.D. Moses de León had only found it. The time for its revelation to the world had come, because the Messianic Age was drawing near. The work was to be called the *Zohar* — meaning "Light" and connoting "Splendor." In centuries to come this one book would come to be regarded as virtually synonymous with the science of Kabbalah.

We can rightly consider this masterwork in the category of Pseudepigrapha (false writings), like the ancient books of Enoch and Jubilees. The language of the *Zohar* was not Hebrew, but Aramaic, which was, supposedly, the language increasingly spoken in the days of Simeon ben Yokhai. The *Zohar* was enormous in size, consisting of several thick volumes. Its contents were largely based on Moses de León's *Midrash ha-Ne'elam* (Hidden Commentary), now re-released as part of a colossal hoax. But hoax or not, the teachings of the *Zohar*, which fall somewhere between a running commentary on the books of Moses and a compendium of kabbalistic lectures, were widely received and believed. Medieval Kabbalah was on a course of explosive growth, and the *Zohar,* the "*Book of Splendor,*" was to profit from the resulting mania.

For a number of years, he labored to circulate the *Zohar,* which he accomplished from his own home in Guadalajara. Moses de León's "home business" became his full-time career, spanning several decades, as his sojourns led him to the cities of Viverro, Valladolid, Avila (which the Christian mystic Saint Teresa would later call home). This stunningly beautiful city, large and prosperous, was located high in the Avila Mountains of Castille-León, and was surrounded by an eleventh-century wall, bearing nine gates and eighty-eight towers. Having been founded in the Roman times, it became an important city in the kingdom of Castille, into which it was incorporated in the year 1088. It was the perfect locale for Moses de León to continue his literary career.

Persisting with the genre of Pseudepigrapha, he wrote several works in Hebrew, on the subject of what we might call "the care of the soul." Later, he attempted to produce a *new* book of Enoch, though it was never released as such. Part of the work ultimately found its way into his *Mishkanha-Edut* (The Tabernacle of Witness), which describes what becomes of the soul after death. Moses de León's other writings, twenty-four in all, include:

• *Sefer ha-Rimmon* (The Book of the Pomegranate) — a discussion of the commandments of the Bible, the reasons behind them being based on Kabbalah, after the fashion of the *Zohar;*

• *On the Act of Creation* — a mystical look at the first six chapters of Genesis;

• *Ha-Nefesh ha-Hakhamah* (The Soul of Wisdom) — a long and rambling discourse on the ten Sefirot (Spheres) of the universe; and

• *Mashal ha-Kadmoni* (The Ancient Parable) — ruminations about the Biblical prophet Elijah, observations on the "Song of Solomon," and a fierce argument against the ancient Sadducees.

Nevertheless, it was the *Zohar* that gained the greatest measure of popularity, and it was for the *Zohar* that he would be remembered.

The Zohar and the "Shroud of Turin"

The many Kabbalists of the enchanted provinces of Spain gloried in the new work, and Moses de León was inundated with orders. His literary career was at last becoming a splendid success. Nevertheless, questions about the origin of the *Zohar* inevitably arose, begging a logical explanation.

Whence did this previously unknown dissertation arise? What was the history of its transmission? Why had no one ever heard of it before? The theory, given in answer, was fantastic, but befitting the medieval wonderland that was Spain. It was alleged that the towering Spanish rabbi, Moses ben Nachman, or "Nachmanides," had dug it up after his journey to Palestine, in the year 1265. He in turn sent it back to his son, who lived in Catalonia. From there it was whisked away by a magical whirlwind to Aragon, descending into the waiting arms of Moses de León. He and he alone now guarded the original text, copying and distributing its secrets.

It was during his residence in Avila, in the year 1305, that Moses de León journeyed to Valladolid, in the hills of north-central Castille. Valladalid was home of one of Moses ben Nachman's disciples, Isaac of Acre. This prominent Kabbalist had grown up in Palestine, in a Mediterranean coastal city, in the intimate circle of Nachmanides' pupils. However, he had never heard any mention of the *Book of Splendor*. When the Jews of Acre were massacred, Isaac miraculously escaped, making his way westward to Spain. Only then did he hear of the *Zohar*. Only then was he shown copies of the work. Only then was he met by Moses de León, who solemnly swore that he possessed, in his own home, a text written by the actual hand of Simeon ben Yokhai. He invited Isaac of Acre back to Avila to see what he called the "ancient original manuscript" of the *Zohar*. Did Moses de León acually possess some kind of artifact, an ancient manuscript of some sort, which he purported to be the earlier copy of the *Zohar*? One wonders what manner of sleight-of-hand or "smoke and mirrors" he intended to use to display for a discerning soul such as Isaac of Acre the kabbalistic equivalent of the Shroud of Turin. Of course, the Middle Ages were replete with Christian artifacts, from pieces of the "true cross" to Mary's tooth to St. Veronica's hair. To be sure, the Shroud of Turin, which first surfaced in

1354, was only one example of multiple forgeries. Holy relics were never as important to Jews, but an ancient copy of the *Zohar*, written by Simeon ben Yokhai himself, must have tantalized even the most skeptical of rabbis.

In any case, Moses de León's oath would never be put to the test. On his way back to his home in Avila, in the year 1305, he became ill and died. Furthermore, his widow and daughter came forward with a stunning revelation. There never was an original manuscript of the *Zohar*. No such artifact existed. In fact, Moses de León had written the work by himself and in his own hand, pulling the contents from the complexity of his own mind. His widow further insisted that she had repeatedly asked him why he was essentially "forging" a text he claimed to have been written by an illustrious Sage of antiquity. He answered that had he continued to write under his own name, he would have gained little notoriety and even less income. However, the very name Simeon ben Yokhai, attached to his masterpiece, would assure that it be hailed widely and become an instant success. Thus, a hitherto unknown writer gained acceptance and proved his mettle by the power of a pen name.

Nonetheless, once the "fraud" had been perpetrated, it created a momentum of its own. Spain's mystics did not believe that the *Zohar* was a colossal hoax because they did not want to believe it. It was too comfortable to believe that the work was authentic. The wonderstruck adherents of Kabbalah virtually went into denial about the prospect that the *Zohar* was a clever forgery. Kabbalah had been around for many centuries, indeed for a millennium or two, but, aside from a few short tractates, it had mostly been the domain of oral teachings and private communication. A comprehensive, multi-volume work like the *Zohar* gave the study of Kabbalah the literary grounding it needed. Moreover, the *Zohar* should have the same status of inspiration and authority as the Talmud and the Bible itself, perhaps even a higher standing!

The damning charges of fraud simply could not be true. It was the widow and daughter who were deceived, not Moses de León himself.

If there had ever been an original manuscript of the *Book of Splendor*, what became of it? Where was it? Indeed, if ever it had existed, Moses de León took the secret to the grave with him. Yet, so persistent was the lore surrounding the "Man of León" that attempts were made, even into the twentieth century, to demonstrate that at least portions of the *Zohar* do indeed go back to the days of Simeon ben Yokhai. The great modern scholar of Kabbalah, Gershom Scholem, investigated such a theory, only to conclude, based on the language and syntactical structure of the work, that it was written entirely by Moses de León. In the final analysis, what we are enticed to believe must bow before the facts.[85]

The Impossible Dream

But what of the legacy of the *Zohar*? Whoever the original author was, is not the value of a work determined by its contents, not by its writer? Is not the message more important than the messenger? Does invalidating the author invalidate the book? The fact remains that the *Book of Splendor* created nothing that was essentially new. It gave voice, in a thoroughly unsystematic way, to a discipline that had always defied codification. It became a textbook for practitioners of the mystical lifestyle. The book itself proclaims, supposedly through the mouth of Simeon ben Yokhai, "Many will range themselves round the book *Zohar*, when it becomes known, and nourish their minds with it at the end of days."[86] This prophecy, whoever first may have uttered it, has certainly come to fruition. The *Zohar* is more widely read and studied than ever, and its impact has spread far beyond Jewish circles.

Many of the questions surrounding Moses de León have never been resolved. How, in hindsight, shall we understand this Quixotic man, obsessed as he was with his vision of the unseen world, with dreaming his impossible dreams? Was he insane, or was his idealistic faith a measure of the insanity of the world about, seeking and struggling in vain for things that have no lasting weight of glory? Perhaps, like Don Quixote de la Mancha, hero of the Miguel de Cervantes classic, Moses de León was really the sane one . . .

The Book of Splendor

In the Beginning . . .

When the King conceived ordaining
He engraved engravings in the luster on high.
A blinding spark flashed
within the Concealed of the Concealed
from the mystery of the Infinite,
a cluster of vapor in formlessness,
set in a ring,
not white, not black, not red, not green,
no color at all.
When a band spanned, it yielded radiant colors.
Deep within the spark gushed a flow
imbuing colors below,
concealed within the concealed of the mystery of the Infinite.
The flow broke through and did not break through its aura.
It was not known at all
until, under the impact of breaking through,
one high and hidden point shone.
Beyond that point, nothing is known.
So it is called Beginning,
the first command of all.[87]

So states the classic mystical commentary on the Bible, the *Zohar,* the *Book of Splendor.* To call the *Zohar* a difficult and enigmatic text would be a gross understatement; for the *Zohar* is deliberately obscure, intentionally ambiguous. Can sense be made of such a book, which cloaks its meaning behind a jumble of kaleidoscopic images?

The Mystical Universe

To begin we must understand that the true purpose of the *Zohar* is to explain the *Sefirot*, the ten spheres of the mystical universe. The highest of the *Sefirot* is called *Keter*, or "Crown." It is the unfathomable Will of God, quite beyond human understanding. Within this sphere the creation began. God did not, however, simply start creating physical matter. He conceived; He ordained. What physicists call the essential laws of the universe Kabbalists referred to as the letters of creation. Are these letters what the *Zohar* refers to as "engravings in the luster on high"?

And what about the "blinding spark" that flashed? A kabbalistic expression of the "Big Bang," perhaps? However, just as astrophysicists have yet to fully grasp the laws which brought about the creation, the *Zohar* maintains that the spark occurred within the "Concealed of the Concealed," that is, the *Sefirah* of *Keter* — which is, after all, unknowable.

"A cluster of vapor in formlessness, set in a ring." The words hearken back to the second verse of the book of Genesis: "And the earth was without form, and void" (KJV).On the one hand, it is another picture of the circular orb of the *Sefirah* of *Keter*, and on the other hand, it is an image of how astronomers would later define the formation of galaxies and of our own solar system.

Of note is the fact that some of the lower *Sefirot* — among the system of ten — bear distinct colors. *Gevurah* is red, *Hesed* is white, *Tiferet* is green and purple, and *Shechinah* is blue and black. But *Keter*, being primordial and co-eternal with the *Ain Sof* (He who has no end), has no color at all. As the lower

Sefirot came forth from the "womb" of *Binah* (Understanding), so were birthed the colors we associate with light. *Binah* yielded a flow of radiant colors; but the flow was not known, not seen, until "one high and hidden point shone." This is the *Sefirah* of *Khokhmah* (Wisdom) — the point of beginning, which "impregnates" *Binah*, which in turn conceives the lower seven *Sefirot*.

World Above, World Below

The *Zohar* consists of three massive volumes in Aramaic, recounting esoteric conversations supposedly held between the ancient rabbi, Simeon ben Yokhai, and his disciples. The first volume covers the narrative of the book of Genesis, elaborating mystically on the story of creation and on the lives of the Patriarchs. A second volume covers the book of Exodus, recalling in mystical terms the flight of the children of Israel out of Egypt. A third volume covers the three remaining books of the Torah: Leviticus, Numbers, and Deuteronomy. Throughout its multifaceted commentary, the *Zohar* develops a central theme — that God in His mystical essence is both hidden and revealed in the text of the Torah — for, according to mystic lore, the fullest and most complete of God's names is the Torah itself, from beginning to end. Consequently, whoever meditates on the Torah is in fact meditating on the divine name.

About the value of the *Zohar* we read the following:

> Rabbi Simeon [ben Yokhai] said, "Woe to the human being who says that Torah presents mere stories and ordinary words! . . . But all the words of Torah are sublime words, sublime secrets!"

Rabbi Simeon continued, saying: "Come and see: The world above and the world below are perfectly balanced: Israel below, the angels above."

The idea of a metaphysical world, of which the physical world is a copy and a shadow, goes all the way back to Plato. It is the common thread which weaves its way through the whole of Kabbalah.

Of course messengers are needed, traveling back and forth between the two worlds, linking them and charging them with holy purpose:

> When [the angels] descend, they put on the garment of this world.
> If they did not put on a garment befitting this world
> they could not endure in this world
> and the world could not endure them.

The *Zohar* goes on to expound that God created the Torah, and the Torah in turn created the lower world. This is why the *Sefer Yetzirah* (the *Book of Creation*) had declared that the world was created with letters. They are the letters of the Torah, as the *Zohar* now explains:

> If this is so with the angels, how much more so with Torah
> who created them and all the worlds
> and for whose sake they all exist!
> In descending to this world,
> if she [the Torah] did not put on the garments of this world
> the world could not endure.[88]

Therefore, it is insufficient to be satisfied with the plain and simple meaning of the Torah, as carried in its many narratives. The stories of the Bible are merely the "garments" which make the holy text capable of being borne. One must look beyond the stories; one must peer under the garment. Only then may one taste of the hidden manna. This process begins with the creation account.

The Zohar on Genesis: Who Created God?

If God created the world, then who created God? This oft-asked question consumes the author of the *Zohar*, just as it consumes many moderns. The *Zohar* ingeniously posits a radically new interpretation of the first verse of Genesis: "In the beginning, God created the heavens and the earth."

The Hebrew of "In the beginning, God created . . ." actually reads: *B'resheet barah Elohim* . . . (בראשית ברא אלהים). The letter *B* (ב), normally translated "in the" can just as well be translated "by," "with," or "by means of." Since the word *resheet* (ראשית) means "beginning," the *Zohar* translates the phrase as "With Beginning. . . ." And "Beginning" is another name for the *Sefirah* called *Khokhmah* (Wisdom). The *Zohar* also notes that the text places the verb "created" (*barah*) before the noun "God" (*Elohim*). The passage may therefore be read, "With Beginning created God the heavens and the earth." While readers of English understand that word order varies in certain languages — such as Hebrew — the *Zohar* speculates that there is a *hidden* subject, which should be inserted before the verb "created." We therefore have: "With Beginning _____ created *Elohim*."[89]

And who is this hidden subject? The *Zohar* declares: "The Concealed One, who is not known, created the palace; this palace is called *Elohim*." In other words, the *Ain Sof*, co-eternal with the first *Sefirah*, *Keter*, used the second emanation, *Khokhmah*, to create the third emanation, *Binah* (=*Elohim*), which is as far as our human understanding will take us.

The question, "Who created God?" is never really answered. The problem is only thrust back a generation, concealed in the realm of *Keter*. In the final analysis, if we think we know God, we know only *Elohim*; no one knows the *Ain Sof*.

The Gender Jumble

Kabbalah has long grappled with gender and sexuality, attempting to explain the presence of male and female attributes throughout the animate world. There must be something more to gender than procreation alone. The *Zohar* states:

> "Male and female He created them" [Gen. 1: 27].
> From here we learn: Any image that does not embrace male
> and female is not a high and true image.[90]

Just as the higher world must be in perfect balance with the lower world, so male and female attributes must be in perfect balance for harmony to prevail. The *Zohar* 's commentary continues:

> The Blessed Holy One does not place His abode
> in any place where male and female are not found together.
> Blessings are found only in a place where male and female are
> found, as it is written:
> "He blessed them and called their name Adam
> on the day they were created" [Gen. 5:2].[91]

The *Zohar* has at this point picked up on one of the most fascinating and enigmatic passages in the entire biblical text. Indeed, the Bible really does not say that God created *man* in *His* own image (Gen.1:26). That level of sexism would take centuries to develop. On the contrary, the account of Genesis declares that God created, not a *male,* but "the *Adam*" in His image. *Adam,* translated "man" in English, is also used to designate the *name* of the first man. But *Adam* is simply a shortened form of the Hebrew *Adamah,* which means the "ground" or "earth," from which the *Adam* was created. In truth, we would be better advised to translate the verse: "And God said,

'Let us make a person — a human being, an "earth-creature" — in our image.'" This *Adam*, this "earth-creature," was to be a reflection of everything that God is. And since God is both male and female, according to kabbalistic lore, with masculine as well as feminine traits, so is *Adam*, the "earth-creature," both male *and* female. This is why the later verse, in Genesis 5 (KJV), states that He called *their name* Adam. As the *Zohar* explains:

> It is not written: "He blessed him and called his name Adam."
> A human being is only called Adam when male and female are as one.[92]

The lesson is that every male must find a balance with his feminine attributes, and every female must find a balance with her masculine attributes. Moreover, the purpose of sexual intimacy is not procreation, but rather the union of male and female traits in created beings, as a reflection of the union of male and female traits in God. The implications of such teachings are by no means lost on modern social commentators.

Of Noah and Abraham

Many additional esoteric commentaries on Genesis are recounted in the *Zohar*. Of Noah we are told that when he came out of the Ark and "offered up offerings" . . . "a triple aroma ascended to God: the aroma of Noah's offering, the aroma of his prayer, and the aroma of his actions." The *Zohar* teaches that one's behavior must be consistent with one's intentions and one's prayers. And yet the *Zohar* tells us that while the righteous of every generation "shielded their generations" from the judgment of God, interceding on behalf of the wicked, Noah "did not care and did not ask for mercy." In an apparent rebuke of Noah, the *Zohar* declares, "He just built the Ark, and the whole world was destroyed."

As part of its commentary on the Patriarch Abraham, the *Zohar* states:

> All soul-breaths of the righteous
> have been carved from the bedrock of the Throne of Glory
> to guide the body like a father guiding his son.
> For without the soul-breath, the body could not conduct itself,
> would not be aware of the Will,
> could not actualize the Will of the Creator.

Recall the early, *Heichalot* mystical tradition of the heavenly palaces and the Throne of Glory, here wedded to the idea of the pre-existence of the soul. And recall that the term "Will" is one more reference to *Keter*, the highest of the *Sefirot*. The *Zohar* goes on to say: "The soul-breath directs and trains the human being and initiates him into every straight path."[93]

The *Zohar* proceeds to deal with the call of Abraham, depicted in Genesis 12, in purely allegorical terms. In the biblical text God speaks to the Patriarch, commanding him to leave the place of his birth, ancient Chaldea, and go to a new land, to be revealed to him along the way. But the *Zohar* understands the text in different terms, i.e., that the pre-existing souls of the righteous are dispatched from the heavenly throne, and sent to inhabit human bodies:

> "To the land that I will show you"
> means to such and such a body, a holy body, an upright body
> . . . .
> Abram [that is, Abraham], the soul-breath, went forth,
> father to the body and high from the place of the highest.
> "As YHVH had directed him" to enter the body that she had
> been commanded to guide and train.

With its kabbalistic stress on the duality of gender, Abraham is called "father to the body" but then is referred to as female. The soul-breath is to enter the body that "*she*" is commanded to guide.

However, once the soul-breath has entered a person's body, there is tension and conflict, as one's "good inclination" combats one's "evil inclination." This is what is taught as the character of Lot is introduced into the story of Abraham:

> Look what is written about her once she has entered the body:
> "And Lot went with him."
> This is the Deviser of Evil,
> destined to enter along with the soul-breath
> once a human is born. . . .
>
> The serpent who seduced Eve was the Deviser of Evil.
> We know that he was cursed, as it is said:
> "Cursed are you above all animals" [Gen. 3:14]
> Therefore, he is called Lot, Cursed.[94]

In the *Zohar*'s extended allegory, evil is not a devilish external entity, pitchfork in hand, seeking to cast the righteous into hell. Evil is equivalent with one's own "evil inclination," having entered the body, along with the soul-breath, the "good inclination," at birth. The temptation of Eve therefore becomes another allegory, of every person's temptation by his or her own evil impulses. The serpent represents, on a symbolic plane, the "evil inclination," as does Lot (a later "incarnation" of the serpent), who strives with Abraham and ultimately takes up residence in a city doomed by its own wickedness, Sodom. It is all inevitable and pre-ordained, and human beings should therefore not be surprised by the internal struggle they find being waged within themselves. For the "evil inclination" is destined "to mislead the human being and challenge the soul-breath."

So it was, in another biblical account, that when Abraham journeyed down to Egypt, he was, figuratively, descending into hell, into the depths of evil, in order to come forth refined and purified:

> If Abram had not gone down into Egypt
> and been refined there first,
> he could not have partaken of the Blessed Holy One.
> Similarly with his children,
> when the Blessed Holy One wanted to make them unique,
> a perfect people,
> and to draw them near to Him:
> If they had not gone down to Egypt
> and been refined there first,
> they would not have become His special ones.[95]

"Descent," in life experiences, is therefore prerequisite to ascent. Pain and travail is prerequisite to heights of joy. Similarly, the experience of Israel's great dispersion among the nations is a symbolic type of descent, which precedes a great day of redemption. As long as Israel is in exile, the "opening of the tent of Righteousness" is obscured and unknown.

> But when Israel comes forth from exile,
> all the soaring spheres [*Sefirot*] will touch down upon this opening, one by one.
> Then human beings will perceive wondrous, precious wisdom never known by them before.[96]

As the *Zohar* states, "It is all one mystery."

The *Zohar* goes on to speak of Isaac, the son offered by Abraham as a sacrifice, who was "arrayed in his own sphere alongside Abraham." It also speaks of Jacob, who saw the heavens opened and angels ascending and descending on a mystical ladder. It was Jacob whose name was changed to Israel, as he wrestled with an angel — unnamed in the biblical account, but called by the *Zohar* "Sama'el" — the male consort of the female Serpent. Sama'el is another name for the Angel of Death. Interestingly, the Hebrew root word *sam* means "poison." Further, the Hebrew word *smol* means "left," and may refer to the left side of the ten *Sefirot*, from whence the "evil inclination" emanates. Moreover, the Hebrew verb *samay* means "to blind," which is, after all, the role of the great Deceiver.[97]

Next the *Zohar* speaks of Joseph, who received from his father Jacob the notorious "coat of many colors," for which he became the object of his brothers' hatred. It was Joseph who was sold by his envious brothers into slavery in Egypt. And it was Joseph who dreamed dreams (such as one in which the sun, moon, and stars bowed down before him) and received their interpretations. The *Zohar* speaks of another angel, Gabriel, who is appointed over dreams. "Everything is contained in a dream," declares the *Zohar*. But the *Zohar* also warns: "You cannot have a dream without false imaginings intermingling. . . . Therefore, parts are true and parts are false."[98]

This is why it is important, on climbing into bed, first to "accept the Kingdom of Heaven":

> For when a person sleeps in his bed
> his soul leaves him and soars up above. . . .
> For nothing is revealed
> while the person is still under the spell of the body. . . .
> Rather, an angel tells the soul,

and the soul, the person,
and that dream is from beyond.[99]

The story of Joseph additionally teaches that a dream should be told only "to one who loves him," lest the listeners become as the brothers in the biblical tale: "They hated him all the more" (Gen. 37:5 NIV). But the wise are those who carefully guard the secrets entrusted them. A different type of multicolored "dreamcoat" will be given them:

When they leave this world, all their days are sewn together,
made into radiant garments for them to wear.
Arrayed in that garment,
they are admitted to the world that is coming
to enjoy its pleasures.[100]

Such are the lessons of the Patriarchs.

Exodus

In its running commentary on the books of Moses, the *Zohar* takes up the story of Israel's exodus from Egypt, culminating in the crossing of the Red Sea and the giving of the Torah on Mount Sinai. Again, the *Zohar* reinterprets the story on the level of allegory. The biblical account speaks of "a man" who took to bride a woman of the tribe of Levi, who in turn bore a son named Moses. But the mystical commentary speaks of the man as the angel Gabriel, who enters a divine union with the *Shechinah*, also called the "Communion of Israel." *Shechinah* is the heavenly counterpart of Israel below. It is Gabriel who carries the pre-existing souls of the righteous from their abode in the heavenly Eden to bodies of flesh and blood on earth. As for the literal account of Moses' birth, we are told:

Shechinah was present on their [Moses' parents'] bed
and their desire joined with Her.
Therefore Shechinah never left the son they engendered.[101]

In typically kabbalistic terms, sexual desire and sexual relations are seen as expressions of holiness:

A human being who makes himself holy below
is made holy above by the Blessed Holy One.
Their desire focused on joining *Shechinah;*
so *Shechinah* joined in the very act they were engaged in.[102]

The Burning Bush

The baby Moses, enshrouded from birth in the divine presence, is hidden away from the wrath of the pharaoh, who had decreed death for the children of the Israelites. As he grows to manhood, he flees into the desert, to encounter God's presence in a new way, speaking to him from a bush which burns but is not consumed. At this point the *Zohar* speculates on this enigmatically supernatural occurrence:

One who comes close to fire is burned.
Yet Moses came close to fire and was not burned.[103]

How could this be? Quoting the Sages of old, the explanation is advanced that Moses was clothed with all ten of the *Sefirot.* The mystical meaning of the incident is that just as the bush is blazing with fire but is not consumed, so Israel is enslaved to wicked taskmasters in Egypt, yet is not destroyed. On the contrary, a great deliverance is to come through Moses.

When God declares to Moses that He has in the past *appeared* to Abraham, Isaac, and Jacob, when the text might have said "*spoken* to" the meaning is that the colors of *El*

Shaddai, "colors in a cosmic prism," were revealed to the Patriarchs. Likewise, "The enlightened will shine like the *Zohar* [the radiance] of the sky." Who, precisely, are the "enlightened" of our own age?

> The wise one who contemplates by himself, from himself,
> words that human beings cannot mouth.[104]

And what is the method by which they will shine?:

> The secret is: close your eyes and roll your eyeball.
> Those colors that shine and glow will be revealed.
> Permission to see is granted only with eyes concealed.[105]

There is a difference between "seeing" and "knowing," akin to two mirrors, one which shines and one which does not shine. When one looks into a mirror which does not shine, one sees; but when one looks into a mirror which shines, one knows. Moses, we are told, attained "the mirror that shines." All of these secrets are taught by the story of the burning bush.

Angel Bread

The story of the Exodus teaches other mysteries, expounded by the *Zohar*. What is the mystical meaning of the manna, which was sent down from heaven to nourish the Israelites, as they wandered in the wilderness? Each day, declares the *Zohar*, dew flows in a trickle from the Ancient One into the Orchard:

> Some of the dew flows to those below;
> holy angels are nourished by it,
> each according to his diet,
> as it is written:
> "A human ate angel bread" [Ps. 78:25].[106]

Quoting Simeon ben Yokhai, the *Zohar* proclaims, "Some people are nourished by it even now!" Manna, then, is not merely a miraculously provided food for the ancient people of Israel; it is a divine sustenance for people of all ages who delve into the wisdom of Kabbalah. The quest for such wisdom becomes one's portion, one's food:

> Because Torah derives from Wisdom on high,
> and those who engage Torah enter the source of her roots;
> so their food flows down from that high and holy sphere.[107]

Holy Letters, Holy Commandments

From ancient times Kabbalah had taught that the universe was created through the letters of the Hebrew alphabet. The *Zohar,* however, expounds on this concept, equating the letters of creation with the letters on the tablets of stone, which we call the Ten Commandments. When the primordial letters first appeared, they circled about, until a spark was ignited, which in turn erupted as flashes. Comets burst forth, and the heavens glowed with intensity:

> Letters came forth, pure and bright
> from the flowing measure of the spark . . .
> All of Israel saw the letters
> flying through space in every direction,
> engraving themselves on the tablets of stone.[108]

Thus were carved, by the finger of God, the Ten Commandments. Thus is Israel, in mystic communion with God, the "people of the Book."

Leviticus, Numbers, and Deuteronomy

The remainder of the *Zohar* concerns itself, in a single volume, with the last three books of the Torah: Leviticus, Numbers, and Deuteronomy. Among the subjects of mystical speculation, the *Zohar* on Leviticus takes up the nature of Israel's sacrificial system. At the heart of the Torah is the description of an elaborate system for the slaughter of animals, similar to the appeasement offered by the Canaanites and their neighbors to the many deities of the ancient Near East. What was the difference between the daily carnage of blood and sinew and entrails conducted by pagans and that performed at the Tabernacle of Moses by the hands of Israel's priests? A mystical meaning had to be found, and the Hebrew word for "sacrifice," *korban*, provided the point of departure. Quite correctly, the *Zohar* emphasizes the fact that the *root* of the word *korban* is *kirev*, which means "to come close" or "to draw near." Commenting on the first two verses of Leviticus, "When any of you brings *korban* to YHVH. . . " we read:

> The drawing near of those holy crowns,
> drawing near to one another, connecting with each other,
> until all turn into one, complete oneness,
> to perfect the Holy Name. . . .
> The drawing near of those holy crowns is to YHVH
> so that the Holy Name be perfected and united,
> so that compassion fill all the worlds
> and the Holy Name be crowned with crowns
> and everything be sweetened.

From the multiplicity of the system of *Sefirot*, with its ten holy crowns, perfect unity is to come. This is the true essence of sacrifice — not the slaying of animals, but, by living a perfected, compassion-filled life, bringing unity from diversity.

God's attribute of compassion is emphasized in the four letters of the Tetragrammaton — YHVH — emanating from the right side of the *Sefirot*. By contrast, God's attribute of judgment is emphasized in the name *Elohim*, emanating from the left side of the *Sefirot*. The *Zohar* continues:

> All this is intended to arouse Compassion,
> not to arouse Judgment.
> Therefore "to YHVH," not "to *Elohim*."[109]

The divine advice is proffered succinctly: "We must arouse Compassion! We need Compassion, not Judgment!"

The Feast of Tabernacles

The *Zohar* also finds mystical meaning in the yearly autumnal feast of Judaism, called *Sukkot* — the Feast of Tabernacles. Why did the Torah command that the children of Israel should, every year in the fall, build rude huts or booths — "Tabernacles" — of sticks and leafy branches and dwell in them for seven days and nights? As with so many aspects of traditional religion, there is the ancient tradition, shrouded in the hoary past, and there is the inner meaning, of universal relevance, across time and space. In the case of each "booth," the inner meaning suggests a bride, equivalent with the *Shechinah* (also called the "Communion of Israel"), who has followed her beloved — God — into the wilderness. *Shechinah* figuratively *becomes* a bride, just as each booth is traditionally "decorated, crowned, and arrayed . . . like a bride bedecked with jewels." Therefore, even today:

> When one sits in this dwelling, the shade of faith,
> *Shechinah* spreads Her wings over him from above,
> Abraham and five other righteous heroes come to dwell with him![110]

Playing on the meaning and significance of the word *Shechinah*, the *Zohar* also notes that its root, *shakhan* (to dwell), is equally at the root of the word *mishkan* (tabernacle) and the word *mashkon* (pledge). Quoting Leviticus 26:11, "I will place My tabernacle among you,"[111] the *Zohar* expounds the hidden meaning: "My dwelling is my pledge!" Since the Temple of old has long since been destroyed and the people sent into exile, what remains for Israel?

> Even though the Blessed Holy One has removed Himself from us,
> He has left a pledge in our hands,
> and we guard that treasure of His.
> If He wants His pledge, let Him come and dwell among us![112]

The pledge is the *Shechinah* herself, equivalent with the feminine attributes — the feminine half — of God.[113] The Sages of old had declared that when Israel went into exile, the *Shechinah* went with her. Consequently, if God wants His other half, He must come and dwell with Israel in unity.

The Age of Enlightenment

The *Zohar* never loses touch with the sublime image of the *Sefirot*, through which God emanates His divine presence across the universe. Out of the depths of despair, across ages of suffering, woe, and homeless exile, redemption shall flourish, like the primordial sparks themselves, in a new age of enlightenment:

> I have seen that all those sparks sparkle from the High Spark,
> Hidden of all Hidden!
> All are levels of enlightenment.
> In the light of each and every level
> there is revealed what is revealed.

All those lights are connected:
this light to that light, that light to this light,
one shining into the other,
inseparable, one from the other.[114]

It is through deep meditative practice that the reality of the "High Spark" is grasped. The lights are of course the ten *Sefirot*, separate and distinct, yet intimately connected, one to another. There is unity from diversity.

The emphasis at the end of the *Zohar* comes full circle with what it expounds at the beginning — the division in the universe between things hidden and things revealed. As the Torah herself declares: "The secret things belong to the Lord our God; but the things that are revealed belong to us and to our children for ever" (Deut. 29:29). The Torah has revealed herself, putting on "garments" of stories and narratives. But the ultimate goal is to strive with all one's might to approach the *Ain Sof*, "the Eternal One":

The light that is revealed is called the Garment of the King.
The light within, within is a concealed light.
In that light dwells the Ineffable One, the Unrevealed.[115]

The last bit of wisdom taught by the *Zohar* is, interestingly, a commission and a call to action: "Rabbi Hiyya rose to his feet and said 'Until now the Holy Spark has looked after us; now is the time to engage in honoring him!' "[116]

Honoring involves upright conduct, which in turn demands a certain resolution of will. The reader of the *Zohar* is left with something to do, and that something involves making the world a fundamentally better place. Such is the message and the mission of the mystics.

Magical Mystical Tour

Jewish life in Spain had soared, for several centuries, during what has rightly been called a golden age. Never since the days of Solomon's great Temple in Jerusalem had so many Jews risen to such heights of prestige, power, and cultural prominence. Everywhere one looked, there were Jews of influence, such as Hasdai ibn Shaprut, whom an Arab caliph elevated to the role of court physician, director of the customs department, advisor, and emissary. Bear in mind that with the flowering of the Islamic world, there was great intellectual ferment, in which the Jews played a substantial role. Consequently, there was much cross-fertilization between Jewish mystics and Sufi mystics, giving rise to Islam's own brand of mysticism. But that was Arab Spain. Christian Spain (after the great "Reconquest" was a very different animal. For a period the Jews were tolerated, but in the course of time, the tenor of life was destined to change. The Christians who took back the Iberian Peninsula from the Moslem Arabs were not as inclined to allow deviation from the majority faith. Their doctrine was perversely simple. Spain must be one united Catholic land. Dissent must be quashed. How else can Christ come again?

Slowly, the golden age of Spain turned into what the Christian mystic, Saint John of the Cross, described as "The Long Night of the Soul." The Christian overlords of Iberia demanded of their Jewish subjects a high price for residence in their golden realm — conversion. Suffering the painful stigma of being outside the bounds of polite society, many Jews did indeed become "Christians," at least outwardly. But a good number of these continued to practice their Judaism, lighting candles on the Sabbath and observing the festival days quietly and in secret. Having paid the ultimate price for acceptance by their Christian neighbors, they were, nonetheless, viciously ostracized. The Christians of Spain called them *Marranos*, or "Swine." These Jewish "converts" to Christianity were pushed increasingly to the periphery of society, toward final excommunication.

Feminist Kabbalah

Indeed, from the moment the Iberian Peninsula changed hands — from Moslem to Christian — the position of the Jews became increasingly precarious. In the long run, the trauma resulting from the persecution of the Jews of Spain was one more example of how mystical activity and human suffering were interconnected, and how one increased commensurately with the other. In times when hope in the physical world seemed elusive, the mystic elevated hope to a higher level. The Spanish Kabbalist, Kanah ibn Gedor is a case in point. Attacking the pleasures of material existence, which seemed inconsistent with a saintly and spiritual life, he looked to unraveling the "inner secrets" of the Talmud, rather than getting bogged down with its rational dialectic. He was the author of many mystical works, including *Sefer Hakanah*, which grapples with the issue of whether the laws and ordinances of the Bible and Jewish tradition are in effect at all in this new period of exile. The very existence of the Jews as a people, coupled with their unique literary product, the Talmud, was proof enough that the commandments remained in effect.

But something was lacking. Kabbalah had long dealt with issues of gender, seeing the universe charged with sexuality and seeing even God as possessing female characteristics in equal proportion to the traditionally masculine traits. Why, then, had tradition placed the greatest burden of keeping the commandments on men only? Indeed, of the 613 commandments found in the Bible, women were charged with keeping only the negative ones — the "Thou shalt nots" — and were given great leeway on the positive ones — the "Thou shalts." Men, on the other hand, were obligated to keep all 613 commandments, both positive and negative. Ibn Gedor's kabbalistic dictums insisted that women share equally the burden of fulfilling the commandments. The *Sefer Hakanah* queries God: "Why did you create poor woman who has neither reward nor punishment because she is exempt from certain commandments [namely, the positive commandments]?"[117] Since Kabbalah teaches that masculine and feminine characteristics must be in balance in the universe, it stands to reason that women, in keeping the "Thou shalts," should help to bring the female traits into their proper place in the cosmos. In essence, Ibn Gedor created a strongly feminist demand for equality, in mystical tones, centuries before feminism itself was ever conceived.

Inquisition

In the meantime, however, Spain's anti-Semitic drumbeat continued unabated. In due course a mechanism was carefully put in place, the machinery of state-sponsored terror. It was aimed at all deviants from the holy Catholic faith, but it was specifically directed against Jews. The anti-Semitism of centuries past was the work of ignorant mobs of inflamed peasants. This persecution, however, was different. Unlike previous outbreaks of anti-Jewish violence across Europe, its authority derived from Rome itself, by papal fiat. The *Marranos* must be examined, interrogated, as to whether they still practice Judaism. If need be they must be urged, even forced, to "confess" their non-Christian practices. They called it the "Inquisition," at the helm of which was a sadist of notorious infamy. He held the title "Grand Inquisitor," and the very mention of his name struck terror into the souls of his Jewish victims — Thomás de Torquemada. No form of torture was beyond his design. The targets of his inquisition were routinely stretched out on the rack, their limbs being ripped out of their sockets, to induce confessions.

In Fourteen Hundred Ninety-Two . . .

Many confessed, being prepared to say anything that would ease their torment. Many more were killed, being handed over to the civil authorities, who in turn carried out the grizzly executions. The Spanish golden age had turned into an apocalyptic nightmare. It was Thomás de Torquemada who whispered into the ears of two of the most celebrated Spanish monarchs of all time, King Ferdinand and Queen Isabella. It was at his urging that they signed into law a notorious edict expelling all Jews from Spain. It was a time of woe and lamentation. It was the effective end of more than a millennium of Jewish habitation in the Iberian Peninsula. It therefore came to pass that in 1492, the very year in which three modest ships, the *Niña,* the *Pinta*, and the *Santa Maria,* set sail in a voyage which would lead to the discovery of a "new world," another fleet of ships, laden with half a million Jews, set sail in a melancholy voyage of desperation. Banished from their homes, the travelers fanned out across the Mediterrean lands of North Africa and points east, becoming the spores of new Jewish communities everywhere they landed. Among their destinations were Morocco, Tunis, Egypt, Turkey, and of course, the Holy Land.

Long before, the Jewish poet of Moslem Spain, Judah ha-Levi had written:

My heart is in the East and I am at the
edge of the West. Then how can I taste
what I eat, how can I enjoy it? How
can I fulfill my vows and pledges
while Zion is in the domain of Edom,
and I am in the bonds of Arabia? It
would be easy for me to leave behind
all the good things of Spain; it would
be glorious to see the dust of the
ruined Shrine.[118]

Now the distant dream was becoming, for many Spanish
exiles, a reality. The suffering of the ages had fueled the mystical fires which prompted the Jews of Spain to return to their
ancient home. The dust of the ruined Temple in Jerusalem at
last came within view, as thousands of Jews arrived on the
shores of Palestine.

Kabbalah had driven them, motivated them, buoyed them
up on their perilous journey. But Kabbalah also taught that the
Messiah and the Messiah alone would restore Jerusalem to the
Jewish people. They had come to the Holy Land, but they were
not to live in Jerusalem . . . not yet. They must find another
place to settle, where they would be free to study the mysteries
of Kabbalah while waiting for the imminent appearance of the
Anointed One. They would not settle in Judea. They would
settle to the north, in the rock-strewn hills in the region called
Galilee. They planted roots in a settlement built during Talmudic times, protected and sequestered, where no foreign over-
lord would harass them. It was a town called Safed, and for
these mystics, it was a new Eden. Their mystical tour had led
them here.

Safed is a city lost in time. Nestled high in the hills of northern Galilee, it is a tiny metropolis which has weathered the ages without too much loss of identity. To walk its narrow streets is to journey through centuries of tradition and lore. There are no grand events in history for which this place is noted. No great and mighty deeds done here put Safed on the map. The fame of this town, this jewel of Galilee, is not worldly; it is otherworldly. For Safed, the undisputed seat of medieval Jewish mysticism, became during the long night of the Spanish exiles, a gateway to the world beyond.

In the windswept stillness of the limestone hills, one can almost hear the chanting of the great Hasidic masters of bygone days. The ambiance of the place, which today is the locus of a thriving artists' colony, leaves a distinct impression on the soul of every visitor. The story of Safed is in many ways the story of Kabbalah itself. For when the mystical impulse exploded out of Spain, Safed received this impulse. It was in every respect a Jewish city, and its only inhabitants were Jews. During the 1500s all of Palestine belonged to the Ottoman Turks, but the Jewish Duke of Naxos had found favor in the eyes of the sultan, with the result that the Jews of Galilee were left to run their own affairs, virtually independent. As the fifteenth century rolled into the sixteenth, the Jewish population of the town soared from about three hundred families to seven hundred sixteen. Many prominent Jewish Kabbalists from elsewhere in the world now called Safed their home.

Among them was Jacob Berab, a towering expert in Jewish law. He had been exiled from Spain and fled to Morocco, becoming the chief rabbi of Fez before traveling to the Holy Land. Now he found himself at the helm of the scholarly community of Safed.

Somewhere along the way, around the year 1535, a mystical

master named Solomon Alkabetz turned up in Safed. Alkabetz quickly rose to prominence, moving to nearby Meron, where he headed up a rabbinical *yeshiva*. The significance of Meron was not lost on him, for this was the traditional place of burial of none other than Simeon ben Yokhai, the supposed author of the *Zohar*.

In the year 1536 another giant of Jewish Law and lore appeared in the hills of Galilee. His name was Joseph Caro, and he was destined to attain a monumental stature among the Jewish people, rivaling even the great Sage Moses Maimonides. Prior to his arduous pilgrimage to Palestine, Joseph Caro, like so many of his compatriots from Spanish Jewry, had immersed himself in the broad stream of Kabbalah. His teacher, who preceded him to Safed, was none other than Solomon Alkabetz. Once in the Holy Land, Caro continued to study the deep secrets of the *Zohar*, receiving tutelage from Alkabetz's brother-in-law, Moses Cordovero. After two years of such study, Jacob Berab officially ordained him a rabbi. In time Joseph Caro headed up a *yeshiva* in Safed and ultimately succeeded Jacob Berab as head of the entire community. He also produced a concise yet comprehensive handbook of biblical Law, called *The Prepared Table*, which is accepted down to the present day as an authoritative guide to Jewish life. The fact that Caro was a legal expert as well as a Kabbalist proved, in the eyes of many, that reason and mysticism can go hand in hand, complementing one another.

The Divine Rabbi

The spirit of Safed was contagious, its influence being felt by Jews the world over. Its intoxicating ecstasy fanned out from Galilee as far as Turkey, Poland, Germany, and Italy. Adding to this influence was yet another arrival in this mystical paradise, one who would be called nothing short of "divine": Ha-elohi

Rabbi Yitzhak, "The Divine Rabbi Isaac," more properly known as Isaac Luria. His dedicated followers, who venerated his memory and his spirit, developed an acrostic for his name: Ha-Ari, "The Lion."[119]

He was born in Jerusalem in the year 1534, of German-Jewish stock. The death of his father orphaned him at an early age, whereupon he traveled to Egypt, to reside with his uncle. His study of the Talmud in his youth left him only with dread, and he soon turned to the world of Kabbalah. He left his young wife at home while he went off to meditate in the empty stillness of the broad Nile River valley. He said little, and preferred to speak in the "Holy Tongue," Hebrew. He reveled in solitude; he learned to hear the pain of the world in silence. He returned to his home only for the Sabbath, after which he retreated again to his meditative life. He took to reading the *Zohar,* which, due to the invention of the printing press, was now readily available.

For years the pattern of his life proceeded in this way. He experienced rapturous supernatural visions, encountering the prophet Elijah from ancient Biblical times. Elijah, it was prophesied, would be a forerunner, bringing the Messiah to the Jewish people. Elijah, it seems, had been designated to reveal to Isaac Luria the meaning, the "system," of the *Zohar.* The methodology of mysticism would now be given voice with new clarity and force by the "hermit" of Cairo. Through his meditations, he glimpsed new meaning in the long dispersion of the Jews among the nations of the earth. Israel's dispersion is designed to bring redemption to humanity, for the purified souls of the Israelites are to combine with the souls of other nations, thereby freeing them from impurity and evil.

Everywhere he looked he heard the whispering of spirits. . . in the trees, the grass, the birds, the rushing of water, in the component sparks of pure flame. Though he might well be described as a God-possessed man, he found no favor or recognition in Cairo. In the words of a Hebrew proverb, "A prophet is unrecognized in his own city." Thus, he did what Moses had done in ancient times. He came out of Egypt and returned, with his wife and child, to the Promised Land. In the year 1569, Isaac Luria arrived in Safed.

He was not particularly noticed at first. For a time he studied kabbalistic theories with Moses Cordovero. Then he turned to an alchemist and mystic named Chaim Vital Calabrese, the son of an Italian "Scribe" (a copyist of the holy Torah). As the two collaborated, they regularly journeyed to Meron, to visit the grave of Simeon ben Yokhai and to receive an emanation of the ancient Sage's spirit. They engaged themselves in combat with the powers of darkness, with evil spirits who fled before their righteous presence. Vital, impressed by the spiritual dynamic of his friend, became a "publicist" of sorts for Luria, circulating reports of his spiritual power and the divine gifts with which he was invested. Crowds began to muster, eager to learn of his revelations, his insights into the *Zohar*, the "system" revealed to him by the prophet Elijah. To his new flock of disciples, Luria communicated his insights regarding the "transmigration of souls" — the prior existence of each human spirit, deriving from Adam, until coming to reside in present bodies of flesh.

The Messiah Son of Joseph

Coursing through all of Luria's teaching was an awareness of the Messiah and an expectation of his imminent arrival. He even went so far as to set a date for this momentous event, at the beginning of the second half of the second thousand-year period since the destruction of the Jerusalem Temple, namely 1568 (as he reckoned it). It is the shared burden and responsibility of the Jewish people, he taught, to bring about the Messiah's arrival through their deliberate actions of faithful obedience to the Law of Moses. Many centuries before, the Talmud had made an obscure messianic statement: "Messiah son of Joseph was slain, as it is written, 'They shall look unto me whom they have pierced; and they shall mourn for him as one mourneth for his only son.'"[120] Luria was privately convinced that *he* was in fact the Messiah of the House of Joseph, though how he reconciled this idea with the statement that the Messiah son of Joseph was slain is a mystery. In any case, Luria saw himself as one sent to prepare the people for the coming of the Messiah of the House of David. And prepare them he did.

When the Sabbath day came, his heart turned to rapture. He clothed himself in resplendent white garments of four corners, symbolizing the divine name of God (*Y-H-W-H*, יהוה). He led his disciples as they bobbed and chanted and whirled their way across the Galilean hillsides. Every Friday, as the sun's bright orb began to sink below the horizon, they assembled themselves to intone the ancient chant: *L'khah dodi likrat kalah; penei Shabbat nikabbalah.* "Come, my Beloved, to meet the bride; the face of the Sabbath we will receive." The bride, clothed in brilliant wedding gown, was the perfect metaphor for the Sabbath, and the Sabbath in turn represented the soon-coming Messiah. Luria's disciples were an exotic sight to behold, having wrapped themselves in their long tasseled prayer shawls. Their *tefillin* (the little boxes containing the declaration: "Hear, O Israel; the Lord our God is One!") were affixed on their left arms and on their foreheads by thin leather straps. When the landscape surrounding their bejeweled town of Safed grew dim in the twilight, they retreated to their synagogues, where they huddled together for hours, drinking in the divine light of the Sabbath candles, until at last they extinguished themselves in darkness. It was a ritual enacted over and over again, in seven-day cycles, as kabbalistic yearnings reached a fever pitch.

It is related that on a particular Friday afternoon, as Luria was leading his flock on another venture out of town for their festive reception of the Sabbath, he turned to them and queried whether they wanted to take a trip, immediately, to Jerusalem, and spend the Sabbath in the holy city. They replied that it would be a long journey, that they had wives in Safed, and that leaving their families behind would be impractical. Luria retorted, "Woe to us! We are unworthy; I saw that the Messiah was about to appear in Jerusalem, and if you had agreed to come along right away, we would have been redeemed from our exile in Diaspora!"[121]

But Isaac Luria would never see the Messiah. He died suddenly in the year 1572, at the age of thirty-eight. In death, his stature would only increase, to the point of near deification. A host of disciples, followers of the Holy Ari, would inspire future generations of mystics with the memory of the divine rabbi.

The Lion's Whelps

They were popularly called "Lion's Whelps," the young cubs who would spread the kabbalistic message abroad and take it to new heights — and depths. At their helm was none other than Chaim Vital Calabrese, who claimed that Luria had appointed him successor. Full of enthusiasm, Vital now aired abroad an astounding idea — that *he*, not Luria, was the long-awaited Messiah son of Joseph. This declaration, while it had only limited effect, was a harbinger of things to come. All objections to the contrary, Chaim Vital Calabrese continued his preaching in Jerusalem. His visions were many, his prophesies bombastic. Some, transfixed by the mantle of authority passed to him, claimed to have seen a pillar of fire extending above him as he spoke. Others declared that the spirit of the prophet Elijah had descended upon him. Traveling to Safed, he continued in the ways of Luria, casting out demons and visiting the grave of the beloved master, Simeon ben Yokhai.

He proceeded to Damascus where a pocket of ancient Essenes had once lived, taking up their mystical mantle and prophesying that the souls of various disciples living abroad must be joined to his. Incredibly, they began coming, from Poland, Germany, Italy, and other lands, to play a role in the messianic burden of redemption. Many were anxious to see the manuscript notes left behind by Isaac Luria, which Vital claimed he alone possessed. A scandal erupted when Vital's brother Moses stole into Chaim's house at a time when he was gravely ill and copied the notorious notes, proceeding to sell them at a high price. Chaim, upon his recovery, announced that these were not the authentic notes of Isaac Luria, which he still possessed and would never circulate. Instead, he directed that Luria's secret documents be buried with him at the end of his life.

Nevertheless, when Chaim Vital Calabrese died, his son Samuel Vital — another of Luria's whelps — published the collected visions and dreams of his father in a fresh volume. As the writings circulated, Luria's sparks were fanned. In Holland, a Sage of no small repute named Manasseh ben Israel carried the torch of Lurianic mysticism, while in Germany and Poland, Isaiah Hurwitz (called "the Holy") and Naphtali Frankfurter elevated Luria's system to a new height of popularity. Circular letters, recalling the miracles and wonders of the Lion and his whelps, were widely disseminated. Skeptics and rationalists notwithstanding, the onward march of Kabbalah continued undaunted.

The "Frankenstein"
of Kabbalah

The quaint and ageless beauty of eastern Europe is epitomized in the city called Prague, the capital of what is today known as the Czech Republic. Splendid old Prague sits majestically on the banks of the Vltava River, a branch of the mighty Elbe which skirts across the heart of the city from south to north. The river's eastern flank is fairly flat, but off to the west a set of steeply inclined hills rises, adorned by a magnificent palace from the twelfth century, the Hrad Castle. Adjacent to the palace stands the great cathedral of St. Vitus, dating back to the fourteenth century. Old Prague is equally famous for its Mala Strana, or "Little Quarter," whose narrow and crooked lanes are home to multiple churches and palaces. In the Stare Mesto, or "Old Town," connected to the Mala Strana by a statue-laden bridge, the great Tyn Church dominates the skyline. A huge clock indicates both the time and the season, and an imposing statue of Jan Hus, the martyred Protestant reformer, still stands sentinel, bearing mute witness to the ages-old cultural ferment of this town.

Prague, very much a product of the tumult of the centuries, was, historically, a city teeming with mystics, healers, alchemists, and soothsayers of every variety. Little wonder that the Holy Roman emperor, Rudolf II, spurred by his interest in the supernatural, should move his domicile from Austria (Vienna) to this city of mystic wonder.

Prague was also the home of a strong and sizeable Jewish community, firmly rooted in this part of the world, yet forced to live on the periphery of society. Sequestered as they were behind the stifling walls of a ghetto, the Jews of Prague were often the targets of bitter attacks, leaving their very lives imperiled. One of the most serious threats facing European Jewry in the sixteenth century was the slander hurled by certain hate-inflamed Christians against the Jewish people and their religion. It was the Blood Libel that Jews would kidnap and kill Christian children, using their blood for ritual purposes. This hideous lie had been around for some time on the European continent, but now it took on a new dimension.

As grotesque as the lie was, even more grotesque was the fact that it was so widely believed. In time, "Blood Libel" became an anti-Semitic battle cry and an excuse for attacking Jews across the continent. In many cities, the Jewish inhabitants, barred by law from brandishing weapons, cowered in fear of the rabble, who were more than willing to drain blood for blood. In Prague, however, they often found their escape in their own flights of mystical fancy, otherwise known as Kabbalah.

The Tzadik and the Legend

The year was 1580. The beloved chief rabbi of the Jewish community of Prague, Judah Loew ben Bezalel, was himself a renowned Kabbalist, as well a scholar and judge.[122] He wrote prolifically on many religious matters, and he earned from a number of Christian clerics a great deal of respect. To Rabbi Loew is ascribed one of the most incredible and enduring tales of the long legacy of Kabbalah. The story is told of how the venerable rabbi, seeing his community viciously accused of the slander of Blood Libel, turned to the Almighty for help. After long days of prayer and fasting, Rabbi Loew's sleep was interrupted one night by a vivid and disturbing dream. In the midst of a fiery conflagration, a luminous hand appeared which proceeded to write a single lucent word upon the ashes and the smoke. The word was in Hebrew: *Golem*.

It is an ancient, mysterious word, which connotes the idea of a shapeless mass. According to the Talmud, the word refers to whatever is less than perfect, or not yet complete, such as the newly created Adam, before being brought to life by God: "How was Adam created? In the first hour his dust was collected; in the second hour his form was fashioned; in the third he became a shapeless mass (*golem*); . . . in the sixth he received a soul; in the seventh hour he rose and stood on his feet." But in kabbalistic folklore the word *Golem* meant only one thing — a hulking giant fashioned of clay, brought to life by magical incantation, and controlled by a truly righteous person, a *Tzadik*. There were prior tales of such a *Golem*, originally ascribed to a *Tzadik* of Chelm in Poland named Rabbi Elijah.[123] Now, it fell upon the undisputed *Tzadik* of Prague to breathe life into legend.

The Incredible Hulk

The dream had delivered the message; a *Golem* must be created. The rest was up to Rabbi Loew. In the morning he called for the two individuals he could trust the most, his son-in-law and his most outstanding disciple. He explained how he had awakened with a start, the impression of the dream fresh in his mind. Long ago, he explained, God Himself had created the universe through the power of divine utterance. The time had come, he declared, for words to be invoked once more, to animate a being of clay, capable of defending the Jewish inhabitants of Prague. Kabbalah had taught the inherent power of the divine name. This power must be utilized. The ineffable name of the Almighty must be uttered.

That night, after long prayer and ritual purification in an immersion bath (a *mikveh*), they left the ghetto through a secret hole in the wall, to find themselves walking the forbidden streets of central Prague. Coming to the Vltava River, the three compatriots began digging near the banks, unearthing a steadily growing mound of clay. Hours passed, as the men labored into the night. Rabbi Loew took the clay in his hands and began fashioning a sculpture, bearing human form. At the risk of creating a forbidden "graven image," the *Tzadik* continued his holy travail, until, at last, a giant human visage stood upright, the wet clay glistening in the starry night.

Next, Rabbi Loew took to chanting the incantations — or *Tzirufim* — of Kabbalah, straight from the ancient book called the *Book of Creation,* the *Sefer Yetzirah.* As the *Book of Creation* had stated, it was the letters of the Hebrew alphabet which animated the cosmos, and if that be the case, then uttering the divine name should be able to bring forth life itself. With great awe and rapture, Rabbi Loew spoke the name of the Almighty. In a holy instant the elements of the cosmos erupted in a fury of violent wind and driving rain. A torrent of steam rose from the great mound of clay. Both son-in-law and disciple looked on in utter amazement as Rabbi Loew stretched out his hand and delicately engraved in the forehead of the figure a single word in Hebrew: *Emet* — "Truth."

It was indeed a moment of truth, as inanimate clay became an animate, sentient being. The massive creature moved its chest and inhaled . . . a living breath. Rabbi Loew had become creator and "father" of a new life form. Opening his mouth, he now spoke to the creature.

"Awaken!" he commanded. Obedient, the Golem opened his eyes and beheld his master, his father. Now it was the Golem's turn to open his mouth. The creature's first utterance was to ask his father whether it was wise to have created him. Rabbi Loew commanded his Golem to don a cloak which he had brought along and to follow him back to the ghetto. The Golem complied, pacing deliberately after the three men back to the synagogue, where he followed them up to the darkened attic. Rabbi Loew next explained to the creature why he had been created. There were evil people beyond the walls of the Jewish community, intent on planting "evidence" of the Blood Libel slander in the ghetto. There were flasks of blood, and even the body parts, planted to "prove" that the Jews had kidnapped Christian children. The task of the Golem was simple. He was to serve in the synagogue by day as a *shamash*, or "custodian," while by night he was to guard the Jewish quarter, apprehending those who sought to plant their "evidence." But he was not to harm anyone. He was merely to bring evildoers to the authorities.

According to the folklore, Rabbi Loew even gave his Golem a name — Yosef — Joseph, after the biblical patriarch who saved his people in ancient Egypt. The Golem asked his father how long he might live, and Rabbi Loew responded that he would only remain alive as long as the Jews were in danger. Then he would return to the clay from which he came. The *Tzadik* of Prague next had to explain to his shocked people why he had brought such a being to life. He declared that the Golem would be a great blessing and that he was not to be feared. In keeping with time-honored tradition, Rabbi Loew removed the life-force from the creature every Friday afternoon, so that the Golem would have no mobility by which he might desecrate the Sabbath.

Indeed, as time passed, the Golem proved the value of his existence. For example, he saved a young girl from forced conversion to Christianity, and he discovered — before it was too late — that the Passover *matzas* had been poisoned. Every night he strolled among the shadows of the ghetto, on the lookout for the accusers of the Jews, whom he frequently caught in the act of planting Blood Libel "evidence," and brought to the police. The entire Blood Libel charge was being exposed for what it was — a vicious slander with no basis in truth — *Emet.* The Golem also came to experience another aspect of existence, namely, the awareness of self and the world around him. He began to notice the sunrise and the sheer beauty of the physical universe, which in turn caused him to begin loving life and to cherish being alive.

Full of purpose and "mission," the Golem was quick to respond when the next threat presented itself. The enemies of the Jews, frustrated by the failure of their Blood Libel charge, presently gathered a fearsome mob to attack the ghetto in full force. As a mass of evildoers approached the Jewish quarter, the Golem, on Rabbi Loew's summons, planted himself at the gates. Hurling themselves against the great doors, and unable to knock them down, the crowd pressed into service a battering ram. As the great siege engine progressively weakened the wooden gates, the Golem, standing on the other side, began to grow in size, becoming even taller and more imposing. When the ghetto doors finally collapsed and the enraged mob poured in through the breach, they shrieked in utter horror to see the corpulent figure of the Golem towering over them. With an angry gesture of authority, the Golem swiped the air with the back of his hand, impacting the confused rioters and knocking them off their feet. Blind terror seized them all; the mob turned tail and fled back through the breach and out of the ghetto. The Golem picked up the abandoned battering ram, snapped it like a twig, and flung it after the cowering rabble who were stumbling over each other to get out of the way, leaving their dead and wounded in their wake.

Rabbi Loew, his hands over his eyes for fear of seeing such wanton havoc and bloodshed, had not imagined this. His Golem was to protect his people, not cause death and injury. He feared what the consequences might be.

An Audience with the Emperor

The *Tzadik* was not surprised when, the next day, he received a summons to appear at the great Hrad Castle, perched on the hills to the west to the city. There, on February 23, 1592, Emperor Rudolf II met with the old *Tzadik*, Rabbi Loew. No record of the subject matter of their meeting survives. Skeptical minds suggest that the two may have discussed politics, or astrology, in which the emperor had an avid interest. But folklore has it that Rudolf asked the rabbi for his people to be delivered from the fearsome Golem. He was terrified, as the story goes, that the Golem might subjugate Prague and reduce her inhabitants to slavery.

To this Rabbi Loew responded that his people, the Jews, who yearly (at Passover) celebrate their own deliverance from cruel servitude in Egypt, would never enslave another people. After all, the mission of the Golem was only to protect the Jews, not to harm anyone else. When the emperor wanted to know how long the Golem would live, Rabbi Loew replied that he would only live as long as the Jews were in danger. When the danger passed, the Golem would cease to exist.

At this the mighty potentate gave his solemn promise that the Jews in his realm would be protected and that no harm would befall them. Rabbi Loew promptly agreed that the Golem would henceforth cease to exist; but he added a warning, that should persecution befall his people again, the Golem would be back, even mightier than before.

Rabbi Loew briskly returned to his community and found the Golem, standing in the cemetery, surveying the tombstones with curiosity. The gentle *Tzadik* conveyed to him the news, that his people had been promised safety and that the need for the giant protector had vanished. The Golem, however, was by now far from a mere lump of clay. He had a name. He had experienced life. He asked his father whether he would remember the beauty of the sun, and Rabbi Loew sadly told him no. In a moment's assertion of will, the Golem announced for the first time that in that case he would not obey his father. In a test of wills between a hulking giant and an elderly religious leader, it was by no means certain who would emerge victorious.

The *Tzadik*, however, reached out with his staff, extending it toward the Golem's huge forehead. Touching the very spot on his broad brow where he had at the beginning carved the word *Emet* (Truth), he now scratched out the first letter. He was left with a new, shorter word — *Met* — *"Dead."* A cry of protest issued from the Golem's mouth, "Father, do not do this to me!" But even as he cried, his magnificently sculpted features dried and split with myriad cracks and fissures. The giant stumbled, tottered, and collapsed into a great mound of clay.

All that night Rabbi Loew, his son-in-law, and disciple helped to shovel the clay onto a cart and bring it back to the synagogue. There, in the attic of the structure, they piled the inert matter which had been the Golem. Since there was no such thing as a funeral for a Golem, they gingerly opened hundreds of old prayer books and laid them face down upon the clay mound, covering it completely. When their melancholy task was complete, they reverently recited the *Kaddish* for mourners, "*Yit-gadal v'yitkadash sh'may rabba*" — "May His great Name grow exalted and sanctified." Thereupon, they retreated from the chamber, locking it from the rear, never to disturb the place again.

The Legacy

The story of the Golem did not quite end, however. The wise old *Tzadik* had warned that the Golem might again come to life, should his people ever be threatened in the future. Some commentators have speculated, figuratively, that technological

Golems might arise in the modern age, who, once having been created, will be unwilling to die. Others suggest that the story of the Golem has, in a sense, repeated itself.[53] Indeed, the Jews were attacked again, not once but repeatedly. The culmination of the legacy of anti-Semitism was, of course, the Nazi Holocaust of the 1930s and '40s. Glorious old Prague, like the rest of continental Europe, was gobbled up by the German war machine, the Jews of the continent suffering persecution, degradation, and death. In Prague, however, the old synagogue (the *Altneuschul*), an imposing landmark of the city and the locus of the Golem story, somehow managed to survive the Nazi terror.

The story is told that on the day after German army rumbled into Prague, two generals arrived at the synagogue. The custodian of the building was ordered to lead them up to the attic, that they might see for themselves the place where the fabled Golem was supposedly laid to rest. The generals barked at the old man, that he remove the tattered prayer books from the piled heap that lay before them.

"I cannot! I must not!" shouted the custodian.

The general then ordered one of his soldiers to uncover the mound. Unsheathing a bayonet, the infantryman stabbed into the great pile of prayer books. Inexplicably, the soldier let out a deafening shriek and fell down on the floor, inert and motionless. In blind terror, the Nazi generals fled from the attic, while two other soldiers dragged the corpse from the place in full retreat.

After this incident the *Altneuschul* remained unmolested, and no German dared cross its threshold. The bayonet remained, protruding from the pile of prayer books, as a mute reminder of the presence of the Golem.[124]

This bit of folklore is intended to explain why, of all the synagogues the Nazis destroyed, the *Altneuschul* was spared and survives to this day. And yet, there are other levels of meaning in the Golem story. Some suggest that in a sense, a new Golem has arisen, in response to the Holocaust. In 1948, the modern State of Israel was born. The Jewish state came into existence from the smoke and ashes of the Nazi atrocities, and it has proved to be a regional giant in the Middle East, more than willing to exercise its considerable military might in defense of Jews anywhere in the world. The State of Israel was brought to life in a single day, by a vote of the United Nations, but, like the Golem, it is unwilling to pass into oblivion as soon as the danger is over. Furthermore, it is clear that the Jewish people are in danger today as always. The danger has not passed, and the Golem called Israel still lives!

Golem, Golem, Who's Got the Golem?

The story of the Golem finds many levels of interpretation, including those relating to practical modes of meditation. Some assert that the Golem is more than just a figure of clay; the Golem is a particular type of soul brought down from on high by the practice of meditation. This way of thinking envisions the meditative exercise of drawing down a "pure soul" — creating within oneself a purified consciousness. After all, the Golem has certain traits which, if they could be created afresh, are greatly to be desired. Specifically, the Golem possesses a pure soul, has no fleshly lusts, is incapable of sin, and is therefore immune from illness. Consequently, the meditative goal is to put away impure thoughts and emotions, coming ever nearer to God, to a point of absolute proximity. On this level one is admonished to create a Golem, metaphysically, every day.

It Happened in Smyrna

The New Testament's own book of Kabbalah, Revelation, contains a cryptic message to a certain city called Smyrna, in modern-day Turkey, on the deeply indented coast of the Aegean Sea: "Do not be afraid of what you are about to suffer. I tell you, the devil will put some of you in prison to test you, and you will suffer persecution" (Rev. 2:10 NIV). To the early Christians, Smyrna was a cauldron of tension. But perhaps Smyrna's greatest test of faith came far later, in the seventeenth century.

Smryna is home to abundant landmarks from the classical world, from a spectacular marketplace — the Agora — to the ancient aqueducts of Kizilcullu. Snugly situated on a small delta plain, Smyrna is one of the oldest cities of the Mediterranean world. Off to the east, the great Anatolian Plateau covering almost all of Asia Minor looms upward, to over two thousand feet. Far to the north, the Pontic Mountains course along the shore of the Black Sea, while, to the south, the taller ranges of the Taurus and Anti-Taurus Mountains stretch skyward to nearly thirteen thousand feet. As the enormous mesa slopes westward toward the Aegean, it is transformed into a belt of bluffs and headlands. It is a region of scattered lowlands interlaced with hillocks. There are no active volcanoes in this part of Turkey, but the whole peninsula is geologically unstable and known for massive earthquakes. One earthquake of a different variety occurred when a particular expression of Kabbalah got out of hand, in the form of a young rabbi of piety and sincerity, if somewhat illusory vision.

The end was near. Surely a better day was about to dawn. It was a hope shared by Jews as well as Christians. For the latter, it took the form of a fervent longing for the return of Jesus — the "Second Coming" — to put things right in a universe torn by human waywardness. It would amount to a completion of the process of redemption which the "First Coming" only began. For Jews, however, the Messiah had not come at all. How could the Anointed One have come as long as war and bloodshed reigned supreme, as long as the lion lay not down with the lamb, as long as the people of Israel remained in lonely dispersion, as outcasts among the nations of the earth? The agony of the expulsion from Spain heightened and compounded the longing for redemption, as did a horrific series of events in Poland and the Ukraine that culminated in the year 1648.

The Poles had sent many of the Jews of their lands (called Rendars) east into the Ukraine, as "colonists," to develop an efficiently bureaucratic system of farming and to send the proceeds back home. The Ukrainians, being Eastern Orthodox, bitterly resented the Catholic Poles, and they took out their rage against the visible symbols of Polish presence on their turf, who happened to be Jewish, not Catholic. A huge uprising, headed by a fierce and murderous Cossack named Bogdan Chmielnicki, was launched against the Jewish Rendars, who fled west by the thousands, across the Dnieper River and back into Poland. Over three hundred Jewish towns and villages were decimated in what turned into a horrific two-year tide of bloodshed. By the time it was over, more than one hundred thousand Eastern European Jews had lost their lives. It was by anyone's estimation a mini-Holocaust, as a direct consequence of which a pallor of despair descended across the whole of Jewry.

The terrible suffering of these times appeared to many as a sign that the "end of days" was finally near, that the promised redemption was on its way. The present torment must surely be what prophets and Sages had long spoken of as "the pangs of the Messiah." Just as every birth is accompanied by the pains of labor, so the travail of the people heralds the birth of the Messianic Age. This was not a time for despondency; it was a time for jubilation and hope that the Deliverer would come to gather the exiles and sit firmly on the throne of David.

In the year 1648, on the heels of the mass slaughter in Poland and the Ukraine, the Messiah came. The *Zohar* had indeed predicted that in this very year — a year which had in reality produced unspeakable horror — the age of redemption would dawn. A cryptic passage reads:

> At the conclusion of the twelve tribes (twelve hundred years) there will be darkness over Israel, until the *Vav* [a Hebrew letter and reference to the Messiah] shall arise at the time of sixty-six years after twelve hundred years of exile. And after the conclusion of the sixty-six years of the night-darkness, the words "And I shall remember my covenant with Jacob" will begin to come to pass. . . . After that King Messiah shall fight against the whole world, aided by the Right Hand of the Holy One. At the end of another sixty-six years the letters in the Holy Name shall be seen perfectly engraved above and below in manner due. After a further one hundred and thirty-two years He will begin "to take hold of the ends of the earth and shake off the wicked." The Holy Land will be purified, and the Holy One will raise the dead there and they shall rise in their hosts in the land of Galilee. At the end of a further hundred and forty-four years the remaining dead of Israel in other lands shall be raised, so that after altogether four hundred and eight years the world shall be re-inhabited and the evil principle (the "other side") driven out of it. . . . Then the holy spirits of the people

of Israel at the fullness of time will be invested with new, holy bodies, and be called "Saints". . . . These are the veiled mysteries.[125]

According to the *Zohar*, Israel's exile began 3828 years after the creation of the world. Adding twelve hundred and another sixty-six years to that, the *Zohar* arrives at 1306 A.D. The signs of redemption are to be manifest in another one hundred ninety-eight (66 + 132) years, or in 1504 A.D Add to that yet another one hundred forty-four years, and one arrives at the year 1648 A.D. This was when the Redeemer would come.

The Redeemer's name was only now revealed, as Shabbetai Zvi, and he would create a phenomenon that would verge on mass hysteria. Humanly speaking, he was a man of fine physique, comely and tall, sporting a neatly trimmed beard, with Cimmerian hair. His eyes had a "far-off" look of mystery about them. His voice, both in speaking and in song, was said to be melodious and enchanting. His enthusiasm was contagious. Though of Spanish lineage, his home was the city of Smyrna in Asia Minor. As a child he avoided the company of others, shunning playmates and developing a solitary bent. Like his compatriots, he studied the Talmud in school, but he gravitated to its more esoteric elements, turning ultimately to the enigmatic lessons of Kabbalah. Quite precocious throughout his youth, Shabbetai received ordination as a rabbi when he was just eighteen years of age.

The young mystic married a beautiful young wife, but, being of an ascetic nature, tended to ignore her and even shunned physical intimacy with her in search of a higher truth. Such indiscretions are not allowed in Judaism, and in time, Shabbetai's wife sought a writ of divorce. A similar fate awaited a second marriage, which also ended in divorce. It was said that he seemed to lack an instinctual attraction to the opposite sex.

He was still quite young when he found himself the leader of a devoted band of mystical souls in Smyrna. He would sing to them the verses of Kabbalah — the very words of Isaac Luria — in the original Spanish. He uttered many mysteries, including the divine name of God, which, contrary to all established tradition he would vocalize fully. His fame and legacy began to grow. "The Kingdom of Heaven is at hand!" So had proclaimed Isaac Luria, the "Divine Rabbi," and his kabbalistic disciples; the familiar chords of this refrain surfaced anew in the teachings of Shabbetai Zvi.

The plan of the redemption to come was magically and marvelously complex. The scattered shards of the "primordial soul," which are found in every person, need to ascend from the shackles of "primordial evil." But when the evil inclination takes hold of human nature through the fall of the "divine elements," the upward ascent of these shards is impeded. Since human souls are thereby held in bondage, a continual transmigration of souls from body to body is required. However, the moment the spirit of evil is made impotent, the kabbalistic order will reign supreme. Streams of mercy will flow forth unimpeded upon the "lower world," to restore it through miraculous agency. Moreover, every truly righteous person — or *Tzadik* — can bring about this great redemption. The mystical strains of the teaching were compelling indeed.

"John the Baptist"

It was in Smyrna that Shabbetai Zvi first heard of the massacres in Poland and the Ukraine. Not long afterward, around the year 1651, he and his disciples were placed under a rabbinic ban, exiled from the city of Smyrna. He wandered from place to place and made his way to the Turkish capital, where a preacher named Abraham Yakhini showed him what he claimed to be an ancient parchment, written by the father of the Jewish people, Abraham. It read:

> I, Abraham, was shut up for forty years in a cave, and wondered that the time of miracles did not make its appearance. Then a voice replied to me, "A son shall be born in the year of the world 5386 [corresponding to 1626], and be called Shabbetai. He shall quell the great dragon; he is the true Messiah, and shall wage war without weapons."[126]

Deeply believing in his own mission Shabbetai traveled on to the Holy City, Jerusalem, where he devoted himself to prayer, shedding floods of tears. In time he went on to Cairo in Egypt, where he sought aid from a prominent supporter.

Then came the young Kabbalist's "true love," an enchanting fellow mystic named Sarah. She, like Shabbetai, was a desolate soul. An orphan from the massacres of 1648, she had subsequently eked out a living as a prostitute. But never mind her dubious occupation; had not the biblical prophet Hosea married a prostitute? Besides, Sarah had steadfastly maintained that she was to become the bride of the Messiah; she could make no other marriage contract. It was all part of the divine plan. Furthermore, Sarah's beauty and charming manner galvanized the support of a growing train of followers, including many young males who would otherwise have had no interest in mystical messianism.

It was on the way back to Jerusalem that Shabbetai and his "magical mystery tour" encountered a young rabbi, scholar, and mystic named Nathan of Gaza. He was a man of flawless reputation, and he was said to be able to exorcise demons and to read people's souls. Deeply involved in the world of esoteric speculation, Nathan the Kabbalist, over the course of the next two years, came to be convinced that he was in fact a prophet and that his particular mission and task was to announce the arrival of the Anointed King of Israel. He was a "reincarnation" of Elijah the prophet, preparing the way for the Messiah. And the Messiah, as revealed to him by a supernatural vision, was none other than Shabbetai Zvi. Just as John the Baptist had announced Jesus, just as Rabbi Akiva had proclaimed the messianic stature of Simon bar-Kochba, Nathan was to declare Shabbetai.

The moment of truth came on the last day of May 1665, when the two men appeared at Gaza and made the awesome announcement. Who would have thought the impact that such an announcement would have? Who would have imagined that large numbers of people would soon begin to believe that this eccentric man, known for practicing extreme asceticism and self-denial, was the one they had been waiting for? But the message was surprisingly well received and was followed up by a number of circular letters, directed to the entire Diaspora — the scattered Jews of every land. Shabbetai began to parade about on horseback. In a manner resembling Jesus of Nazareth, he summoned twelve disciples who were deemed fit to become judges of the twelve tribes of Israel.

The next events in this bizarre tale are almost beyond belief. Shabbetai Zvi came home to Smyrna, even though he had been banned by the rabbis fully ten years earlier. When he appeared there in the synagogue, the *Shofar* (the ram's horn) was publicly blown, and the throng shouted, "Long live our King, our Messiah!" Shabbetai took hold of the scroll of the Torah, cradled it in his arms, and proceeded to chant to it, in his melodic voice, an old Castillian love song. After some days, the enthusiastic believers deleted the name of the Turkish sultan from the prayers for the welfare of the ruling authorities and substituted a prayer for Shabbetai Zvi, the Messiah and King of all Israel. A new crop of seers walked the streets of Smyrna, proclaiming visions of Shabbetai enthroned in glory. Nathan of

Gaza next sent another circular letter, in which he prophesied the shape of things to come. He wrote the following:

> A year and a few months from today, Shabbetai will take the dominion from the Turkish king without war, for by the power of hymns and praises which he shall utter, all nations shall submit to his rule. He will take the Turkish king along to the countries which he will conquer, and all the kings shall be tributary unto him, but only the Turkish king will be his servant.[127]

Moreover, a new doctrine began to crystallize. A new divine personage had sprouted forth from God, who would restore Divine Perfection in the world. This person was the Messiah, "Holy King" and "Primordial Man." He would destroy corruption in the world and make streams of grace to flow in the desert. He was not only Messiah; he was God incarnate. Yet another circular letter was issued:

> The first-begotten Son of God, Shabbetai Zvi, Messiah and Redeemer of the people of Israel, to all the sons of Israel, Peace! Since you have been deemed worthy to behold the great day and the fulfillment of God's word by the prophets, your lament and sorrow must be changed into joy, and your fasting into merriment, for you shall weep no more. Rejoice with song and melody, and change the day formerly spent in sadness and sorrow into a day of jubilee, because I have appeared.[128]

In an incredible development, multiple Jewish communities in many different lands began to prepare themselves for the ultimate redemption of the people. From Egypt to London and a host of places in between, the true believers rushed to the immersion baths, to cleanse their souls for the day of salvation. For a people bowed under a yoke of oppression, the very idea produced ecstasy. They watched and waited for a mystical, supernatural sign, that would bid them to set sail for the Holy Land. Many began selling their worldly belongings, even their homes. From London a letter, written to the great Jewish philosopher of Amsterdam, Baruch Spinoza, bears witness to the mania:

All the world here is talking of a rumor of the return of the Israelites, dispersed for more than two thousand years, to their own country. Few believe it, but many wish it. . . . Should the news be confirmed, it may bring about a revolution in all things.[129]

The long waiting for the "confirmation," however, proved to be in vain. The signal did not come. A record from a Yiddish chronicler of the town of Hamlin, in Germany, reads as follows:

Many sold their houses and lands and all their possessions, for any day they hoped to be redeemed. My good father-in-law left his home in Hamlin, abandoned his house and lands and all his goodly furniture, and moved to Hildesheim. He sent on to us in Hamburg two enormous casks packed with linens and with peas, beans, dried meats, shredded prunes, and like stuff, every manner of food that would keep. For the old man expected to sail any moment from Hamburg to the Holy Land. . . . For three years the casks stood ready and all this while my father-in-law awaited the signal to depart. But the Most High pleased otherwise.[130]

Across the lands of their dispersion, many were spurred on by the mystical impulse and decided to wait no longer. Even as Shabbetai Zvi himself made preparations to journey from Smyrna to the capital of the Turkish empire, Constantinople, the true believers from across Europe and North Africa set out on a massive exodus toward Palestine. This was the messianic ingathering of the exiles. The "end of days" had come. On the part of the Turks, it was hard to ignore the fact that thousands of people had physically uprooted themselves and crowded onto ships bound for the eastern flank of the Ottoman empire. The sultan was amazed and bewildered. What could this "citizen army" be up to? Might they pose a threat to the very stability of the Turkish government? Whatever their true intentions, the sultan decided that they must be stopped and that he must act. On his specific orders, Shabbetai Zvi was captured somewhere off the coast of the Dardanelles and brought to his destination, Constantinople, not as the conquering Messiah, but as a prisoner bound in fetters.

Prometheus Bound

Thrown into prison, the now notorious messianic pretender nonetheless received numerous visitors, who doggedly persisted in believing in him. There were reports of miracles performed at his hands, proving that, even in confinement, God's grand design was being accomplished. It was all part of a divine plan. This, clearly, was not what the Turks had in mind for Shabbetai's fate. If we execute him, reasoned the sultan, we will make him a martyr to the throngs of his followers descending on our eastern flank. Better to make him an example of folly and misplaced faith.

Shabbetai was dragged before a Turkish tribunal in September 1666. In the presence of the sultan himself, he was given a clear choice: "Choose Allah or die!" Shabbetai chose Allah. In a state of deep melancholy, and betraying at least a modicum of blind terror, Shabbetai Zvi had done the unthinkable. He had officially converted to Islam. In return for being promised a daily stipend of one hundred fifty piasters, he even changed his name to Aziz Mehmed Effendi — a far cry from the promised Redeemer of Israel.

But the mania, once it had begun, simply would not die. In stunned disbelief, Shabbetai's followers could not accept that their hopes for deliverance were once more in vain. Perhaps even this was part of the divine order. Are not such setbacks all a part of the "pangs of the Messiah"? Nathan of Gaza developed the notion that the Messiah's apostasy was the ultimate phase in the process of redemption. In descending to the pit of evil, he was in fact raising up the last of the sacred sparks. Indeed, reasoned others within the movement, if the Messiah had converted to Islam, so would they! Suddenly, the sultan had droves of new converts to Islam on his hands. Still others, who chose not to follow Shabbetai in conversion, simply believed that it would all become clear in good time. Perhaps this was all part of a ruse. Perhaps the real Shabbetai had been spirited off to heaven, and this fellow, Aziz Mehmed Effendi, was merely an impostor. The mass hysteria waned, but was not extinguished.

The flotilla bearing down on Palestine slowly dispersed, conveying many hapless and brokenhearted Shabbateans back home, to consign themselves to more long years of patient waiting. The founder of the movement, Shabbetai Zvi, died on the Day of Atonement, in 1676, a broken and disillusioned man. But even after his death, many of his most prominent devotees would not give up their messianic longings. Nathan of Gaza, in particular, spent the rest of his days as a vagabond and wanderer between the great cities of the Mediterranean world, fanning the embers of the dying movement, trying to keep Shabbetai's magic alive. Nathan died just three years after Shabbetai's death, but small clandestine pockets of followers carried on the odd legacy. Someday, they reasoned, the Redeemer will return, bringing his redemption with him. Like a virus that lives on residually in the human body, Shabbetai

Zvi's stubborn brand of magical mystery messianism was never quite extinguished. It lived on in trace amounts, only to be reinvented in one form or another down to the present day.

Jacob Frank: Prometheus Unbound

One more outcropping of the Shabbatean frenzy exploded a full century after the original movement crystallized. Small secret Shabbatean societies had continued to come together from the late 1600s to the early 1700s, from the Middle East to continental Europe, involving some of the most prominent rabbinic dynasties. By the middle of the eighteenth century, a charismatic figure of enormous ego named Jacob Frank came to the fore in southern Poland, proclaiming himself the heir of Shabbetai Zvi's legacy. He had encountered followers of Shabbetai during his youthful travels in Turkey, and now he was prepared to reinvigorate the movement in his homeland. Physically strong and a megalomaniac, Frank became the central figure for Shabbateans in Poland, Hungary, and the Ukraine.[131] He announced the creation of a veritable army of Jews, sufficient to carve out an independent Jewish state within the borders of Poland.

He had a particularly erotic constitution, and his sexual indulgence was a bond held in common with other members of the Shabbatean brotherhood. They were said to have engaged in all manner of orgiastic rites as part of their spiritual practice. Sin and evil, they insisted, was to be made holy. It was to be sanctified. The practice of sin by "holy men" served to redeem it. What about the commandments of the Law — "Thou shalt not . . . "? Kabbalistic lore had long maintained that the Law would "wither away" in the Messianic Age. And since the Messianic Age had clearly arrived, such commandments no longer applied.

Clearly, the leaders of traditional Judaism were not amused.

Accusing Jacob Frank of gross ignorance, they formally excommunicated him in the year 1756. They even went so far as to approach the venerable Rabbi Jacob Israel Emden with the idea that the Christians should be asked to burn the Frankists as heretics. Emden replied that such a scheme would be impractical and too costly. Moreover, invoking the aid of the Holy See would be no easy task. Under mounting pressure, Frank, like Shabbetai Zvi before him, converted to another faith, in this case Christianity. One more nail had been driven into the proverbial casket of the Shabbateans; one more outcropping of Kabbalah — perhaps the most bizarre in history — had gone by the wayside.

Christian Kabbalah

Welcome, all ye noble saints of old
As now before your very eyes unfold
The wonders of so long ago foretold
God and man at table are sat down.[132]

This popular eucharistic song of modern Christian liturgy sums up the longing of the mystics, who asked the "Great Question" from ages past: How can the infinite God, who is beyond space and time, be intimately involved with mortal human beings, trapped in frail bodies of flesh and blood and sinew? Jewish prophets, Sages, and rabbis had from time immemorial found the answer in the interwoven threads of Kabbalah, coursing through the tapestry of the culture of their people. For Christians, however, the answer was expressed in the person of Jesus of Nazareth, who celebrated the mystical union of God and humanity in the sharing of bread and wine. The apostle Paul had written, "He is the image of the invisible God, the first-born of all creation" (Col. 1:15). And the Gospel writer declared, "No one has ever seen God; the only Son, who is in the bosom of the Father, he has made him known" (John 1:18). For Christians it was Jesus who bridged the gap between individuals and their Creator. Infinite Deity was "explained" in the life of a single man. Since Jesus, Paul, and other New Testament personages were, in a sense, Kabbalists in their own right, it was perhaps inevitable that Christianity would one day gravitate toward its common roots with Judaism in the realm of mysticism. It was only natural that Christian mystics of a later age would turn to Kabbalah in their deep yearning to express their faith in the Man of Galilee.

In spite of serious misunderstanding and mutual hostility between Jews and Christians, explosions of Kabbalah and Christian mysticism sometimes occurred in lockstep. Moreover, the mystical movements of both faiths were certainly related, not only to each other, but to grand currents in cultural history swirling about them. Sometimes Jewish mystical writings seemed to contain distinctly "Christian" themes. For example, the *Zohar* proclaimed certain concepts which sounded hauntingly "Christian" in tone, including a peculiar proclamation of the "Holy Trinity": "Three there were! Turned back into one!"[133] Did this statement refer to three rabbis mentioned in the *Zohar,* as some contended, or did it reference, in mystical tones, the Christian proclamation of the Father, Son, and Holy Spirit?

The famed Dominican mystic, Meister Eckhart, while he was not familiar with the *Zohar* itself, was nonetheless fascinated by Jewish writings. And this fascination colored his meditations on Christ. Another Christian cleric of the Middle Ages, Saint John of the Cross, wrote his famous poetic work, *The Dark Night of the Soul,* in a state of "perfection," namely the union of pure love with God. Through his many trials, in which he was kidnapped, publicly flogged, and half-starved, he found his rapturous union with God. But it fell to others to fully develop the Christian link with Jewish mysticism.

Renaissance Mystics

There was for example Pico della Mirandola, of Florence, Italy, who became intoxicated with kabbalistic thought during the period shortly before the expulsion of the Jews from Spain. Thanks to Pico's interest in Kabbalah, Jewish influence on

European culture — which was already growing as the Jews fanned out from Spain — was all the more intensified. Of course, Pico studied the techniques of Jewish Kabbalah from a particularly Christian vantage point, supplying uniquely Christian interpretations. He was convinced that Kabbalah verified the truth of Christianity and that, based on the mystical manipulation of letters and names, he could prove that the name of the Messiah is in fact "Jesus." He declared, "No Hebrew Kabbalist can deny that the name IESU (Jesus), if we interpret it on Kabbalist principles, signifies the Son of God."[134] He believed that the ancient text of the Hebrew Bible (the Old Testament) could, through Jewish mysticism, enhance and sanctify the fabric of Christianity.

Pico divided Kabbalah into two branches: the combination of Hebrew letters to transmit mystical messages, and the capturing of power from higher realms, that is, the power of angels and spirits. But he warned about dangers inherent in kabbalistic practice. If the use of Kabbalah is pure and holy, the results will be good. But if the two branches are combined, through the unholy use of magical arts, the end will be great evil.

In the end, Pico's greatest contribution was the introduction of Christian Kabbalah into the heart of the Italian Renaissance. As a result, the Renaissance — the "rebirth" of western culture through the rediscovery of its ancient and classical past — would grow to include not only the rational arts and sciences of Michelangelo, Léonardo da Vinci, and a host of others, but also a sizable mystical and "occult" component, fed by Christians interested in Kabbalah.

As the "rebirth" spilled across Italy's northern borders, the stream of Christian Kabbalah was picked up by Johannes Reuchlin, one of the greatest scholars of the German Renaissance. Reuchlin traveled to Italy as a young man, where he met Pico della Mirandola and others involved with interpreting Kabbalah in a Christian light. Inspired by Pico's work,

Reuchlin began studying Jewish mysticism himself. He wrote books pertaining to Kabbalah and the Hebrew language, taking the new discipline of "Christian Kabbalah" to a higher level. Unfortunately, while he was writing his second work, *De Arte Cabalistica*, a fierce eruption of anti-Semitism transpired, instigated by a Jewish convert to Christianity named Johann Pfefferkorn. Reuchlin held his ground, however, entering into a controversy with Pfefferkorn which catapulted him to fame all across Europe. Reuchlin was seen as victimized by rigid conservatives and was hailed as a hero of the "New Learning" which the Renaissance epitomized. Furthermore, Reuchlin advanced the idea that Christian Kabbalah was at the very heart of the New Learning. As Renaissance Christians increasingly turned to Jews to help them translate and appreciate the Hebrew scriptures (Old Testament), Reuchlin announced that the new Hebrew studies were just as important for Renaissance Christians as the study of Greek.

The Crucible

Nevertheless, the spirit of tolerance fostered by the Renaissance was not destined to last. The sixteenth and seventeenth centuries saw a marked increase in anti-Semitism, accompanied by various witch hunts. Anything "supernatural," including Kabbalah and Christian Kabbalah, was, during these centuries, held in deep suspicion.

One so-called sorcerer and practitioner of "black magic," who happened to survive the crucible of the age, was the notorious Henry Cornelius Agrippa. He penned his famous *Occult Philosophy* (or *Three Books of Occult Philosophy*), with the objective of combining "natural magic" and the kabbalistic magic of Pico della Mirandola. This voluminous work played an important role in the spread of Renaissance Neoplatonism (the division of the universe into physical and metaphysical realms), with its magical core. The function of Kabbalah, according to Agrippa, was to gain access to the highest supercelestial magic — "white magic" — and to fortify individuals for spiritual encounters. He wrote:

> Seeing there is a threefold world, elementary, celestial, and
> intellectual, and every inferior is governed by its superior . . .
> wise men conceive it no way irrational that it should be possible
> for us to ascend by the same degrees through each world, to the
> same very original world itself, the maker of all things, and First
> Cause, from whence all things are, and proceed.[135]

But Agrippa failed to convince critics that they should appeal to a philosophy more profound than intellectual scholasticism.

The French in particular believed Agrippa to be the most pernicious of black magicians, which led to the spread of the witch hunts in Europe. Not a few practitioners of metaphysics were now accused of witchcraft and burned at the stake, among them many innocent women. The subsequent witch trials of Salem, Massachusetts, owe their inspiration, at least in part, to the European "crackdown" on Christian Kabbalah.

Reformation

Also influenced by the growing Christian interest in kabbalistic speculation was the famous German artist, Albrecht Dürer, a compatriot of the great Reformers, Erasmus of Rotterdam and Martin Luther, as well as the mystic Henry Cornelius Agrippa.[136] Dürer saw art as power, and he believed that the root of artistic power is to be found in numbers — the domain of kabbalistic *gematria*.[136] The deeply religious Dürer was impressed by Luther and became a Lutheran Protestant. Consequently his designs were characterized by faultless geometrical precision as well as profound religious meaning. His widely hailed engraving of Melencolia I was inspired by Agrippa's *Occult Philosophy* and Reuchlin's *De Verbo Mirifico*.[137] Dürer's work as a whole centered on the idea of religion made stronger through a mystical link with the world beyond. His engravings are the stuff of inspired trance, in which the visionary is protected from demonic dangers by the presence of angels. Arguably, to the extent that Christians have been interested in angels and the angelic realm, they are being more or less directly influenced by Jewish mysticism, and by the likes of Pico della Mirandola, Reuchlin, and Agrippa.

Some time afterward, another Reformation artist, Lucas Cranach, produced a group of paintings in turn influenced by Dürer. In Cranach's work, the visionary is not protected from demonic powers, but is rather at the mercy of witches. Christian Kabbalists, intent on preserving a wholesome spirituality, warned of the inherent danger in Cranach's art, which turned the imagery of Dürer's melancholy in the direction of witchcraft. But the growing interest in the supernatural, which they had unleashed, apparently had a mind of its own and would not be easily harnessed by well-meaning admonitions.

Of Witches and Fairies and William Shakespeare

The Elizabethan Age was profoundly affected by the metaphysical impulse, in its occult philosophy, its magic, its melancholy, and its goal of penetrating the circles of knowledge and experience, both scientific and spiritual. In Elizabethan England, the philosopher John Dee, son of an official at the court of King Henry VIII, rose to prominence.[138] When Queen Elizabeth I came to the throne, he was immediately accepted into her court. The extent to which Dee's philosophy, and with it all of Elizabethan philosophy, was affected by Kabbalah is apparent from the content of his library. On its shelves were writings of Pico della Mirandola, Johannes Reuchlin, and several copies of Agrippa's *Occult Philosophy*. While believing himself to be a zealous Reformed Christian, John Dee was in reality a Christian Kabbalist. He had a fascination with the supercelestial world of angels and divine powers. He believed he had the power, personally, to summon angels. He wrote of attending seances with his assistant, while Agrippa's book was present on the table.

In 1589, Dee traveled to Prague, where the occultist emperor Rudolph II held his court. It was in Prague that he came into contact with the illustrious Rabbi Loew of the Golem story. The Christian metaphysical philosopher and the Kabbalist rabbi must certainly have had a great deal to talk about. From Prague Dee journeyed to Bohemia, staying with a noble family who were themselves interested in the occult. Dee and his associate went forth attempting to summon angels via the incantations of Practical Kabbalah. His overarching mission was to proceed to higher levels of Christian Kabbalah as a means of encouraging great religious revival.

Things did not materialize as he had hoped. By the time Dee returned to England, none of his supporters remained in the court, and the Queen no longer favored his philosophical inquiries. Shunned and isolated, Dee was also confronted by a growing witch hunt. He never regained prominence, though other prominent Elizabethans expressed their own versions of Christian Kabbalah. There was, for example, Edmund Spencer, who was described as a Neoplatonist and who inclined toward elements of Christian Kabbalah, as found in the writings of Reuchlin and Agrippa. Like John Dee, Spencer advanced the idea of a higher philosophy which would bring on a worldwide movement of rebirth, with Queen Elizabeth I, of course, at the helm.

Then there was William Shakespeare, who has been hailed for many reasons, though rarely is he understood for his role in expressing various aspects of Christian Kabbalah and occult philosophy. *Hamlet*, for example, contains several melancholy and prophetic visions. Shakespeare's work as a whole is laced with elements of the supernatural, from ghosts in *Hamlet* to witches in *Macbeth* to fairies in *King Lear*.[139] Although Shakespeare did not directly have a hand in Christian Kabbalah or occult philosophy, he was, nonetheless, greatly influenced by it.

God and Man at Table Are Sat Down

Christian Kabbalah did not in the end bring forth a new age of understanding, either between Jews and Christians or of the doctrines of Christianity itself. Jews, who were targeted by the Church as "Christ killers," continued to be vilified and scorned, officially and unofficially, as Europe's eternal pariahs. Some Christian Kabbalists, eagerly anticipating the Second Coming of Christ, as Messiah, deliberately befriended Jewish mystics, who were just as eagerly anticipating the Messiah's First Coming. But the undertow of mistrust remained, and no amount of theosophical speculation could bridge the gap. Was the growth of Christian Kabbalah a unique opportunity for Judeo-Christian dialogue? Was it a chance for theological adversaries to come together in a common aim of finding a mystical unity with the Infinite God? If so, it was an opportunity lost. Perhaps in the modern eucharistic hymn the hope for mutual understanding lives on:

> Elders, martyrs all are falling down,
> And prophets, patriarchs are gathering round,
> What angels long to see now man has found.
> God and man at table are sat down.

The Master of a Good Name

The 1700s were, to be sure, interesting times, spiritually. In England a fiery preacher named George Fox began charging into the cathedrals of the Anglican Church, denouncing the priests as "empty professors of religion." Dubbed the "red hot Quaker," he spearheaded a movement of sincere followers who gathered across the hillsides, awaiting the stirrings of the Holy Spirit that caused them to "quake." Hence was born a revival of common folk, the Quakers. In Wales, a disparate Christian sect began to jump in frenzied dance, and became known as the "Jumpers." And in America, another group crystallized, the "Shakers," establishing communal settlements where they practiced their peculiar form of semi-delirious prayer. Little wonder that numbers of Christians began to be interested in a great master of Kabbalism, who stepped out of obscurity in eastern Europe to become one of the driving forces of Jewish spiritual renewal.

Israel ben Eliezer was a remarkable man indeed. In sleep he seemed almost ordinary. Yet, when he spoke to disciples, when his eyes locked on theirs, he became far more striking, more wise, more powerful, more compelling, than anyone they had ever known. For had not many astonishing miracles been done by his hands? Did he not have the secret knowledge of the name of God, which, when he uttered its letters in proper sequence, effectuated miraculous cures? Indeed, he knew their very thoughts, as if empowered by some sublime perception.

They called him a *Baal Shem*, a "Master of the Name." Many *Baalei Shem* (Masters of the Name) had come before him. They were miracle workers, this class of teachers, at whose hands the works of God were accomplished. They expelled demons; they brought divine health beyond the abilities of physicians. When the world round about was bleak and gray and anti-Semitic, the *Baalei Shem* held the heart of the people at their bosoms. Of Israel ben Eliezer it is said, "He knew the secret, full name of God, and could say it in such a way that — with its help — he was able to effect strange things and especially to heal men in body and soul."[140]

To be sure, this man was beyond all his predecessors. In an environment dominated by rational skepticism, he brought unbounded joy. His detractors claimed that he was but an *Am ha-aretz* (an ignorant man) who had no legitimate claim to authority. Such criticism, however, fell on deaf ears. For this man's authority derived not from the number of years he had studied in rabbinical *yeshiva*, nor from the nature of the ordination he had received, but from his personal level of devotion and his ability to communicate that devotion to his admirers. Like the ancient mystic, Khoni the Circle-Drawer, his authority was a measure of his popularity, and on this ground, he was virtually unassailable.

Consequently, *Baal Shem* was not the whole of his nomenclature. It seemed only fitting that he should also be called a *Shem Tov*, one who has a "good name." In other words, he was hugely admired by his compatriots and by the people at large. He was not only well thought of, but adored, almost to the point of being worshipped. He who began as a relatively unlearned man in the ghettoized communities of eastern Europe rose to prominence, becoming a cultural icon among Jews around the world. Thus, the two designations of his name, *Baal Shem* and *Shem Tov*, were fused, and he became the *Baal*

Shem Tov, "Master of a Good Name." The first letters of the three words of this title were also fused, as an acrostic, so that he was also called simply "the Besht."

The Besht wrote down nothing during his lifetime, though the stories about him are legion. He was born in the mountains of southern Poland, in a village called Okopy, around the year 1700. In folklore, we read: "Israel's father died while he was still a child. When he felt death drawing near, he took the boy in his arms and said, 'I see that you will make my light shine out, and it is not given me to rear you to manhood. But, dear son, remember all your days that God is with you, and that because of this, you need fear nothing in all the world.' Israel treasured these words in his heart."[141]

Education has always been highly valued in Jewish culture, but the Baal Shem Tov, perhaps because of being orphaned and poverty-stricken, was a poor student. After all, the dimly lit, narrow hovels in which children studied in those days were hardly conducive to learning, nor did they inspire restive souls such as young Israel's. He would often run away from the study hall and find solace in the woods, meditating on the things of nature. We read, "Now, Israel studied diligently enough, but always only for a few days running. Then he played truant and they found him somewhere in the woods and alone."[142] Indeed, he loved nature, and he saw God in nature, for everything in nature points to God — a theme which courses through Kabbalah from beginning to end. For him the greatest aim of life was understanding the tongue with which nature speaks.

He held several odd jobs during his early years, among them being that of a teacher's assistant. He was charged with gathering up the local children and leading them off to school via the woods, where he would teach them to listen to the chirping of the birds. "While he walked with them, he sang to them and taught them to sing with him."[143] Conventional study of rabbinic Law, represented in the Talmud, interested him little.

Instead, he found another job, which involved being a watch-man in a *Bet Midrash* (House of Study) by day, while by night he threw himself into the study of Kabbalah. In mysticism he found his true passion, his love, his calling.

The Lure of the Mountains

At some point in his early life he journeyed to the moun-tains, to contemplate life and God and human existence. The rocky spurs and babbling mountain streams whispered their secrets to those who had ears to hear. The simple peasants of the region were skilled in the use of herbal remedies, which Kabbalah had embraced from the very beginning. To the reme-dies themselves he added prayer — not just the liturgical bene-dictions he was accustomed to pray in synagogue, but intense, fervent groanings, evidence of his deep *kavanah,* the inclina-tion of his heart. Such prayer reverberated across the moun-tains, as he threw his entire body into motion, rocking and bobbing and swaying with fervor. It has been said that *kavanah* is the mystery of a soul directed to a goal.[144] Such was the soul of Israel ben Eliezer.

He was in general a man of few words, not given to the argumentative fury that characterized much of his generation. He spoke deliberately, almost pensively, but with a gentle con-fidence that caught his hearers in a spell of unabashed opti-mism. There was a sense of calm about him, a steadiness and sensitivity. In due time he married a rabbi's daughter, and together they eked out a livelihood. "They came to a little town in the Carpathian Mountains, where the woman found a place to live. Israel went to the nearby hills, built himself a hut, and quarried clay. Two or three times a week, she went to him, helped him load the clay in the wagon, took it into the town and sold it for a small sum. When Israel was hungry, he put water and flour into a little pit, kneaded the dough, and baked it in the sun."[145] All the while he lived for the ecstasy of his life with God. Sometimes during his prayer he would catch a glimpse of eternity, his soul flying heavenward to be embraced by light. He once declared, "A glance can flood the soul with great light, but the fear of men builds walls to keep the light away."[146]

Later, he and his wife became the proprietors of an inn, but they continued to live in dire poverty. The bulk of the income derived during his wanderings he gave away as an expression of *Tz'dakah* — "charity." Above all, he maintained ritual purity, dunking himself every day in a ritual immersion bath — a *mikveh*. Then, on his thirty-sixth birthday, the time came for his "unveiling," the revelation of his divine calling. He triumphantly announced his true vocation — as a teacher and faith healer. Israel ben Eliezer had become the Baal Shem Tov.

A period of wandering began, during which time the Besht began to manifest his remarkable gifts of healing. He prayed, "Lord, it is known and manifest to you how much rests in me of understanding and power, and there is no man to whom I could reveal it."[147] Miracles were wrought at his hands. He imparted his healing virtue to everyone he met on trek across southern Poland, from ordinary workers in the fields to tax collectors. Like ordinary "physicians" of his day, he practiced bloodletting and the application of leeches. But beyond "conventional" medical techniques, he reveled in the miraculous. He exorcised demons of insanity, and many people were returned to their right minds. He resorted to the use of Practical Kabbalah, employing spells, magical incantations, and special amulets in the service of the divine will.

A Kabbalistic "Sermon on the Mount"

When he opened his mouth to teach, his audience was mesmerized by his smoothly melodic voice. In a sort of "transfiguration," people barely recognized this man, who suddenly spoke with boldness and authority. Was this the same wagoner, the same horse-trader, who had wandered through their country as a vagabond? Much of what the Baal Shem Tov taught was certainly distorted. When the Besht was handed a transcript of his orations, he took one look and exclaimed, "There is not *one* word here that I have spoken!"[148] But we can at least imagine what his teaching must have sounded like, as he stood before his devoted little band of disciples, inhaling periodically through the pipe in his mouth:

"God is everywhere, in everyone and in everything. Kabbalah teaches that the sparks of the divine presence scattered at the moment of creation, and that the burden of humanity is to collect them, elevate them, and bring about redemption. But I tell you that the sparks fill the world and everything in it with holiness, with the light of the *Shechinah*.

"The scholars and Sages have told you to fear Satan and demons and forces of evil. But I tell you that the world is full of light, not darkness, that good is greater than evil. I tell you that God may be found in the simplest acts of life . . . in eating, drinking, marital relations, even in tying your shoelaces!

"You have been taught that keeping the commandments is the most important thing in life. But I tell you that the emotions, the feelings that derive from keeping the commandments are more important than the commandments themselves. Therefore, you are to feel the presence of God — the *Shechinah* — in your worship and in every commandment you keep, from the least to the greatest.

"You have been taught to flee the power of the evil inclination, the *Yetzer ha-Ra*. But I tell you that nothing is evil by itself. What you call evil is only a void, an absence of goodness. It is a measure of the fact that God himself is in exile, just as we, his people, are in exile. Therefore, evil is only the bottommost rung on the ladder of goodness. Moreover, the greater a man, the greater his 'evil inclination.'

"Kabbalah teaches of the chariot-throne of the Most High. I tell you that you should make of your evil inclination a chariot for God. You must feel your urges in their depths and take possession of them.

"You must learn to know pride and not be proud, know anger and not become angry. You shall become whole in all qualities. The wise person may glance at anything at all and not stray.

"The fate of an individual is only an expression of the soul: one whose thoughts roam about among unclean things finds the unclean in life; one who submerges oneself in the holy experiences finds salvation. The thought of a person is one's being; therefore think of the upper world. All outward teaching is only an ascent inward; the final aim of the individual is to become, personally, a teaching.

"You have heard it said that we must wait for the Messiah to bring us redemption. But I tell you that the world is to be redeemed, every day, through joy. It is for joy that you have been created. I teach you, not of the end of days, but of the luster of ordinary life. Therefore, dance with joy, even as I have danced.

"You have been taught to pray, fervently and with *kavanah*. But I tell you prayer is far more than you know. It is a marital union between the individual and the *Shechinah*, and you must enter it in a state of excitement. As a man 'cleaves' to his wife, so must you 'cleave' to God; and this 'cleaving' (*d'vikut*) is the essence of prayer. As the smoke ascends from burning wood, but the heavy part cleaves to the ground and becomes ashes, so from prayer only the will and the fervor ascend, but the external words crumble to ashes. It is a great grace of God that human beings remain alive after prayer. By nature one ought to die, having buried one's strength and entered into prayer for the sake of the *kavanah* that is fostered.

"God needs his people; for what good is a king if He has no kingdom? Likewise, what would there be to pray for if the world were sinless? The Sages teach that adultery begins in a glance of the eye. But I tell you that if you should look at a beautiful woman, remember that all beauty comes from God, and that thought transforms your glance to goodness.

"Each morning presents a new calling. One rises eagerly from slumber, being made holy and becoming, as it were, another person. One is found worthy to create, imitating God himself by shaping his own world. Creation does not cease with the Sabbath; but human beings join God in continuing the works of creation. Indeed, the individual joins God in one's *own* creation."[149]

"Think and believe with perfect faith that the Divine Presence is near you and is watching over you. Always be happy!"[150]

The Messiah

There was a sense of ecstasy in the teaching of the Besht. It was sublime and powerful, beyond anything his disciples had ever heard. Granted, there were many "faith healers" in Germany and Poland in the eighteenth century; they were the "physicians" of the people. But none was like the Besht. It was as if light and fire emanated from his very person, especially during his fervent prayers. So busy was he in dispensing cures to all in need — even to non-Jews — that he slept a scant two hours a day. Yet, even in his sleep his ministry went on. For in supernatural dreams he was privy to the future as well as the past, and nothing, either of good or evil, was hidden from him.

Around the year 1745, the Baal Shem Tov ended his wanderings, settling in the town of Medzibosh. Among his visitors were a number of rabbis from the north, whom he convinced of his radical doctrines. He was never granted official rabbinic ordination (called *s̆michah*), but he counted among his compatriots the son of a prominent rabbi, whose family was nothing short of a rabbinic dynasty. Many followers came to him, joining him in the frenzy of dance, the clapping of hands, the bowing and the jumping. As congregations were drawn together around his charismatic personality, the ultimate claim was made: Enough patient waiting for the advent of the Messiah; the Baal Shem Tov *is* the Messiah! The Besht never made the claim for himself, though he once claimed that the Messiah had helped him with a particularly difficult cure.

For some the Messianic Age had dawned; for others this claim was the final outrage. Many false Messiahs had come before. The memory of Shabbetai Zvi persisted, along with the determination not to let such folly be repeated. Detractors began to assemble, denouncing these strange new teachings and the entire Hasidic movement. One scholar in particular approached the Baal Shem Tov and queried, "What of the rabbis who call your teachings false?" The Besht answered with a parable: "Once, in a house, there was a wedding festival. The musicians sat in a corner and played upon their instruments, the guests danced to the music and were merry, and the house was filled with joy. But a deaf man passed outside the house; he looked in through the window and saw people whirling about the room, leaping and throwing their arms. 'See how they fling themselves about,' he cried. 'It is a house filled with madmen!' For he could not hear the music to which they danced."[151]

In keeping with his "messianic" calling, the Baal Shem Tov made plans to journey to the Land of Israel, the ultimate pilgrimage for a devout Jew. On one occasion he had to turn back, having already set out on the journey. "God knows," he wrote, "that I do not despair of traveling to the Land of Israel; however, the time is not right."[152] But the time was never right, and his burning desire was never to be fulfilled.

In the year 1760 the Baal Shem Tov died. His circle of devotees was small but growing. Who could succeed such a person as this? Who could keep his teaching alive? Who was worthy to carry the torch of Kabbalah? Deep bickering ensued. For six years the Hasidic faithful quarreled. Finally, a preacher (a *maggid*) from a town called Mezhirech — north of Medzibosh — stepped forward to assume the mantle of the Besht. His name was Dov Baer, a man with rich insight into the human psyche. While Dov Baer lacked the charismatic vision of the Besht, he became an anchor for the Hasidic movement, which now began commissioning disciples.

The Sparks Scatter

The message of the Baal Shem Tov and his Hasidic band began to explode, scattering the magical sparks of ecstasy across the land. The next generation of Hasidim would set forth on their own wanderings, spreading their teachings, from central Poland to Lithuania, and as far as the forested tracts of the Ukraine.[153] Hasidic communities, self-contained and well integrated, cropped up everywhere, generally revolving around devoted little groups who would gather for prayer. In ramshackle buildings dotting old Europe they would sit at rude tables, pondering their esoteric doctrines. What erupted in the end was a firestorm of controversy.

The teaching of the Besht was branded as heresy, and for all its popularity, an equally determined group came forward to fight it with the tools of reason. They were known as the *Mitnagdim* — the "Opponents." Chief among them was a powerful intellectual from the Lithuanian town of Vilna. His name was Rabbi Elijah ben Solomon Zalman, also known as the *Gaon* (Genius) of Vilna. Reclusive by nature, Rabbi Elijah saw himself establishing a bulwark in defense of the Torah. And every expression of ecstasy, even prayer, which lessened the authority of the Torah or interfered with its study, he perceived as a menacing threat. He not only hailed the study of the Talmud (a practice much less emphasized by the charismatic Hasidim), he personally studied for such long hours that he soaked his feet in ice water to keep himself from falling asleep.

What of the miracles said to have been worked by the Baal Shem Tov and his disciples? What of the dreams, the visions, the private communication from God? Delusions! The folly of pagans! Deceptive phantasms which hinder the soul from truer pursuits. He shunned all contact with the new ecstatics, even when leaders from the movement sought out his company. In the year 1772, Rabbi Elijah formally banned Hasidim from the town of Vilna. Bonfires were lit, and the writings of the Hasidim were consigned to the flames. By 1781 the ban turned into formal excommunication. It was written: "They must leave our communities with their wives and children. . . . It is forbidden to do business with them and to intermarry with them or to assist at their burial."[154]

What was the response of the Hasidim to Rabbi Elijah and his ban? They issued their own ban, against the *Mitnagdim*. Ban was met with counter-ban. They organized their own book burning, of works printed against them. They entrenched themselves in their experiences, dug in their heels, and gave no quarter. Rabbi Elijah died in 1791. It is said that after his death, overjoyed Hasidim engaged in yet another dance of ecstasy — at his tomb in Vilna.

The Hasidic movement, empowered by an inner fire, refused to die. The *Mitnagdim* notwithstanding, Hasidic leaders sat on their mystical thrones, aloof, unassailable, and almost worshipped. An additional criticism was that the Hasidim engaged in "rabbi worship," creating hereditary dynasties of unimpeachable paragons of power — demigods. These rabbis (*rebbes*, as they were called) drew their authority from their association with the Besht himself, from having known him personally or from having sat at the feet of one of his disciples.

Thus were the secret teachings transmitted, from *rebbe* to *rebbe*, in a lineal descent. One such dynasty, begun in the *shtetl* communities of Russia (known for their endearing portrayal in *Fiddler on the Roof*), was known as Lubavitcher Hasidism.

The Lubatchivers sought to tone down some of the ecstatic practices of their predecessors in Hasidism, becoming decidedly less demonstrative in their dancing, their clapping, and their bobbing. They also began to place a greater stress on learning, on study, on the pursuit of knowledge, both Talmudic and secular. These Hasidim began forming their own *yeshivahs*, for the training of *rebbes* to perpetuate their movement. As if incorporating the criticism of Rabbi Elijah, they made room in their ecstasy for the study of the secular sciences. (What they could not have known is that one day the secular sciences would sound increasingly like Kabbalah.)

The Legacy

Slowly, the rift between Hasidim and *Mitnagdim* began to shrink, and the despised sect began to be tolerated, even attaining an air of respectability. The Lubavitcher movement became, over time, the most prominent and visible expression of Hasidic Judaism, its black-coated followers becoming worldwide emissaries of their *Tzadik* — their "Righteous One" — as their venerable *rebbe* was known. Down to the present day the Lubavitcher movement dominates the Hasidic world, having turned parts of contemporary Brooklyn into a veritable Hasidic fiefdom. Their aged *rebbe* who died in late 1993 became the most illustrious of them all. His name was Menachem Mendel Schneerson, and, like the Besht himself, he was rumored to be the Messiah. The fires he fanned continue to burn among his tenacious followers. They still carry the banner of a movement they call *Chabad*, an acronym which stands for "Wisdom," "Understanding," and "Knowledge." They have even taken to the airwaves to proclaim, in ever-growing numbers, their message of spiritual renewal. Such is the enduring strength and legacy of Kabbalah.

Modern Hasidim are most readily recognized by their distinctive garb, which is really a carryover from their years in the villages of western Russia. Their coats and shoes are black, their shirts white. They wear wide-brimmed, fur-lined hats, picking up the black of their coats. Extending from beneath their belts the fringed tassels of their prayer shawls, which they wear as undergarments, are clearly visible. Whatever the weather, and regardless of the temperature, the Hasidic "uniform" is unchanging. Occasionally, they are made objects of ridicule. Some secular Israelis, noting the conspicuous presence of many Hasidim in today's Jewish state, often disparagingly refer to them as "penguins." They are seen as rigid, inflexible practitioners of long-outdated religious strictures. Few understand their unique legacy, the persecutions they have endured, or the inner fire of Kabbalah. Few witness them in prayer, in their dance, or in their ecstatic celebration of God. But those who catch a glimpse of the inner life of these piously orthodox souls are aware that Kabbalah is still alive and well and thriving on several continents. The spirit of the Baal Shem Tov lives on.

A Very Narrow Bridge

The test of any movement of great impact is not necessarily what it achieves or proclaims during the brief years of its founder, but whether it has achieved a level of dynamism — or "critical mass" — sufficient to outlive its founder and be carried on to succeeding generations. The most powerful ideas are not only embraced by their original advocates; they must experience a continual rebirth for ages to come. If this is the ultimate test of ideologues and their ideologies, then the sparks ignited by the Baal Shem Tov certainly pass with flying colors.

Indeed, the Besht became the patriarch of a dynastic line of *rebbes,* who would carry his message of spiritual renewal far beyond the confines of Poland, scattering the sparks across the globe. One such *rebbe*, born in 1772 in the town of Medzeboz in the Ukraine, had the distinction of being the great grandson of the Baal Shem Tov himself. He was called Rabbi Nachman of Bratzlav.

He not only carried the rabbinic mantle of his great grandfather; he was a towering Sage in his own right, as well as a powerful storyteller. He is also considered the last great Kabbalist. In his youth he was known to prostrate himself for long hours at the grave of the Baal Shem Tov, seeking to imbibe the spirit of the great master. He gave himself to asceticism, embarking on long and frequent fasts. His kabbalistic yearnings prompted him to undertake a long and perilous voyage to Palestine, but, feeling unworthy, he decided to return to Europe just an hour after his arrival. He was ultimately persuaded to stay on for a period of a year, though he left the Holy Land immediately thereafter. Returning to the Ukraine in the year 1802, Rabbi Nachman took up residence in a city called Bratzlav, whereupon he collected and edited his own teachings, setting them down in writing.

Rabbi Nachman, who was only thirty-eight when he died, said at the end of his life, "My light will glow till the days of the Messiah."[155] Certainly, his life represents an important link in the continuance of the Hasidic revolution. He had moved to the town of Uman only months prior to his death, and his tomb remains a place of pilgrimage for many devotees of his teachings. Not a single picture of this Hasidic master survives, but his synagogue in modern Israel contains a chair — a seat of honor symbolizing his spiritual presence. Along with the *Chabad* movement, the school established by Rabbi Nachman continues to define modern Hasidic thought and practice.

Chief among the ideas propagated by Rabbi Nachman's "Bratzlaver" tradition is that the goal of life, a completely simple faith, is achieved through traveling an arduous course. One meets with mortification, sorrow, and loss. But by accepting the pain in silence, one experiences the "root of repentance," which in turn is transformed into healing — the "mending power" of life. Every descent is the predecessor of an ascent; the way down is the way up. Such is the life of the truly righteous person, the *Tzadik*.[156] Of the *Tzadik*, he once declared, "Though the Land of Israel appears to be just like any other land, it is actually great in its holiness. So it is with a righteous person. The *Tzadik* may look like everyone else, yet the inner being is entirely holy and completely different from the ordinary person."[157]

Rabbi Nachman was once asked, "What in reality is the power of choice?" He responded, "It is simple. If you want, you do, if not, not. Too many people become trapped in their habits. But if they will it, they may easily overcome them. For no one is given an obstacle too great to be overcome."

If we were to imagine Rabbi Nachman's version of the "Sermon on the Mount," it would likely have sounded something like this:

"It isn't the way things turn out that is most important; it is the way things begin. The key, then, is in beginnings. Every beginning is difficult, for at the start of any endeavor, you are trying to turn things around, to reverse course and plow again in a new direction. Expect hardship. But once you have made a sound beginning, the burden eases and things become less of a burden. Therefore, treat every day as a new beginning, as if the entire world is being created afresh. Look backwards, toward the start, and drink deeply from its well.

"Let your soul be filled with a sense of awe, all through the day, in everything you do. Let your awe consume your prayer, as you vocalize words with such power that they become thunderbolts in your mouth.

"Observe God's commandments, not out of dread, but from a sincere joy which stems from the commandments themselves. It is a holy commandment to be happy.

"Taste of the hidden light; talk to your Creator, emptying your heart's contents. Savor this light. Meditate before God, for meditation is the highest level of life. Empty yourself of clutter; learn to see the world in a new perspective.

"You must also judge yourself, examining your thoughts, motives and intentions. Weigh everything in the balance. Cling to that which is true; discard the rest.

"If you believe that you can do damage, believe also that you can repair.

"For the pleasure of a quarter of an hour, a person can lose his or her portion in this world as well as in the World to Come.

"Expel your fears; banish them to the wilderness. Transform them. Elevate your fears, converting them into the true fear of heaven. For when things seem to be at their worst, the situation can turn around to one's full advantage.

"Never give up hope, for there is no such thing as despair.

"The whole world, and everything in it, is a very narrow bridge. And the important thing ... is not to be afraid at all."[158]

This last phrase of Rabbi Nachman became his most famous, being immortalized in song and chanted in Israel and throughout the Jewish world to this day. What, exactly, is Rabbi Nachman's "narrow bridge"? It is different for everyone. It is the path each of us must travel, parts ordained for us, other parts the fruit of our own choices. Those who fear are those who lose their way on the bridge, perhaps never reaching the other side, perhaps never realizing that the goal is not really the other side, but the path itself. Those who transform their fears are also those who, kabbalistically, transform their "evil inclinations" into chariots for God.

The Seer of Lublin and the Man on a White Horse

For many centuries, up until the destruction of the Jews of Europe in the Holocaust, the locus of Jewish life and culture in the entire world was Poland. And within Poland a particular city in the east called Lublin was known as a hub of Jewish mysticism. Lublin was home to Rabbi Jacob Isaac, also known as the "Seer" (1745-1815). He was an honored *Tzadik* — a "righteous person" — as well as being a leading practitioner of Practical Kabbalah, the magical arts connected with the mystical impulse. The Seer of Lublin helped to establish the Hasidic movement in Poland and in the region in the south of Poland called Galicia.

At the same time, in the early nineteenth century, the entire European continent was rocked by a man on a white horse, who "went forth conquering, and to conquer" (Rev. 6:2 KJV). Napoleon Bonaparte, a diminutive Corsican general and unlikely candidate for emperor of France, held forth the idea of "liberty, equality, and fraternity" for all people within his expanding realm. Everywhere he went, Napoleon dismantled the ghettos where Jews had been forced to live. In Italy, throngs of Jews rushed out to meet him, bearing the tri-color rosette, the symbol of the French Revolution. Nevertheless, the most pious and orthodox of Jews questioned how Napoleon should be perceived. Was this deliverance, this liberation, the beginning of the Messianic Age? Or was this a false hope — a mere delusion — since only the Messiah could bring true deliverance, and since the man on the white horse was no Messiah! The Hasidic rabbis of Lublin and the nearby town of Koznitz went so far as to pray for Napoleon's defeat, believing that redemption is for the end of days, and that the end of days had not yet arrived.

In one of the most bizarre tales of Jewish folklore, we are told that while Napoleon was sojourning through Koznitz, he stripped himself of his general's attire and donned the raiment of a simple man. Entering the home of a *Tzadik*, the rabbi whose house it was suddenly recognized him. Raising up a scroll of the book of Esther (which recounts the victory of the Jews in ancient times over their enemies), he declared: "You will surely fall, Napoleon, you will surely fall!"[159] Such were the sentiments about the French "deliverer" among many pious Jews.

The Seer of Lublin agreed with his colleagues at first, withholding his support for the Corsican general and preferring to wait for a thoroughly Jewish Messiah. In time, however, he reversed his opinion, as Napoleon's fortunes began to change for the worse. In 1813 the French army, which had captured

Moscow, was forced to retreat, in what was the beginning of the end of the dream of deliverance. The Seer decided to put his magical mysticism to work, with spells and incantations on behalf of Napoleon. But all mystical powers notwithstanding, the French deliverer met an untimely defeat at Waterloo. The dream died, and the hope of a better day was extinguished with it.

The Rebbe of Brooklyn

M any epithets describe the gigantic megalopolis of New York City, widely known as the greatest city on earth. It is also the greatest Jewish city on earth, bearing the imprint of multitudes of Europe's oppressed Jews, who came streaming through the gates of Ellis Island during the long decades preceding the Holocaust.

> Give me your tired, your poor,
> Your huddled masses yearning to breathe free,
> The wretched refuse of your teeming shore.
> Send these, the homeless, tempest-tossed to me.
> I lift my lamp beside the golden door.

This inscription, adorning the base of the Statue of Liberty, was, not coincidentally, penned by an American Jewish poet named Emma Lazarus. It expresses the hopes and dreams of millions of immigrants of every extraction to the United States, whose port of entry and initial domicile was the city of New York.

The polyglot character of the great metropolis is reflected in a patchwork of boroughs, fanning out from the sliver called Manhattan. The so-called outer boroughs, including the Bronx, Staten Island, and Queens, form a crescent around what New Yorkers refer to as "the city." The most Jewish of New York's boroughs is located across the East River from

Manhattan — Brooklyn. Its own expression of the "melting pot" that characterizes the United States, Brooklyn is home to some of the most ethnically diverse communities in America. Among them are certain pious, ultra-orthodox neighborhoods, transplants of European Hasidism, where valid expressions of modern Kabbalah may yet be found. The story behind these pockets of Jewish piety could well fill volumes.

The dominant personality of Jewish Brooklyn to arise in modern times was born in Nikolaev, Russia, in the spring of 1902. He was Menachem Mendel Schneerson, whose name derived from the rabbinic dynasty that included the famous "Alter Rebbe," Rabbi Schneur Zalman of Liadi (hence he was called "Schneerson").[160] He was almost Solomonic in his appearance. Still strikingly handsome as he was in his youth, his wise and compassionate eyes peered from under the thickly rimmed black hat that typifies Hasidic dress. His vision was for a perfected world, redeemed by a goodness that comes from God. A clear prodigy from childhood, he was educated by a private tutor in his early years. He was married in 1928 to the daughter of his rabbinic predecessor, Rabbi Yosef Yitzhak Schneerson. The years prior to the Second World War found him in at the University of Berlin and later in Paris, where he pursued secular studies, including science and mathematics, at the world-famous Sorbonne. His fluency in many languages was one more expression of his scholastic genius. In Menachem Mendel Schneerson the simple faith of the Baal Shem Tov was thus combined with great intellect and the pursuit of broad-based learning.

With the march of the Nazis across continental Europe, Schneerson and his wife made their way, in June of 1941, through the gates of Ellis Island, to safe refuge in the United States. It was in Brooklyn that the Rabbi Yosef Yitzhak, who had escaped the Nazi tide a year before, passed to Menachem Mendel the mantle of leadership over the educational, publishing, and social service efforts of the ultra-orthodox "Lubavitch" movement. With the death of Yosef Yitzhak in 1950, Menachem Mendel Schneerson became the undisputed leader, the Rebbe of Chabad, an international outreach to Jews of every continent. The mission of the Chabad was to restore a spiritual dynamic to a people decimated by the murder of six million human beings during the Holocaust. The Herculean task was nothing less than to establish in the United States a "center" for the study of Torah that would replace the destroyed Jewish centers of learning of Europe.

The Teaching and the Action

Whereas the Baal Shem Tov had long before demonstrated how everyone can serve God, the impetus of Chabad would be to teach how everyone can serve God. The chords and strains of this teaching were familiar to Kabbalists of ages past and characterize the Kabbalah of today:

Nothing in life happens by accident. Our actions are dictated by reasons which are often beyond reason. There are deeper patterns, reaching in their divine purpose beyond our narrow vision. Therefore, when we encounter struggles and difficulties in carrying out our appointed tasks, we must strive to overcome them in a direct and unswerving manner. Some seek to avoid problems by going around them. It is better, however, to confront them head-on and to do so from the start.

Goodness and godliness, he taught, are inherent in the world, and are lodged within every individual. There are unifying principles, he declared, which bind the physical universe to the spiritual, and which energize human beings to maximize their potential, to impact the whole world, beginning with their immediate spheres of influence, via the smallest of their acts of *gemilut hasadim* — "lovingkindness."

A prolific writer, the Rebbe composed over two hundred

volumes of discourse and commentary, dealing with issues that confront the world in a post-Holocaust climate. His burden was not confined to philosophy, but intimately related to the performance of "commandments" — *mitzvas* — as a means of redeeming the world, act by act. His teachings were steeped in ancient tradition, but his tactics were radical for an ultra-orthodox Jew. Never had the Jewish world seen anything like it. He stressed family and individual purity, disseminating information about traditional Jewish life in every way possible. He commissioned a special van, called the "Mitzvah Mobile," which would show up in Jewish neighborhoods, arousing curiosity and wonder. Sabbath candle lighting kits were passed out to Jewish women. Jewish men were asked, "Have you put on *tefillin* today?" They would then be instructed in the performance of the ancient ritual, wrapping their forearms and foreheads with leather straps, securing the small boxes containing the "Hear, O Israel" declaration.

He saw to the establishment of "Chabad Houses" in cities across the United States and around the world, wherever substantial Jewish populations were to be found. The Chabad House is basically an ultra-orthodox bastion of study, worship, and communal life, where the spirit cultivated by the Rebbe could be transmitted to other Jews. Emissaries were dispatched, linking Chabad House with Chabad House and establishing new ones in places as far flung as South Africa and the Philippines.

Kabbalah Goes High-Tech

Before long, the Rebbe's host of Hasidics took to the airwaves, buying time on radio and television to further the message of Jewish renewal. It was not unusual to see a black-coated "Chabadnick" in front of a TV camera propounding the mysteries of Kabbalah on cable networks, via satellite. Every high-tech means, including the Internet, would be utilized to elevate the sparks globally.

Among the Rebbe's innovations was the practice of calling, actively, for the joyous observance by Jews the world over, of the ancient feast of Hanukkah. It was Hanukkah that celebrated the victory by the Israelites of old over the wicked Syrians, who had outlawed the Jewish faith. It was during the dreaded persecution preceding Hanukkah that the early strains of *Merkavah* mysticism were first heard. And it is that mystical message (a divinely inspired "We shall overcome") transmuted into modernity, that the brightly burning menorahs of Hanukkah convey. And so it came to pass that Chabadnicks across the globe set about the kindling of giant nine-branched Hanukkah menorahs in public places, linking their observances through live television broadcasts.

But the Rebbe's pronouncements were not aimed at Jews only. While encouraging Jews to observe the ancient precepts of the Law of Moses, he perceived that God's message of hope applies to people of all faiths and in all lands. He pronounced that non-Jews should be encouraged, not to keep Jewish Law, but to keep a series of seven "common-sense" principles, in tradition transmitted to the sons of Noah after the Great Flood. Called the "Seven Laws of the Sons of Noah," or "Noachide Laws," they include prohibitions against:

- idolatry
- blasphemy
- bloodshed
- sexual impurity
- theft
- eating the flesh of a living animal,

and a positive commandment:

• the establishment of a system of justice.

It is all part of *Tikkun Olam*, the kabbalistic "repair of the world," in advance of the Messianic Age. In other words, non-Jews are to do their part in bringing the Messiah, just as Jews are to keep the 613 commandments of the Torah. For this reason, Chabadnicks in Israel began affixing banners to buildings all over the country, framing the question: "Are you ready for the coming of the Messiah?" It was a question they posed quite seriously. Indeed, it appears that with every fresh expression of Kabbalah, throughout history, the focus returns to the Messiah. And the Chabad-Lubavitch movement is no exception.

The rumors began to spread that the Messiah was not only at hand; he was here, among us, in the person of the Rebbe, Menachem Mendel Schneerson. Back in his Brooklyn fiefdom, the Rebbe himself said nothing about such speculation, either to confirm or deny what was being aired abroad. It was noted, however, that in spite of a strong Chabad presence in the modern State of Israel, Menachem Mendel Schneerson had never in his long and illustrious lifetime set foot in the Holy Land. Even after he was well advanced in years, his followers thought perhaps the time would come when the Rebbe would embark for the ancient homeland and bring about the final redemption of Israel, and indeed the whole earth.

His personal traits seemed to back up the contention. As the "elder statesman" of modern Hasidism, the Rebbe seemed indefatigable, even as he aged. Pressed with responsibilities, as a cultural icon and a stateless "head of state," Schneerson never slowed down and never took a day off from his labors, in more than forty years. He slept little and fasted much, all the while praying for people who came in mass numbers for an audience with him. Even in his nineties, he had the habit of standing for seven hours each Sunday, handing out dollar bills to be donated to charitable causes to multitudes who made pilgrimage to see him. Yet, he still found time to organize an enormous grass-roots effort to free Soviet Jews and help them in their struggles to emigrate to Israel. It was said of him, "He saw what others did not and did what others saw not."

The Messiah Is Dead! Long Live the Messianic Hope!

The world of Chabad therefore went into deep shock when their leader was stricken, in the fall of 1993, with a severe brain hemorrhage. Unconscious and hospitalized, the Rebbe slipped into a deep coma, while followers around the world watched, waited, and prayed. Even the non-Jewish world was mesmerized, as rumors abounded that he would be restored to health by miraculous intervention. Days dragged into weeks, then into months, and the condition of the Rebbe grew increasingly grave. His flock went into deep denial. In spite of his advanced age, no one was prepared for this event, and none had expected it. His stature was too towering, his presence too overwhelming. But alas, there was to be no miracle. The Rebbe would never regain consciousness.

On June 12, 1994, Menachem Mendel Schneerson, the Rebbe of Brooklyn and of Hasidics around the world, died. According to Jewish tradition, he was buried within twenty-four hours. As with previous expressions of Kabbalah, the messianic elements of the movement were not easily to be extinguished. New speculations arose. The Rebbe will yet be restored. This will be the mark of his Messiahship. He will be brought back to life. He will be resurrected. Leaderless, the Chabad-Lubavitch seemed to lose its way. There was wonder over whether the movement would survive at all.

But survive it has. The Chabad Houses have continued to grow and flourish in recent years, the Rebbe's spiritual presence bidding the faithful to continue their work. The message remains. The world is yet in need of restoration. The task is incomplete. The world will be redeemed; it must be redeemed. And individuals who understand their own role in the process, both Jew and non-Jew, represent the messianic, kabbalistic hope for the future of humankind.

The Angel of History

An enormous winged angel is the subject of a painting at the Israel Museum of Jerusalem. The artist, a Russian Jew named Paul Klee, depicted his angel looking back over his shoulder at the viewer with a look of blind horror on his face, utterly aghast. On closer inspection, it becomes clear that the wings are not wings at all, but two torn and damaged scrolls of the Bible, the Torah. Why is the angel so horrified? Is it horror in the abstract, or is he horrified by us — by who we are, what we have made of ourselves, what we have done to humanity and to our planet? We ask ourselves, as viewers and "art critics" where we have come and where our history is taking us. And we hear — from the angel — a cosmic warning.

The story of Kabbalah clearly dovetails with the story of human society, with our onward march, as we struggle to find our way. The mystical thread courses throughout history, as individuals seek to find meaning in a heartless world. Moreover, mysticism teaches that we must find lessons in history, that we must learn from the mistakes of the past, lest we be condemned to repeat them. The painting by Paul Klee was purchased by a modern Jewish philosopher with his own kabbalistic bent named Walter Benjamin, who claimed that it gave him a divine "spark" of inspiration. That "spark" would manifest itself in a concept that Benjamin would call "the Angel of History."

Walter Benjamin, who became one of the most influential philosophers and critics of the twentieth century, was a close, personal friend of one of the major scholars of Kabbalah in modern times, Gershom Scholem. In the days of Weimar Germany (between World War I and World War II), young Gerhard Scholem, an assimilated Jew with little formal religious education, was a mathematics student working toward his doctorate. But he found himself lured into the study of Jewish mysticism, just as so many Kabbalists of ages past had felt strangely drawn into "the Orchard."

By the early 1920s the transformation was complete. Gerhard Scholem, the mathematics student, had become Gershom Scholem, the Hebrew student, pursuing his Ph.D. on the subject of Kabbalah. With the emphasis of Kabbalah on mathematical codes found in the Bible, called *gematria*, Scholem later declared, "All of mathematics is found in Kabbalah!"

A confirmed Zionist, his plan was to go to Palestine before the 1920s were over, and he did. He enrolled at the Hebrew University of Jerusalem, ultimately founding the literary study of Kabbalah as a formal academic discipline. It was Scholem who spearheaded the literary study of the *Zohar*, concluding that the work was entirely the product of Moses de León, rather than Simeon ben Yokhai. He also arranged an academic stipend to be sent to his friend Walter Benjamin in Paris, so that he too might come to the Land of Israel and study kabbalistic thought.

But Benjamin was not a Zionist and never went to Palestine. Instead, he spent the money in Paris, mainly on coffee. He was never awarded a Ph.D. He never wrote a "proper" book. He never held a job. He was supported by his parents and by his wife well into his thirties. He was content with doing his own research, which nobody would fund. But because of his friendship with Scholem, he brought mysticism into his writings, seeking an interdisciplinary "universal theory." Scholem commented that he never knew anyone so obsessed with investigating detail and finding significance in minutiae.

Benjamin believed that inspiration comes in flashes, which do not derive from reason or rationality. They are "sparks," like the sparks of the primordial explosion in the Lurianic system. We think in fragments, Benjamin explained in his writings. And we should let the fragments be our inspiration, setting them down, even if they are disjointed and unconnected. Let our sparks of inspiration be "unprostituted." Like the multiple glass arcades in Parisian architecture, we need a certain transparency, which lets our insides out, and the outsides in. This is how we elevate our sparks, bringing us back to our "original state," before the Fall of humanity in the Garden of Eden.

In one of his flashes of inspiration, Benjamin saw the painting of Paul Klee as an image of something profound. He developed a motif of the "Angel of History," surveying the whole of human life and civilization. And the Angel has something very important to teach us. History, says the Angel, is, sadly, little more than a series of catastrophes brought about by class war and by human beings in their fallen state not being able to understand one another.

Moreover, if human history amounts to a series of disasters, there are only a finite number of options. It can carry on in that manner, with one more or less minor disaster following on the heels of another. It can proceed inexorably toward a major disaster, or cataclysm — the "end of the world." Or, we might conceivably learn from history, with the Angel of History's help, so that a new age might dawn and a better world might arise.

The Rubbish Heap and Human Choice

Indeed, the Angel is watching humanity's onward march as a spectator rather than a participant. He sees, far better than we do, that what history has created up until now amounts to a giant "rubbish heap" (in Benjamin's words), consisting of the tragic experience of wars, famine and deprivation, suffering, and woe. Unfortunately, humankind is blind to the rubbish heap, being unable to see it at all. Only the Angel of History — who is not a part of humankind — beholds the danger. It is a danger expressed in a humanity gone mad, utterly out of control.

In the end the Angel provokes questions, leaving the answers up to us. Since we must move forward and cannot move the clock back, what are we to do? Do we let the rubbish heap grow higher and higher, like a towering wall, behind us? If so, as the rubbish continues to pile up, it might fall on us, in a cataclysmic disaster. Or, are we prepared to look around, see it, and respond? If we do, the result will be horribly frightening, as shown in the look of horror on the face of the angel. But we will, nonetheless, have to come to terms with what we see. And what we see in the twentieth century, through the horror of the Holocaust and other episodes of genocide across the globe, from the "killing fields" of Cambodia to "ethnic cleansing" in Bosnia, should give all of us pause for thought.

Perhaps one of the greatest lessons of Kabbalah is expressed by another twentieth century philosopher, Emmanuel Lévinas, a Lithuanian Jew who lost his entire family in the Holocaust. Lévinas was quick to recognize that the universe can be a very cold and lonely place, with very little hope or help for pain. In the Holocaust in particular, God's face has been hidden. Whereas Benjamin's Angel of History looks toward us, God has looked away, especially through the anguish of the Holocaust years, giving us free will to determine our destiny as a species.

We can, in the end, choose the way we prefer to view the world around us. We can see everything in cold, impersonal terms, or we can choose to see the "sparks" in everything. In that sense, we choose to invest the world with meaning and value. We invest a painful world with comfort — a comfort found through God and religious observance.[161] We become, in the final analysis, the sum total of the choices that we make.

This is a modern way of expressing the teaching of the great Hasidic masters of centuries past. The burden is clearly on us to elevate the sparks that have landed about us, to help release them back to God, to bring about a "repair of the world." The choice is ours, in multitudes of decisions that we make every day. We may add more rage and rancor to the world environment, or we may choose to perform random acts of kindness. We may abdicate our human responsibility for the conduct of individuals and of nations, or we may awaken to the message of the Angel of History and struggle to change the planet for the better. As the rubbish heap continues to pile up behind us, the task has never been more urgent.

Cosmic Kabbalah

A t the Fermi Laboratory outside Chicago an impressive statue rises called *Broken Symmetry*. Three enormous arks representing the fundamental forces in the universe intersect at the top, though imperfectly. The struggle of these arks suggests the struggle of astrophysics to find a unified theory, uniting the laws of nature. To date no such theory has been found. The attempts have come close — very close — but questions persist: Did the universe have a beginning, and if so, what happened before then? Where did the universe come from, and where is it going? How much freedom — how much "will" — did God have in creating the universe?

Such questions are at the very heart of the realm — the *Sefirah*, if you will — of scientific inquiry. Historians are in general agreement that monotheistic faith is directly responsible for the rise of modern science; for monotheism proposes that an all-knowing Creator promulgated a basic code in the universe capable of being unlocked. As Einstein commented, "Science without religion is lame, religion without science is blind."[162] In fact Einstein's General Theory of Relativity is predicated on the idea that rational laws govern the physical universe. "It is hard to sneak a peek at God's cards," he once wrote. "But that He would choose to play dice with the world . . . is something that I cannot believe for a single moment."

Einstein's erudition notwithstanding, his fellow physicist, Niels Bohr, rebuked him with a quip, "Stop telling God what to do!"[163] In recent years Einstein's immutable theories have in fact been called into question. Stephen Hawking comments, "God not only plays dice; he sometimes throws them where they cannot be seen." Yet more questions have surfaced. "How real is time? Will it ever come to an end? Where does the difference between the past and the future come from? Why do we remember the past but not the future?"[164] It all comes back to the creation of the universe, and the creation of the universe is the realm of Kabbalah.

The Big Bang

In the beginning . . . was the Big Bang.

An initial cosmic event — a Big Bang — is theorized because the galaxies making up the universe are all moving away from each other. We know this because the light refracted from distant stars, when its constituent colors are broken down in a spectroscope, is shifted to the red end of the spectrum. This is a direct result of what is called the Doppler Effect, which tells us that waves — light or sound — emitted from objects moving toward us are compressed, and that the same waves emitted from objects moving away from us are lengthened. On an everyday level, this results in the change in pitch of train whistles as they move past us. On a cosmic level, it results in the red side of the rainbow shifting away from the rest of the spectrum. There can be only one reason for this — the galaxies comprising the universe are hurling away from each other at incredible rates of speed. There is no question about it; the universe is expanding.

The mystics of course had no spectroscopes. But one thing they knew: It is light, in the end, which tells us everything. It might be quite coincidental, but in Kabbalah we find a passage which could well be describing the very red shifts first observed by Edmund Hubble in his telescope:

> By embellishing substance with imagination, we can liken the first power to the concealed light. . . . The fifth power can be likened to red light. The sixth power is composed of whiteness and scarlet. The seventh power is the power of scarlet "shifting" (or "tending") toward whiteness. The eighth power is the power of whiteness shifting toward scarlet. The ninth power is composed of whiteness and scarlet and scarlet shifting toward whiteness and whiteness shifting toward scarlet. The tenth power is composed of every color.[165]

Coincidence perhaps. Science tells us, however, that if the universe is expanding, then this expansion is traceable back to a single "happening" — an explosion — a Big Bang. "The expansion of the universe suggested that it had a beginning at some time in the past," notes Stephen Hawking. "An expanding universe does not preclude a creator, but it does place limits on when He might have carried out his job."[166]

Incredibly, Kabbalah also describes a cosmic explosion. We are told that God created the world *yesh m'ayin* — "being from nonbeing." So great was God's presence, filling all in all, that He had to contract himself in order to make room for the universe. This "contraction" is called in Kabbalah *Tzimtzum*. It is the primordial creation event. Astronomers tell us that it is a fallacy to think that there is empty space beyond the known universe. What is there beyond the boundary of the universe? Certainly not "emptiness," for such concepts are merely the product of the laws governing the space-time continuum in which we operate. As a matter of fact, the space which comprises the known universe is not really empty at all, but is full of "dark matter" and "light matter"; and we might well conceive of God contracting Himself to make room for it.

According to the *Zohar*, "Primordial nothingness brought forth beginning and end."[167] Astrophysicist Christopher Isham comments: "The concept of creation out of nothing is, of course, a fascinating one; it's something which interests people enormously. The . . . picture of creation from nothing is actually a very graphic way to describe mathematics in nontechnical terms."[168] Indeed, Kabbalah and quantum physics in many ways dovetail, in conceptualization if not in specific language. Kabbalistically, the ten "spheres" begin with the single point in the center — which modern astrophysicists call a "singularity."

This "singularity" in the minds of the Kabbalists consists of nothing less than the letters of the alphabet. Letters, they insist, are the fundamental building blocks of the material world. However outrageous and unscientific this may sound, think, by analogy, of the universe as a book, a volume of writing, governed by complex mathematical codes — equations. What is a book? What is the Great Book, the Torah? Is it so much ink on a page, or is it the ideas formed from words which come from vocalizing (giving breath to) the letters? Taken literally, the idea that the creation stems from letters (Hebrew letters at that) is absurd. But on another level, the letters may be compared with the equations of astrophysics, the elementary laws by which the universe operates. Equations, like letters have no substance of themselves, no weight, no matter. Neither do letters, which, in their purest form, consist of ink from a quill. They have shape; yet they are truly "of nothing."

Stephen Hawking writes: "Because mathematics cannot really handle infinite numbers, this means that the general theory of relativity predicts that there is a point in the universe where the theory itself breaks down. Such a point is an example of what mathematicians call a singularity. . . . The universe could have had a singularity, a big bang."[169] Elsewhere, Hawking observes: "A star collapsing under its own gravity is trapped in a region whose surface eventually shrinks to zero size. And, since the surface of the region shrinks to zero, so too must its volume. All the matter in the star will be compressed into a region of zero volume, so the density of matter and the curvature of space-time become infinite. In other words, one has a singularity contained within a region of space-time known as a black hole."[170]

Kabbalistically speaking, the "spheres of nothing" found in the *Book of Creation* might be the rough equivalent of how the ancients understood black holes: "For that which is light is not-darkness, and that which is darkness is not-light."[171]

The What and the Why

Kabbalah as a discipline is perhaps uniquely suited to bringing together theoretical physics, philosophy, and theology. For Kabbalah not only approaches the mysteries of creation, but draws out the ethical implications of the Big Bang — namely, that we are all truly brothers. Astronomer Allan Sandage observes, "[The universe] is the machine that has created you. Every single atom in your body was once inside a star. We are all brothers in that sense."[172] Kabbalah, likewise, strains to describe the "creation event," but takes a giant leap beyond to delineate the human task. We must bring about the "repair of the world."

Contemporary astrophysics goes so far as to speak of the planet itself being "alive." From the gases which form our atmosphere to the waters comprising our oceans, the entire character of the earth is a direct product of living things. An enhanced appreciation for the environment is one of the by-products of modern science, and it is also a fundamental principle of the earliest threads of Kabbalah. The earth itself, as the whole universe, contains sparks of the divine.

A Universe of Small Things

To fully appreciate the natural world it is important to understand the fundamental forces comprising its immutable laws. There are four forces in all: gravity, electromagnetism, the "weak force," and the "strong force." But why are there four, and why do they differ fundamentally in character? Why is there not a single force which energizes the universe? Einstein spent his life in search of an elementary picture of the cosmos, a single underlying principle. "What really interests me," he wrote, "is whether God had any choice in the creation of the universe." Einstein also observed, "The Lord God is subtle, but malicious He is not."[173] There must be in nature a certain beauty and symmetry, which, while difficult to understand, is nonetheless marked by simplicity.

Atomic theory is itself quite old, going back as far as Aristotle. The Roman poet Lucretius in his day popularized an early form of atomic theory. But it was Einstein who formally postulated the interchangeability of matter and energy, theorizing that energy is actually composed of particles, which he called "quanta." Do these particles — a kind of primordial "ether" — precede the universe itself? Kabbalah puts it like this:

> For before the celestial world — known as the 377 compartments of the Holy One, blessed be He — was revealed; and before mist, electrum, curtain, throne, angel, seraph, wheel, animal, star, constellation, and firmament — the rectangle from which water springs — were made; and before the water springs . . . before all these things there was an ether, an essence from which sprang a primordial light refined from myriads of luminaries; a light, which, since it is the essence, is also called the Holy Spirit.

There is a precise order here, "ether," "mist," and "electrum" being the kabbalistic equivalent of earliest atomic and sub-atomic particles from which the universe formed — a "primordial light." The next several entities, "curtain," "throne," "angel," "seraph," "wheel," and "animal," hearken back to Ezekiel's grand vision of the throne of glory and the angelic beings surrounding the Almighty. Only after God's throne is established (which we may liken to the fundamental laws of physics) do stars and constellations congeal, finally producing the "firmament" we call the night sky.

Linking the cosmos with flesh and blood, we note that all life, plant and animal, is composed of carbon atoms, which compose DNA, and which are even older than planet earth. The outer regions of each atom are inhabited by a shell of particles carrying negative charges — electrons. Their kabbalistic equivalent is "electrum." Between the electron shells we find "photons," which carry the "electromagnetic force." The nucleus of each atom is fashioned of protons and neutrons. Even older and more fundamental particles — "quarks" or "nuclear forces" — have left trails from which the protons and neutrons are made.

The Four Forces

As cosmologists struggle to find a unified theory, they wrestle with the idea that the four elemental forces in the universe might ultimately be one. Kabbalah also speaks of four forces, or "four lights," instrumental in the creation of the cosmos. It is interesting to compare the contemporary "four forces" with the "four lights" of Kabbalah. They include:

• THE STRONG FORCE:

the force which holds quarks together within protons and neutrons and holds the protons and neutrons together to form atoms. It is the strongest of all the forces, without which the universe would be little more than a "quark fog" – which Kabbalists would call *Tohu v'bohu* — "formless and void." Carried by "gluons" (the most perfect imaginable "glue"), it is short in range. Themselves invisible, gluons weave webs of energy into forms we call matter. In Kabbalah we find: "By embellishing substance with imagination, we can liken the first power to the concealed light."[174]

Kabbalah declares: "*Come and see: There are four lights. Three are concealed and one is revealed. A shining light . . .* "[175]

• ELECTROMAGNETISM:

the force deriving from particles which carry an electric charge. It is the second strongest of the four forces, infinite in range and carried by photons, which in turn carry light from the sun and stars.

Kabbalah states: "*A glowing light; it shines like the clear brilliance of Heaven.*"[176]

• THE WEAK FORCE:

the power which mediates the process of radioactive decay. It is the third strongest of the four forces, very short in range and carried by "weak bozons." The weak nuclear force helps power the sun and stars by releasing tremendous amounts of energy bound up in nuclei of each atom.

Kabbalah states: "*A purple light that absorbs all lights.*"[177]

• GRAVITATION:

the universal attraction of all massive particles toward one another. This is the weakest of the forces, though infinite in range. Gravitation always attracts; never repels; and is carried by "gravitons."

Kabbalah states: "*A light that does not shine but gazes toward the others and draws them in. Those lights are seen in her as in a crystal facing the sun. The first three are concealed, overseeing this one, which is revealed.*" [178]

Four forces, four "powers," fuel the universe. But is it possible that they might, at some point in the beginning, have all been one? To be sure, finding ultimate unity is still a daunting task.

Grand Unified/ Super Unified Theories

Astrophysicist Leon Lederman has stated that the greatest flaw in the existing theories about the universe and its laws is aesthetic — there are too many parameters. It is all too complex. Another renowned physicist, Steven Weinberg, states, "We haven't come to bottom level yet, but we pick up intimations of underlying beautiful theory, whose beauty we can only dimly see at the present time."[179] It is the drive and desire for unity that, more than anything else, fuels the work of today's scientists. The desire to see unity is as old as Kabbalah itself: "Everything that Moses stated was said so . . . that the knowledge regarding Him would be true and unified."[180]

Yet another astrophysicist, John Archibald Wheeler, states, "There must be at the bottom of it all not a simple equation, but an utterly simple idea; and when we finally discover it, it will be so compelling, we will all say to each other, 'How could it have been otherwise?'"[181]

Attempts have made, for example, to bring together electromagnetism and the weak force as aspects of a single "electroweak force." The idea is that under conditions of extreme heat (such as existed at the creation of the universe), a new particle would appear — a "Z particle" — capable of knitting together electromagnetism and the weak force. The Z particle decays and recombines to form a photon, the carrier of electromagnetism. The photon in turn decays to form a pair of "weak bozons," carriers of the weak force. The bozons then transform themselves back into a Z particle. What had been two forces is now one electro-weak force. This reduces to three the number of fundamental forces in nature.

In an attempt to confirm the theory, protons were accelerated in the giant Serne Ring in Switzerland. The careening protons were systematically collided with "anti-protons" — matter meeting anti-matter — resulting in mutual annihilation. The experiment resulted in observable traces of Z particles, confirming the hypothesis. What was witnessed was nothing less than "little bangs," simulating at least in part the original Big Bang. Again, science sounds hauntingly like Kabbalah, and Kabbalah sounds like science, for the collision of matter and anti-matter is what Kabbalah calls "synthesis":

> The nature of the *Sefirah* is the synthesis of every thing and its opposite. For if they did not possess the power of synthesis, there would be no energy in anything.[182]

The statement sounds amazingly Hegelian: Thesis + Antithesis = Synthesis. Beyond rhetorical dialectic, there is in this statement a collision of sorts with the world of astrophysics. The synthesis of matter and anti-matter — protons and anti-protons — yields the synthesis of the electro-weak force.

Grand Unified Theories

It is postulated that at still higher energy levels, three of the four forces would function as one. Yet another particle, called the "X particle," would do the work of unification. A gluon (carrier of the strong force) would strike an X particle and be transformed into a photon (carrier of electromagnetism). Conversely, a gluon striking an X particle would be transformed into a weak bozon (carrier of the weak force).

In the final analysis, even the first law of thermodynamics, stating that matter can be neither created nor destroyed, breaks down.

The Marriage of Earth and Universe

One of the by-products of modern science has been to marry the earth to the universe, for all are ultimately of the same substance. More recently, however, the picture becomes increasingly tenuous. It is now believed that all matter in the universe is just a passing fancy, a single phase in the ongoing dance of energy. If electromagnetism and the weak force are united at high energies and the strong force joins them at still higher energies, then might not all four forces ultimately be one? Kabbalah, in language somehow reminiscent of "relativity" (the theory that matter and energy are interchangeable) states: "This is the one matter which stems from the primeval light and points towards form, creation and change of form."

The Large-Scale Universe

Speculating on the fundamental forces of nature leads to another question. Does the universe have an edge — a boundary? Stephen Hawking postulates the following: "The boundary conditions are: The universe has no boundary." Super-symmetry physicist Nick Warner says of this (tongue-in-cheek), "It all sounds rather Zen, doesn't it?"[183] Perhaps he should have said, "It all sounds rather Kabbalah. . . ."

Consider the observable universe, as we know it. Our own sun is but one of a few hundred million stars comprising the major spiral galaxy in which we find ourselves, the Milky Way.

The Milky Way is in turn part of a "Local Group" of galaxies, a cluster comprised of the Milky Way and dozens of others. The Local Group belongs to the Virgo Super-cluster, which is roughly 100 million light years wide. Furthermore, all of them are expanding, moving away from each other.

Astronomer Alan Sandage (Edwin Hubble's pupil) observes, "It is not as if the galaxies are expanding into a space that's already there; the space itself is expanding; the expansion creates the space. It is somewhat like the surface of a balloon. Put yourself on any dot and all the others seem to move away. Every place is center of expansion. Every place and every time was identical in the beginning."[184]

But when was the beginning? To the extent that time is real and not an illusion, most astronomers place the Big Bang about fifteen billion years ago. Kabbalah puts it like this:

> The gushing forth was sudden, not unlike the sparks which fly and burst forth when the craftsman forges with a hammer.
> After the first light another fountain was drawn out from which flows darkness.[185]

In scientific terms astrophysicists speak of "quasars" — incredibly bright and incredibly distant objects which may have been the nuclei of galaxies going through a violent youthful phase. Quasars are so distant from our own galaxy that to detect them through giant telescopes is to look back billions of years, toward the beginning.

Yet, before there were even quasars, there must have been ancient photons (left over from the Big Bang, before stars and galaxies were born) which spread out across the universe as infinitesimal traces of the original explosion and which may yet be seen as background "noise" on TV screens. Kabbalah postulates that after the "contraction" (*Tzimtzum*) by which God made room for the universe, there came to be a second event, called *Sh'virat ha-kelim* (Breaking of the Vessels). As the emanation of God proceeded from the central point, some of the vessels were unable to withstand the power of the light and shattered. While most of the light returned to the infinite source, the remainder scattered as sparks, along with the broken shards of the vessels. The sparks subsequently were entrapped in material existence, waiting for human beings to liberate them and restore them to divinity.

The First Instant

The heat of our sun represents just a tiny fraction of energy stored in the nuclei of atoms at the beginning, when the universe would have worked in a marvelously simple way, beyond what even the unified theories can project. The question remains: How could a single kernel of energy have become everything that is?

Astrophysics dovetails with Kabbalah as we follow the sequence of events in the creation from the perspective of the Kabbalists and from that of twentieth-century cosmologist Michael Turner:[186]

Kabbalah: "For we have already said that the two flows are really one matter coming from the primeval darkness, alluding form."[187]

Turner: During the first instant — the "threshold of creation" — a single primordial law operates.[188] What this law is, however, we do not and may not ever know. Astrophysicists looking for a unified theory of quantum mechanics are sometimes well aware that the intellect can take us only so far.

Kabbalah: "At that moment Moses began to observe the primeval light, the root of all. And he found it to be a darkness composed of two entities stemming from two sources, one flowing with light, the second with darkness."

Turner: During the first ten-to-the-minus-thirty-fifth second: The electro-weak force has not yet diverged from the strong force. X particles and free quarks sail the sub-nuclear seas. Only two forces operate: gravity and the electro-nuclear (Grand-Unified) force.

Kabbalah: "Now this flow extends and gushes forth by way of channels, and the flow again becomes weak like a stream, and the stream again becomes minute, turning into a thread. And in this exiguity it extends and is directed until it becomes small, tiny droplets."

Turner: During the first one-ten-billionth of a second: The electromagnetic and weak forces are still welded together as the electro-weak force. Z particles are created, and only three forces are at work.

Kabbalah: "These droplets grow and become fragmented entities."

Turner: During the first one-tenth to one-hundredth of a second: Even "neutrinos" (extremely light, possibly massless, elementary matter particles affected only by the weak force and gravity) are bound up in a broth of matter and energy.

Kabbalah: "And the fragments continue to grow until they burst forth in great strength, mingling and interacting one with another, expanding and conjoining until a sap pours forth from them."

Turner: During the first second: The heat is so intense that it overwhelms strong force. Free quarks fly about in a primordial soup.

Kabbalah: "Now this sap flows and extends and is congealed."

Turner: During the first 100 seconds: Helium nuclei are formed. The universe cooled sufficiently so that protons and neutrons could get together and form the nuclei of atoms. "Triplets" are formed, two of which are thrown off, producing a stable helium nucleus. One-fourth of these congealed into helium gas, representing the fact that about one-quarter of the universe today consists of helium.

Kabbalah: "And through this coagulation they are polished, purified, and clarified such that the original fragments that we mentioned are utterly disintegrated."[189]

Turner: During the first million years: the dawn of light — the birth of the first atoms. Photons could fly freely without hitting other particles, because matter in the universe had sufficiently thinned out. Furthermore, electrons could settle down around atomic nuclei, resulting in stable atomic structures.

Kabbalah: "Know and comprehend that before all the above-mentioned entities there was nothing but this ether. And this ether darkened because of two things, each having different sources. The first issued an infinite, inexhaustible and immeasurable light."

Turner: During the first billion years: galaxies are formed, as the primordial gas is still thick enough for the swirling interstellar clouds to congeal. The only two elements present in the first-generation stars are hydrogen and helium.

Returning to the very beginning, we wonder whether we will ever understand that "first instant," the "threshold of creation." With regard to the highest of the ten *Sefirot* (*Khokhmah*), Rabbi Azriel declares, "It is elevated above the probing of an investigator."[190] Kabbalah also states:

> It is at the level of *Khokhmah* (Wisdom) that the laws of creation first appear. It is here where the paths take on substance.[191]

Will a single, sublime, "grand unified theory" ever be found? Will "God's mind" ever be known? Or will the impenetrable realm of "Crown" (*Keter*) remain, ever and always, above and beyond the grasp of the combined gray matter of the human species? In the final analysis, we find our senses limited, our understanding small. And we feel . . . alone.

Alone in the Void?

Ever since the true magnitude of the universe became known, not too many decades ago, people have in general grown very disturbed at the idea that we are alone. When human beings thought that the earth was the center of all things, it somehow made sense that life on this planet is the only life that exists . . . anywhere. But now that we know that the earth is but a tiny speck in a vast cauldron of swirling stellar formations, we realize that in all of our billions, the "human race" represents barely a blip on the interstellar radar screen of the cosmos. For all of our progress and achievement we seem rather inconsequential in the overarching scheme of things. Therefore, we want to believe in worlds beyond our own, with which we someday might forge a link, as if to invest with meaning our corporate existence.

The idea that other worlds exist in our universe wherein intelligent life may be found is persistent in modern folklore and speculation. Interestingly, this idea, prevalent in the pop culture of print, television, and film, is not without support in the writings of the mystics. One passage from the *Zohar* postulates the following:

> When the desire arose in the Will of the White Head to manifest its Glory, It arrayed, prepared, and generated from the Blinding Flash one spark, radiating in three hundred seventy directions. The spark stood still. A pure aura emerged whirling and breathed upon the spark. The spark congealed and one hard skull emerged, emanating to four sides. . . . Inside this skull lie ninety million worlds moving with it, relying upon it.[192]

On one level, the *Zohar* is again speaking of the ten "spheres" (*Sefirot*) of God's emanations into and through the universe. The "White Head" is "Will" (*Keter*), through which the *Ain Sof* (He who has no end) is manifest. The "one spark" is "Wisdom" (*Khokhmah*), the first point of creation. The "hard skull" is "Understanding" (*Binah*), coming forth from the spark. On another level, however, we can think of the most modern theories regarding stellar formation. Great formations of gas and cosmic dust, emanating from the Big Bang, began to congeal, resulting in a myriad of nuclear furnaces — stars — contained within galaxies, in turn contained within the "skull" we call the universe. The *Zohar* was certainly correct in postulating millions of worlds inside the "skull," although the figure "ninety million" is far too conservative; for there are, as Carl Sagan said, "billions and billions" of galaxies, containing trillions and trillions of stars.

Taking up the same theme, a later Kabbalist, Rebbe Menachem Mendel, declared: "There are many myriads of worlds, each of which is divided into many dimensions, each of which is like a whole organic being. Upon each world hangs many thousands of individual worlds in numbers without measure, each of which is different than and of a superior order to its neighbor."[193] No, we are by no means alone. Each "particular" in the world around us is linked to every other "particular" in the universe as a whole. Consequently, meaning and purpose, while it sometimes eludes us on the most immediate, "micro-level" of our lives, can certainly be found on the "macro-level" of the interconnected cosmos. While postulating the existence of worlds beyond, perhaps the healthiest aspect of Kabbalah is its insistence that there is much about the universe beyond our ability to comprehend. Therefore, people should take care not to delude themselves with speculations about other worlds that are impossible for them to understand. As the *Zohar* states, "Infinity does not abide in being known."[194]

Of Einstein and "Spinoza's God"

At a very important point Kabbalah and modern astrophysics seem to be saying precisely the same thing — God, or at least God's "emanations," may be found in the universe itself. And perhaps the clearest expression of God is in the immutable laws by which all things operate. As I have stressed, modern astrophysics is increasingly at a loss to explain the workings of the universe without resorting to God. In a sense at least, God is one with the universe; God *is* the universe. While it sounds rather pantheistic, it is very much the stuff of Kabbalah.

Going back a few centuries, there is little doubt that kabbalistic ideas strongly influenced a certain Jewish philosopher who believed that the entire universe is governed by a set of complex mathematical laws. His name was Baruch de Spinoza, and the ideas he promulgated were to change profoundly the way philosophers and ordinary people would view the cosmos. When Albert Einstein was asked whether he believed in God, he responded in a telegram to a Jewish newspaper: "I believe in Spinoza's God, who reveals himself in the harmony of all that exists."[195] According to Spinoza, the whole universe, the individual things it contains, and the powers they exert, are not just the offspring of God; they are "of God." The particulars in the universe represent a variety of patterns by which God is revealed. Everything is in God; everything moves in God. Moreover, the entirety of nature is alive. Though the creation's individual entities are perishable, not eternal, they are certainly not defined by the whim of chance, but by the divine nature. As a result each thing in the universe acts within its smaller or larger "sphere" (*Sefirah*). The eternal character of God works in them, via the eternal laws communicated to them. Consequently, things could not be other than they are, since they are manifestations —

emanations — of God's own character. At the end of the day, Spinoza's speculations earned him the title of a "God-intoxicated man."

Where did Spinoza get these ideas, which so influenced the God-concept of the father of astrophysics? Clearly, Spinoza departed from the mainstream of Judaism in his age, casting doubt on traditional notions of religious dogma. He was in fact formally excommunicated from the Jewish community of Amsterdam. But Spinoza's unorthodox approach was certainly influenced by the ideas of the Kabbalists, who also asserted a certain oneness between God and the universe. The line of influence is unmistakable. There were many Kabbalists in Amsterdam, and among Spinoza's fellow students were the Kabbalist leaders Moses Zacut, Isaac Naaar, and Abraham Pereira, all of whom became followers of none other than the mystical messianic pretender, Shabbatai Zvi. One of Spinoza's friends in London was a distinguished German savant named Heinrich Oldenburg, who also became intoxicated with Shabbatai Zvi's kabbalistic doctrines. And like the Kabbalists, Spinoza believed that a new messianic kingdom might someday be established in Israel, bringing about the redemption for which the Jewish people longed.

Thus, it is clear that the ideas of the ancient Jewish mystics were not only transmitted, but reinvented repeatedly, through the likes of Shabbatai Zvi, Spinoza, and eventually Albert Einstein. In the obituary of the latter, Einstein was quoted as saying, "My religion consists of a humble admiration of the illimitable superior spirit who reveals himself in the slight details we are able to perceive with our frail and feeble minds."[196] It may be no overgeneralization to say that if there is a "religion" behind modern astrophysics, we can call it Kabbalah. "Spinoza's God" lives on in the cosmos.

Contemporary Kabbalah

In a technological age, in which human beings often see themselves as little more than incidental units in the whirring machinery of an impersonal society, there is increasing impetus to reach beyond ourselves, to find communion with the world beyond and with the universe as a whole. In contemporary culture, Kabbalah is finding new adherents. High-profile names from the world of television and film are being added to the rosters of devotees of the ancient mystical art. With good reason, many modern people, disenchanted with traditional forms of spirituality, are reaching for a link with the *Ain Sof.* Indeed, cold rationality can feel confining, even stifling, while Kabbalah affords its adherents a boundless adventure to an undiscovered country.

But the contemporary adventure is not confined to esoteric speculations. It is fleshed out in today's marketplace of ideas with practical advice on how to live deeper, richer, more fulfilling lives.

Awareness . . .

The nature of Kabbalah, which after all means "receiving," is the cultivation of a deeper awareness of the world beyond ourselves. At the end of the day, discovering the world means discovering ourselves. One doesn't suddenly stumble upon "awareness"; one must carefully cultivate a sensitivity for one's own flesh. The journey to a higher realm starts with feet planted firmly on the ground.

On a practical level there are a number of "tips" contemporary Kabbalists give to those just entering "the Orchard," or contemplating such a move.[197]

- ### FIND THE BODY AND INFUSE IT WITH CONSCIOUSNESS.

Among all the individual things in the world, each human being is closest to him- or herself. Ironically, however, each human being is also the most distant from him- or herself. Self-awareness invariably builds self-esteem, and self-esteem is foundational for mental and emotional health.

- ### CONNECT WITH WONDER.

One of the most difficult tasks in a technological age is to rediscover the sense of awe, the unbridled curiosity we had about the world around us when we were children. When we lose the quality of wonder, we lose our keen edge for living; when we rekindle the wonder within us, we restore our zest for life itself.

- ### ENTER INTO A NEW DIMENSION.

Recognize that there is much more to the universe than what we can observe with our senses. Cultivate an awareness of the unseen world by studying its various aspects. Then, learn to enter that realm through the regular practice of meditation.

- ### CONNECT WITH LOVE.

Love is another word for "connectedness." It means recognizing our interdependence with everyone around us. It also means acting on that awareness, to enrich, in a very personal way, the lives of those we touch.

- DISSOLVE ALL ROUTINE PATTERNS AND BOUNDARIES.

"Routine" is the enemy of creative experience. It is important to open oneself to new experience, to take "the road less traveled by," to listen to a higher voice in the minute details of daily life.

- CONSIDER THAT WE ARE FREE.

Real freedom, it is argued, is not a matter of rights or laws or unhindered actions, but a state of mind. It is a matter of the way we conceive of ourselves, understanding that each day, we have an almost infinite number of choices to make. Our lives are in fact the sum total of those choices. Making wise ones is the essence of freedom.

- TALK TO THE UNI-VERSE.

We must learn to recognize our interconnectedness — our oneness — with the universe (observing that the prefix "uni-" means "one"). We must learn to hear the universe speak. And we must learn to talk back. Our relationship with the world around us is not to be one-sided; it is to be a dialogue.

- RE-INTEGRATE AS AN INDIVIDUAL "SELF."

Interconnectedness is not the goal and the end of mystical experience. Kabbalah in its contemporary setting urges that the "higher awareness" we cultivate must be refocused on the individual. Since the meditative experience removes us from ourselves, we must learn to return to and ultimately restore the "self."

- INTEGRATE THE "DIVINE MEETING" WITH OUR HIGHER MIND.

The meditative experience is to change us, to make us better human beings. This involves integrating that which is experienced in the realm beyond ourselves with our own self-consciousness. The appeal is not so much to gray matter — our rational capacity — but to the "inner self," the "Higher Mind."

- COME INTO A NEW INTEGRATION WITH THE ATTACHED SPARKS OF OUR SOUL.

Recognize the concept of the divine sparks, with respect to our own souls. Sparks from the primordial explosion have indeed landed in us, and our task is to find an internal harmony with those pieces of the divine presence. As we elevate the sparks within ourselves, we bring the world one step closer to redemption.

In short, kabbalistic speculation must not be left in the domain of abstract esotericism. Kabbalah has no function but to make people better and, ultimately, to make the planet better. To this extent there is nothing more practical than contemporary Kabbalah.

Kabbalistic Commandments[198]

Adopting yet another approach to providing practical kabbalistic advice, I have drafted a series of commandments — ten to be precise — which incorporate the best kabbalistic maxims regarding how and how not to live:

1) Thou shalt not be idolatrous about or bound to any doctrine. No system of thought represents absolute truth. Therefore, do not think that the knowledge you possess is changeless or perfect. Be ready to learn throughout your life and to observe reality at all times. Do not force others (including children) to adopt your views. Help others to renounce fanaticism and narrowness, through compassionate speech.

2) Thou shalt not avoid contact with suffering. Awaken yourself and others to the reality of human misery. Find ways

to be present with those who suffer, through personal visits and conveying positive images to people in need.

3) Thou shalt not accumulate wealth while millions are hungry. Do not adopt, as the goal of your life, fame, wealth, or sensual pleasure.

4) Thou shalt not maintain rage or rancor. Strive to understand those causing anger and hatred. Learn to look at other beings with the eyes of compassion.

5) Thou shalt not utter words that create discord and cause the thread of community to break. Make every effort to reconcile and resolve conflicts, however small. Do not say untruthful things that cause division and hatred. Always speak truthfully and constructively. Have the courage to speak out about matters of injustice, even when doing so may threaten your own safety.

6) Thou shalt not practice a vocation that is harmful to humans or to nature. Seek employment which helps you realize your ideal of compassion.

7) Thou shalt not kill nor acquiesce to killing. Find whatever means possible to protect life, including animal life, and to prevent war.

8) Thou shalt not possess anything that rightfully belongs to others. Seek to prevent individuals and companies from enriching themselves by taking advantage of others.

9) Thou shalt not mistreat the body. Learn to handle it with respect. In sexual relationships be compassionate and tender. Respect the rights and commitments of others.

10) Thou shalt meditate for the sake of the world around you. Learn to practice "conscious breathing" in order to regain composure of body and mind. Do not become lost in your surroundings. Become a conduit of life.

There are of course yet other approaches to contemporary Kabbalah, other "schemas," which provide a framework by which mystical practice may be integrated into daily life. Another program for spiritual development crystallizes Kabbalah into ten principles to guide one's affairs.[199] They include:

1) "Cancellation." This is another word for the practice of meditation, which of necessity involves "canceling" the clutter that fills our minds. Meditation involves focusing down, within ourselves, becoming one both with ourselves and the world beyond ourselves. But meditation is also a discipline that can be learned. Therefore, one should determine to sit in absolute stillness for at least half an hour a day, concentrating on deep, cleansing breaths. But in order to focus one's thoughts properly, a second principle is required.

2) "*Gerushin.*" This is the kabbalistic equivalent of a "mantra," a word or brief phrase which is meaningful to the individual. This helps us to cancel the external world, and it has the effect of refocusing our thought on the meditative process. The modern Kabbalist, like the mystical masters of bygone days, will usually choose a Hebrew expression or phrase, such as Ha-Rakhman (the Merciful One), but in theory any helpful "mantra" will suffice.

3) "*Intention.*" Also called *Kavanah,* this term describes the very ancient practice of letting go of the self and setting one's full attention on a higher reality. From earliest times, Kavanah was linked with focused prayer, but contemporary extensions of the principle involve slowing down our pace, living a more relaxed life, eating slowly, stopping every hour and a half during the day and breathing deeply, and making time to smell the roses.

4) "Charity." The regular practice of giving is not to be thought of as an exercise of pity, but as benefiting the donor, the giver. It is a matter of seeing oneself within the larger circle of life, recognizing the interdependence of all living beings. Thus, giving is transformed from grudging duty into a moral obligation to a natural expression of one's spiritual nature. The individual giver becomes a "vehicle of transfer," in bringing the blessings of God to the corporeal world. One is encouraged to establish specific times for giving, adding to a "charity box" before going shopping, before eating, or before welcoming the Sabbath day.

5) "Acts of Kindness." Practicing random acts of kindness is by no means a new concept. On the contrary, generations of mystics understood the positive value of placing others before oneself. Kindness therefore involves the humble recognition that everything we enjoy in life is a product of the labor and love of someone else. Kind behavior amounts to simple repayment of the care and compassion of others. One is urged to write thank-you notes to people who have been helpful, to tell store managers about good employees, or to pay the toll at the turnpike gate for the car following!

6) "Interpretation of Dreams." Freud's work in the field of dreams, though bold and pioneering, was not the first of its kind. Indeed, people have sought insight from dreams from prehistoric times. Dreams have always played a role in decision-making, and this role should not be relegated to unenlightened superstition. One may choose to keep a dream journal, placing it by the bed and dutifully recording the contents of one's nocturnal visions, as soon as possible. Next comes seeking out interpretations from friends and compatriots, embracing the one which most seems to "click." Finally, one must implement the meaning of the dream in life and experience. But beware... dreams must always lead the dreamer toward greater goodness.

7) "Eco-Kosher." This concept implies consumption, in the broadest sense, as an ethical act. It is the principle that "matter matters." "Kosher" of course applies to what is eaten, but "Eco-Kosher" suggests that all of our consumption must involve sensitivity to the earth and all its inhabitants. Since everything in our universe, animate as well as inanimate, is in some sense a manifestation of God (carrying the divine sparks), then great care must be taken to protect those very things. One must not damage the natural environment or cause needless suffering to animals. Interestingly, many modern Kabbalists are vegetarians. Furthermore, today's kabbalistic voices caution us about investing in companies which harm the planet or its inhabitants. And of course those same voices encourage us to maintain proper diet, healthy exercise, and hygiene.

8) "Repentance." This broad principle means not only feeling sorry, but taking action to undo the harm we may have caused others, intentionally or unintentionally. It is recommended that we should learn to become like a shopkeeper at the end of the day, reviewing the ledger of our deeds. We should strive to keep short accounts with other people in our lives, recognizing that while everyone makes mistakes, no one need make the same mistake twice. Three questions should be asked at bedtime: What did others do on my behalf today? What did I do on behalf of others? What trouble, what harm, what injury did I cause today?

9) "Ethics." This is not merely an abstract principle. It refers to a body of literature which elevates the individual to a higher ground of morality and goodness. Ethics, like so many things, can be learned; but has to be studied. This is why reading is one of the most important pastimes in which a person might engage. One must, however, carefully select the right kind of literature, material of ethical value, capable of edifying and fortifying one's inner being. One is urged to carry a book

of ethics during one's daily affairs, to read when free moments present themselves. Reading is about "becoming," which in turn implies transformation for the better!

10) "Fellowship." The ancient Sages counseled: "Find thyself a friend." This means that the individual needs someone with whom to be close, with whom to share camaraderie, with whom to develop, spiritually. The right kind of friend is one with whom to converse for at least half an hour a day, sharing weakness and failure as well as strengths and accomplishments. However, fellowship also means developing a kinship with a larger community of faith. It means finding a spiritual community, capable of giving unified expression to the faith of individuals. In pop terminology, it amounts to "a bunch of fellows in the same ship"!

Men from Mars, Women from Venus?

Kabbalah has always had a certain feminist "ring" to it. But with the modern emphasis on feminist thought and philosophy, there seems to be a newfound relevance to the age-old mystical discipline. Feminism is coming into its own, from the ivory halls of university campuses to the think tanks that help formulate government policies. Little wonder that some Kabbalist teachers and lecturers have quite a bit to say in the brave new world of gender issues. A case in point is the Australian rabbi, Laibl Wolf, who travels the international lecture circuit explaining the kabbalistic contribution to gender studies.

The entire cosmos, Wolf declares, contains both male and female characteristics. Consequently, rather than seeing men and women as binary opposites, we should recognize that each possesses some latent attributes of the other. Kabbalah, he teaches, shows us how an "inner balance" between the two may be arrived at. Individuals must look within themselves to find their own masculine and feminine sides. Tension and conflict between the sexes arises when people fail to come to grips with the opposite gender in themselves, making the "inner balance" unachievable. Perhaps men are from Mars and women from Venus, or perhaps, with a little help from Kabbalah, long-held stereotypes may give way to a more enlightened, egalitarian society. Perhaps men and women, when they reach to the core of their "inner being," may find that they are not so different after all.

Is That All There Is?

This is the stuff of contemporary Kabbalah, some of it sounding new, fresh, and different, some sounding as old as the proverbial hills. We might call it "Common Sense Kabbalah." But however we choose to designate the phenomenon, there is no doubt that the mystical impulse is growing as the second millennium rolls into the third. Doubtless, it is one more example of the fact that people today, as always, want something more. People do not want to come to the terminus of their lives asking, "Is that all there is?"

If this cosmic speck we call earth, teeming as it is with life, has any meaning at all in a universe of trillions of stars, spiraling across billions of galaxies, then, just conceivably, the disciplines of the mystic masters can help us find it. Perhaps most important of all is the fact that Kabbalah doesn't stop with diagnosing the problem — a cosmic explosion that left the world broken. It gives us something to do . . . a duty, a task, a work of repair. It counsels spirituality without narrow dogmatism. It admonishes reaching for the stars while keeping one's feet planted firmly on the ground.

The ultimate legacy of Kabbalah is that it does indeed point the way to the future, all the while preserving a living link with the wisdom of the past. It sets us on a new adventure, but does not cast us adrift without anchor. Pointing as it does both backward and forward, Kabbalah is more than mere mental exercise. It is, a vital bridge to the twenty-first century.

A Personal Footnote

As a scholar and researcher, I frequently find myself addressing groups of various sizes and composition on the subject of antiquities, the Dead Sea Scrolls, insights from the ancient Sages, and, more recently, Kabbalah. I find, however, that I employ a bit of Practical Kabbala in my own lectures, never failing to wear a small pendant, consisting of an ancient coin. It was found in the mid-1960s on top of a rocky plateau jutting up from the wilderness of Judea, not far from the Dead Sea. The name of the plateau is Masada, home to some nine hundred sixty Jewish freedom fighters who maintained a heroic last stand against the legions of Rome in the first century of the common era. There among the ruins the coin I now wear was excavated. It bears the simple inscription (struck in paleo-Hebrew): "The freedom of Jerusalem." On the same plateau, not far from where my coin was found, the mutilated remains of an ancient parchment were also discovered — the mystical poetic hymn, *The Song of Sabbath Sacrifices* — stunning proof that whoever occupied the top of the plateau in their last gasp of freedom also took care to preserve the oldest definitive document of Kabbalah known to exist in the world.

Every now and then I look down at the coin dangling from my neck and I think about what freedom — real freedom — meant to them. And I think about the certain transcendental something that motivates great people to do great things . . . like a few hundred brave souls holding off the might of Rome. And I am brought back to the strange mystical document that first fueled my interest in the realm of esoteric speculation. For me and for so many others, the journey is just beginning . . .

References

"A Brief History of Time," a film produced in assocition with NBC, Tokyo Broadcasting System, and Channel Four, U.K., A Brief History of Time, Inc. 1991.

Agrippa, Henry Cornelius, *Three Books of Occult Philosophy*, Donald Tyson, ed., St. Paul, MN, Llewellyn Publications, 1993.

Ben-Sasson, H.H., ed., *A History of the Jewish People*, Cambridge, MA, Harvard University Press,1969.

Buber, Martin, *Hasidism and Modern Man*, Maurice Friedman, ed., New York, Harper & Row, 1958.

_____, *The Origin and Meaning of Hasidism*, Maurice Friedman, ed., New York, Harper & Row, 1958.

_____, *Tales of the Hasidim: The Early Masters*, New York, Schocken Books, 1975.

_____, *The Tales of Rabbi Nachman*, Bloomington, IN, Indiana University Press, 1962.

Calaprise, Alice, ed., *The Quotable Einstein*, Princeton, New Jersey, Princeton University Press, 1996.

Carmi, T., ed., *The Penguin Book of Hebrew Verse*, Middlesex, England, Penguin, 1981.

Clulee, Nicholas, *John Dee's Natural Philosophy*, London and New York, Routledge, 1988.

Cohen, A., *Everyman's Talmud*, New York, Schocken Books, 1990.

Dan, Joseph, *Jewish Mysticism and Jewish Ethics*, Northvale, NJ, Jason Aaronson, Inc., 1996.

Denburg-Levine, Rachel, ed., *Spiritual Renewal Recipes*, Boca Raton, FL, 1996.

Eban, Abba, *Heritage: Civilization and the Jews*, New York, Summit Books, 1984.

Epstein, Perle, *Kabbalah: The Way of the Jewish Mystic*, London, Shambala, 1988.

Farina, John, ed., *The Early Kabbalah*, New York, Paulist Press, 1986, p. 94.

Ferris, Timothy, "The Creation of the Universe," Northstar Associates, 1985.

Flusser, David, *Jewish Sources in Early Christianity*, New York, Adama Books, 1987.

_____, *Judaism and the Origins of Christianity*, Jerusalem, The Magnes Press, 1988.

Gaster, Theodor H., *The Dead Sea Scriptures*, Garden City, New York, Anchor Books, 1976.

Glotzer, Leonard R., *The Fundamentals of Jewish Mysticism*, Jason Aronson, Inc., Northvale, NJ, 1992.

Graetz, Heinrich, *History of the Jews*, Vol. 4, New York, DeVinne-Hallenbeck Co., Inc., 1927.

Hawking, Stephen, ed., *Stephen Hawking's A Brief History of Time: A Reader's Companion*, New York, Bantam Books, 1992.

Hawking, Stephen W., *A Brief History of Time: From the Big Bang to Black Holes*, New York, Bantam Books, 1988.

Holder, Meri, *History of the Jewish People: From Yavneh to Pumbedisa*, New York, Mesorah Publications, Ltd., 1986.

Hutchinson, Jane Campbell, *Albrecht Durer: A Biography*, Princeton, NJ, Princeton University Press, 1990.

Idel, Moshe, *Golem*, Albany, N.Y., State University of New York Press, 1990.

Kaplan, Aryeh, *Sefer Yetzirah: The Book of Creation (in Theory and Practice)*, York Beach, Maine, Samuel Weiser, Inc., 1997.

_____, *The Light Beyond: Adventures in Hassidic Thought*, New York, Maznaim Publishing Corp., 1981.

Levinas, Emmanuel, *Difficult Freedom: Essays on Judaism*, London, the Athlone Press, 1990.

Luzzatto, Moshe Chaim, *The Way of God (Derech Ha-Shem)*, Aryeh Kaplan, trans., Jerusalem and New York, Feldheim Publishers, 1983.

Margolies, Morris B., *A Gathering of Angels*, New York, Ballantine Books, 1994.

Mendes-Flohr, Paul and Reinharz, Judah, eds., *The Jew in the Modern World*, New York, Oxford Univ. Press, 1995.

Mindel, Nissan, *The Storyteller: Selected Short Stories*, Volume One, New York, Merkos L'inyonei Chinuch, 1986.

Payne, Richard J. ed., *Zohar: The Book of Enlightenment*, Ramsey, NJ, Paulist Press, 1981.

Potok, Chaim, *Wanderings*, New York, Fawcett Crest Books, 1978.

Scherman, R. Nosson and Zlotowitz, R. Meir, eds., *The Complete Artscroll Siddur*, Mesorah Publications, Ltd., New York, 1985.

Schiffman, Lawrence H., "Merkavah Speculation at Qumran," in Alexander Altmann, *Mystics, Philosophers, and Politicians: Essays in Jewish Intellectual History*, Durham, NC, Duke University Press, 1982.

Scholem, Gershom, *Kabalah*, New York, Quadrangle/ The New York Time Books Co., 1974.

_____, *Major Trends in Jewish Mysticism*, New York, Schocken Books, 1954.

_____, *On the Kabbalah and its Symbolism*, New York, Schocken Books, 1996.

Schonfield, Hugh J., *The Original New Testament*, New York, Harper & Row, 1985.

Shapiro, M., *Minyan: A Ten-Point System of Jewish Spiritual Practice*, Miami, Rasheit Institute for Jewish Spirituality, 1995.

Sperling, Harry; Simon, Maurice; Levertov, Dr. Paul P.; trans., *The Zohar*, vol. III, London, Soncino Press, 1978.

Steinzaltz, Adin, *The Talmud: A Reference Guide*, New York, Random House, 1989.

Vermes, Geza, *The Dead Sea Scrolls in English*, New York, Penguin Books, 1995.

_____, *Jesus the Jew: A Historian's Reading of the Gospels*, Philadelphia, Fortress Press, 1983.

Weiner, Herbert, *9 1/2 Mystics: The Kabbalah Today*, New York, Macmillan Publishing Co., 1991.

Willis, Deborah, *Malevolent Nurture*, Ithaca, NY, Cornell University Press, 1995.

Wise, Michael, Abegg, Martin, Jr., and Cook, Edward, *The Dead Sea Scrolls: A New Translation*, San Francisco, Harper Collins Publishers, 1996.

Wisniewski, David, *Golem*, New York, Clarion Books, 1996.

Yates, Frances, *The Occult Philosophy in the Elizabethan Age*, Boston, Routledge and Kegan Paul Pub., 1983.

Notes

1. A. Cohen, *Everyman's Talmud,* New York, Schocken Books, 1990, p 27-28.

2. Michael Wise, Martin Abegg, Jr., and Edward Cook, *The Dead Sea Scrolls: A New Translation,* San Francisco, Harper Collins Publishers, 1996, p. 375.

3. This and subsequent English translations of the Bible, unless otherwise noted, are taken from the Revised Standard Version.

4. See Gershom Scholem, *Major Trends in Jewish Mysticism,* New York, Schocken Books, 1954, pp. 7-10.

5. Moshe Chaim Luzzatto, *The Way of God (Derech Ha-Shem)*, Aryeh Kaplan, trans., Jerusalem and New York, Feldheim Publishers, 1983, p. 75.

6. Some are inclined to pronounce these letters "Yahweh," though as I will explain, the Almighty's name is not pronounced at all in Jewish tradition.

7. G. Vermes, *The Dead Sea Scrolls in English,* New York, Penguin Books,

1995, p. 73.

8. Ibid.

9. Ibid.

10. Ibid., p. 76.

11. Ibid., p. 70.

12. Ibid., p. 73.

13. Ibid., p. 72.

14. Ibid., p. 73.

15. Ibid., pp. 73-74.

16. Ibid., p. 74.

17. Ibid..

18. Martin Buber, *The Origin and Meaning of Hasidism,* Maurice Friedman, ed., New York, Harper & Row, 1958.

19. Theodor H. Gaster, *The Dead Sea Scriptures,* Garden City, New York, Anchor Books, 1976, p. 164.

20. Ibid., p. 97.

21. G. Vermes, *The Dead Sea Scrolls in English,* p. 208.

22. See Lawrence H. Schiffman, "Merkavah Speculation at Qumran,"

in Alexander Altmann, *Mystics, Philosophers, and Politicians: Essays in Jewish Intellectual History,* Durham, NC, Duke University Press, 1982, pp. 15-47.

23. Theodor H. Gaster, *The Dead Sea Scriptures,* p. 289.

24. Ibid..

25. Ibid..

26. Ibid., p. 291.

27. G. Vermes, *The Dead Sea Scrolls in English,* p. 73.

28. Ibid.., p. 134.

29. Ibid.., p. 125.

30. Ibid..

31. Ibid.

32. Ibid.

33. Ibid..

34. Ibid., p. 127.

35. Ibid., pp. 127-128.

36. Ibid., p. 137.

37. Mishnah, Taanit 3:8; see David Flusser, *Jewish*

Sources in Early Christianity, New York, Adama Books, 1987, pp. 33-34.

38. Geza Vermes, *Jesus the Jew: A Historian's Reading of the Gospels,* Philadelphia, Fortress Press, 1983, p. 19.

39. David Flusser, *Jewish Sources in Early Christianity,* pp. 33-34.

40. Ibid., pp. 34-35.

41. See Hugh J. Schonfield, *The Original New Testament,* New York, Harper & Row, 1985, p. 516, n. 7.

42. Talmud Chagigah 12a-b; cf. A. Cohen, *Everyman's Talmud,* p. 30.

43. Talmud Berakhot 34b; cf. A. Cohen, *Everyman's Talmud,* pp. 283-84.

44. Talmud, Berakhot 33a; cf. David Flusser, *Judaism and the Origins of Christianity,* Jerusalem, The Magnes Press, 1988, pp. 536, 543.

45. Talmud Chagigah 14b; cf. A. Cohen, *Everyman's Talmud,* pp. 27-28.

46. Talmud, Berachot 3a; cf. A. Cohen, *Everyman's Talmud,* p. 282.

47. For an excellent discussion of the background of the Talmud, see R. Adin Steinzaltz, *The Talmud: A Reference Guide,* New York, Random House, 1989.

48. Talmud, Shabbat 34b; cf. Meri Holder, *History of the Jewish People: From Yavneh to Pumbedisa,* New York, Mesorah Publications, Ltd., 1986.

49. Talmud, *Baba Metzia* 59b; Eliezer ben Hyrcanus, end of first, beginning of second century, A.D.

50. Cf. A. Cohen, *Everyman's Talmud,* pp. 46-47.

51. Kiddushin 81a-b; cf. A. Cohen, *Everyman's Talmud,* p. 55.

52. Cf. A. Cohen, *Everyman's Talmud,* pp. 54-55.

53. Deuteronomy Rabba, 11:10; cf. A. Cohen, *Everyman's Talmud,* p. 54.

54. Eruvin 100b; cf. A. Cohen, *Everyman's Talmud,* p. 55.

55. Pesachim 111b; cf. A. Cohen, *Everyman's Talmud,* p. 266.

56. Leviticus Rabba, 24:3, cf. A. Cohen, *Everyman's Talmud,* p. 264.

57. Taan. 21a; cf. A. Cohen, *Everyman's Talmud,* pp. 80-81.

58. Uktz III, 12; cf. A. Cohen, *Everyman's Talmud,* pp. 387-88.

59. Aryeh Kaplan, *Sefer Yetzirah: The Book of Creation (in Theory and Practice),* York Beach, Maine, Samuel Weiser, Inc., 1997, p. IX.

60. Leonard R. Glotzer, *The Fundamentals of Jewish Mysticism,* Jason Aronson, Inc., Northvale, NJ, 1992, p. 3.

61. For an insightful discussion of the Sefer Yetzirah, see Aryeh Kaplan, *Sefer Yetzirah: The Book of Creation (in Theory and Practice).*

62. Glotzer, *The Fundamentals of Jewish Mysticism,* p. 11.

63. See John Farina, ed., *The Early Kabbalah,* New York, Paulist Press, 1986, p. 94.

64. Glotzer, *The Fundamentals of Jewish Mysticism,* p. 17.

65. R. Nosson Scherman and R. Meir Zlotowitz, eds., *The Complete Artscroll Siddur*, Mesorah Publications, Ltd., New York, 1985, p. 125.

66. Glotzer, *The Fundamentals of Jewish Mysticism*, p. 24.

67. Ibid., p. 36.

68. Author's translation.

69. Author's translation.

70. Glotzer, *The Fundamentals of Jewish Mysticism*, p. 54.

71. Ibid., p. 58.

72. Ibid., p. 105.

73. Ibid., p. 109.

74. See Joseph Dan, *Jewish Mysticism and Jewish Ethics*, Northvale, NJ, Jason Aaronson, Inc., 1996, p. 49.

75. See *The Early Kabbalah*, p. 28.

76. See *The Early Kabbalah*, p. 63. The biblical quotation of Proverbs 3:35 is the author's.

77. Ibid.

78. Ibid., pp. 61-62.

79. Ibid., p. 59.

80. Ibid., pp. 31-33.

81. Ibid., pp. 34-35.

82. Ibid., pp. 36-37.

83. See Gershom Scholem, *Kabalah*, New York, Quadrangle/ The New York Time Book Co., 1974, pp. 53-57.

84. See Herbert Weiner, *9 1/2 Mystics: The Kabbalah Today*, New York, Macmillan Publishing Co., 1991, p. 65.

85. Ibid., p. 66.

86. Cf. Heinrich Graetz, *History of the Jews*, Vol. 4, New York, DeVinne-Hallenbeck Co., Inc., 1927, p. 21.

87. Richard J. Payne, ed., *Zohar: The Book of Enlightenment*, Ramsey, NJ, Paulist Press, 1981, p. 49.

88. Ibid., p. 43.

89. Ibid., p. 50.

90. Ibid., p. 55.

91. Ibid., p. 56.

92. Ibid.

93. Ibid., p. 60.

94. Ibid., p. 61.

95. Ibid., p. 64.

96. Ibid., p. 67.

97. See Morris B. Margolies, *A Gathering of Angels*, New York, Ballantine Books, 1994, pp. 119-20.

98. J. Payne, ed., Zohar: *The Book of Enlightenment*, p. 81.

99. Ibid., pp. 81-82.

100. Ibid., p. 94.

101. Ibid., p. 99.

102. Ibid., p. 100.

103. Ibid., p. 102.

104. Ibid., p. 108.

105. Ibid., p. 109.

106. Ibid., p. 113.

107. Ibid., p. 115.

108. Ibid., pp. 119-120.

109. Ibid., p. 145.

110. Ibid., p. 149.

111. Author's translation.

112. J. Payne, ed., *Zohar: The Book of Enlightenment*, p. 154.

113. For a discussion of this concept, see Gershom Scholem, *Major Trends in Jewish Mysticism*, pp. 229-230.

114. J. Payne, ed., *Zohar: The Book of Enlightenment*, p. 186.

115. Ibid., p. 187.

116. Ibid., p. 188.

117. See H.H. Ben-Sasson, ed., *A History of the Jewish People*, Cambridge, MA, Harvard University Press, 1969, pp. 614-17.

118. Cf. T. Carmi, ed., *The Penguin Book of Hebrew Verse*, Middlesex, England, Penguin, 1981, p. 347.

119. The initial letters of each Hebrew word in the term *Ha-elohi* Rabbi Yitzhak spell the word *Ha-Ari* ("The Lion").

120. Talmud *Sukkah* 52a, cf. A. Cohen, *Everyman's Talmud*, p. 348.

121. Cf. Abba Eban, *Heritage: Civilization and the Jews*, New York, Summit Books, 1984, p. 187.

122. See Gershom Scholem, *On the Kabbalah and its Symbolism*, New York, Schocken Books, 1996, pp. 158-204; Gershom Scholem, *Kabbalah*, pp. 351-355; David Wisniewski, *Golem*, New York, Clarion Books, 1996.

123. In truth the Golem story may in fact belong to the town of Chelm and Rabbi Elijah, and it may have been attributed to Rabbi Loew as late as the 1700s; see Moshe Idel, Golem, Albany, NY, State University of New York Press, 1990, pp. 207-212.

124. See Nissan Mindel, *The Storyteller: Selected Short Stories*, Volume One, New York, Merkos L'inyonei Chinuch, 1986, pp. 293-98.

125. Harry Sperling, Maurice Simon, Dr. Paul P. Levertov, trans., *The Zohar*, vol. III, London, Soncino Press, 1978, Shemoth (Exodus), 9b-10a., pp. 28-29.

126. Cf. Heinrich Graetz, *History of the Jews*, Vol. 5, p. 123.

127. Cf. Abba Eban, *Heritage: Civilization and the Jews*, p. 217.

128. Cf. Heinrich Graetz, *History of the Jews*, Vol. 5, p. 143.

129. Ibid., p. 139.

130. Cf. Abba Eban, *Heritage: Civilization and the Jews*, p. 217.

131. See Gershom Scholem, *Kabbalah*, pp. 287-309.

132. Lyrics by Robert J. Stamps, Ph.D.; used by permission.

133. *Zohar: The Book of Enlightenment*, p. 188.

134. See Frances Yates, *The Occult Philosophy in the Elizabethan Age*, Boston, Routledge and Kegan Paul Pub., 1983, p. 19. This source is an excellent overview of the history of Christian Kabbalah.

135. See Henry Cornelius Agrippa, *Three Books of Occult Philosophy*, Donald Tyson, ed., St. Paul, MN, Llewellyn Publications, 1993, p. 3.

136. See Jane Campbell Hutchinson, *Albrecht Durer: A Biography*, Princeton, NJ, Princeton University Press, 1990.

137. See Yates, *The Occult Philosophy in the Elizabethan Age*, pp. 49-59.

138. See Nicholas Clulee, *John Dee's Natural Philosophy*, London and New York, Routledge, 1988.

139. For a discussion of witchcraft in Shakespeare, see Deborah Willis, *Malevolent Nurture*, Ithaca, NY, Cornell University Press, 1995.

140. See Martin Buber, *Tales of the Hasidim: The Early Masters*, New York, Schocken Books, 1975, p. 37.

141.Ibid., p. 36.

142. Ibid.

143. Ibid.

144. See Martin Buber, *Hasidism and Modern Man*, Maurice Friedman, ed., New York, Harper & Row, 1958, p. 98.

145. Martin Buber, *Tales of the Hasidim: The Early Masters*, p. 41.

146. Ibid., p. 42.

147. Martin Buber, *The Tales of Rabbi Nachman*, Bloomington, IN, Indiana University Press, 1962, p. 12.

148. Ibid.

149. Ibid., p. 13-14.

150. See Aryeh Kaplan, *The Light Beyond: Adventures in Hassidic Thought*, New York, Maznaim Publishing Corp., 1981, p. 180.

151. Abba Eban, *Heritage: Civilization and the Jews*, p. 220.

152. See Ben Porat, "Yosef, Korets, 1781," cf. *Encyclopedia Judaica*, p. 1050.

153. See Chaim Potok, *Wanderings*, New York, Fawcett Crest Books, 1978, pp. 466-67.

154. Ibid., p. 467.

155. Herbert Weiner, *9 1/2 Mystics*, p. 198.

156. Ibid., pp. 214-15.

157. See Rabbi Rachel Denburg-Levine, ed., *Spiritual Renewal Recipes*, Boca Raton, FL, 1996.

158. See also Perle Epstein, *Kabbalah: The Way of the Jewish Mystic*, London, Shambala, 1988, pp. 125-27.

159. Paul Mendes-Flohr and Judah Reinharz eds., *The Jew in the Modern World*, New York, Oxford University Press, 1995, pp. 137-38.

160. See Perle Epstein, *Kabbalah: The Way of the Jewish Mystic*, "Rebbe Snheur Zalman: The Intellectual Mystic," pp. 130-39.

161. See Emmanuel Levinas, *Difficult Freedom: Essays on Judaism*, London, the Athlone Press, 1990.

162. Cf. Alice Calaprise, ed., *The Quotable Einstein*, Princeton, New Jersey, Princeton University Press, 1996, p. 153.

163. Ibid., p. 176.

164. Quoted in "A Brief History of Time," a film produced in association with NBC, Tokyo Broadcasting System, and Channel Four, UK, A Brief History of Time, Inc. 1991.

165. Rabbi Azriel; cf. *The Early Kabbalah*, p. 94.

166. *Zohar:The Book of Enlightenment*, p.14.

167. Ibid., p. 147.

168. Christopher Isham,

cf. Stephen Hawking, ed., *Stephen Hawking's A Brief History of Time: A Reader's Companion*, New York, Bantam Books, 1992, p. 127.

169. Stephen W. Hawking, *A Brief History of Time: From the Big Bang to Black Holes*, New York, Bantam Books, 1988, pp. 46, 49.

170. Ibid.

171. Rabbi Azriel; cf. *The Early Kabbalah*, p. 94.

172. Quoted in Timothy Ferris, "The Creation of the Universe," Northstar Associates, 1985.

173. *The Quotable Einstein*, p. 169.

174. *The Early Kabbalah*, p. 94.

175. *Zohar: The Book of Enlightenment*, p. 108.

176. Ibid.

177. Ibid.

178Ibid.

179. Quoted in Timothy Ferris, "The Creation of the Universe."

180. *The Early Kabbalah*, p. 51.

181. Quoted in Timothy Ferris, "The Creation of the Universe."

182. Rabbi Azriel; cf. *The Early Kabbalah*, pp. 94-95.

183. Quoted in Timothy Ferris, "The Creation of the Universe."

184. Ibid.

185*The Early Kabbalah*, p. 50.

186. Timothy Ferris, "The Creation of the Universe."

187. *The Early Kabbalah*, p. 52.

188. A number so small it would be represented by a decimal point with a string of forty zeroes behind it.

189. *The Early Kabbalah*, pp. 51-52.

190. Rabbi Azriel; cf. *The Early Kabbalah*, p. 94.

191. *The Fundamentals of Jewish Mysticism*, p. 5.

192. *Zohar: The Book of Enlightenment*, pp. 165-66.

193. Derekh Mitzvotekha (1850s), p. Bet; cf. Rabbi Rachel Denburg-Levine, ed., *Spiritual Renewal Recipes*.

194. *Zohar: The Book of Enlightenment*, p. 147.

195. Cf. *The Quotable Einstein*, p. 147.

196. Ibid., p. 161.

197. See Rabbi Rachel Denburg-Levine, ed., *Spiritual Renewal Recipes*.

198Ibid.

199. Rabbi M. Shapiro, *Minyan: A Ten-Point System of Jewish Spiritual Practice*, Miami, Rasheit Institute for Jewish Spirituality,

Index

Abraham, Patriarch, 84,
88, 136-140, 142,
146, 176
Abulafia, Abraham ben
Samuel, 120-122
Abulafia, Rabbi Don
Todros, 123
Acher, 67
Adam, 135-136, 163
Adonai, 25
Aggadah, 85
Agrippa, Henry
Cornelius, 187-188,
190
Ain Sof, 92, 101-102,
131, 134, 148, 240,
243
Akiva, Rabbi, 7, 64-70,
72-73, 76-77, 103,
114, 177
Alkabetz, Solomon, 155
Allah, 180
Altneuschul, 169
Am ha-aretz, 193
Amos, Book of, 61
*Ancient Parable, (The
Mashal ha-Kadmoni)*,
125
Angel
of Darkness, 30
of Death, 80, 85-86,
140
of Destruction, 86
of History, 219, 221-
223
of the Presence, 25
of Truth, 34-35, 42
Angels, 22, 27, 34-36,
38-39, 41-43, 45-46,

48, 56, 87, 99, 103,
105-106, 116, 132,
140, 143, 189, 191,
219, 230
of the Face, 39
fallen, 81
Ministering, 38, 105
of the Presence, 39
of Sanctification, 38
(see also Cherubim)
Antiochus, King IV, 17-
20
anti-Semitism, 151,
162, 169, 187, 193
Apocalypse of Baruch, 26
Apocrypha, 17, 81
apocryphon, 17
Araboth, 56-57
Aramaic, 37, 114, 118,
124
archangel, 27, 41
Aristotle, 109, 229
Armageddon, Battle of,
43, 45-46, 48
Ashkelon, 69
Ashkenaz, 109
Hasidei, 108-109, 111,
114
Asmodeus, 119
*Assumption of Moses,
The* 26
Aten, the, 15
Atenism, 15
Avila, 126, 127
Azriel, Rabbi, 119, 238
Baal Shem, 110, 193
Baal Shem Tov, 194,
196, 197, 199-202,
204-205, 212-213

Baal-Shemin, 19
Babylon, 12
Babylonia, 14, 23, 73-
75
Bacchus, 19
Baer, Dov, 201
Balaam, 68
bar Kochba, Simon 69-
71, 177
Beitar, 71
Belial, 30
Benjamin, Walter, 219-
222
Ben Sira, 7
Ben Zoma, 7, 67
Berab, Jacob, 154-155
Besht, the, 194, 196-
197, 199, 201, 203,
205
Bethlehem, 69
Big Bang, 225-228,
233, 235, 240
Binah, 93, 98, 104,
132, 240
Blessings, 38
Blood Libel, 113, 162,
165-166
Bohr, Niels, 225
Bonaparte, Napoleon,
209
Book of Creation, The
88-89, 91, 97-102,
104-106, 117-118,
133, 164, 228
*Book of Secrets, The
(Sefer ha-Razim)*, 83
Book of Splendor, The
124, 128, 130
bozons, weak, 231

Brooklyn, 212, 216
Caesarea, 63
Calabrese, Chaim Vital, 157, 159-160
Capernaum, 6
Caro, Joseph, 155
Cervantes, Miguel de, 129
Chabad, 203, 206, 213-215, 217
-Lubavitch, 216-217
chariot, 26-27, 41, 105, 108, 208
the Works of the, 75
Chebar, the river, 13
Chmielnicki, Bogdan, 172
Christ, 56, 149, 191
body of, 113
Circle, Gerona, 119
Circle-Drawer (see Khoni)
Colossians (Book of), 58, 184
Cordovero, Moses, 155, 157
Corinthians (Book of), 56-58
Cranach, Lucas, 189
Crown, 92-93, 104, 116, 117, 131, 145, 238
Crucible, The 187
Dark Night of the Soul, The 185
D'vikut, 118, 122, 198
Damascus, 55, 160
Daniel, 20-21, 60
Darkness, Sons of, 31, 33-34, 43, 45, 47-48
David, 12, 69
throne of, 173

Dead Sea Scrolls, 8-9, 11-12, 34, 37, 41-42, 48, 90, 253
Dee, John, 189-190
Deity, 14-15, 22-24, 29, 46, 50, 88, 91, 109, 184
female aspect of, 115-116
demons, 81-82, 119, 193
Deuteronomy (Book of), 14, 68, 90, 132, 145, 148
Din, 94-95
Dionysus, 19
Diaspora, 159, 177
Doppler Effect, 225
Dûrer, Albrecht, 188-189
Eckhart, Meister, 185
Eden, 113, 141, 153
Garden of, 56, 87, 221
Effendi, Aziz Mehmed, 181 (see also Zvi, Shabbetai)
Egypt, 15, 43, 71, 139, 141-142, 152, 156-157, 165, 176, 178
Einstein, Albert, 224-225, 229, 241-242
Eleazar ben Judah, 108
Elijah, the Prophet, 77, 84, 86, 125, 157, 159, 177
Rabbi, 163
Elizabeth I, Queen, 190
Elohim, 90, 134, 146
Emden, Rabbi Jacob Israel, 183
emet, 164, 166, 168
Enoch, book of, 21-23, 54, 124

Erasmus of Rotterdam, 188
Esh, 98
Essenes 37, 43-44, 49, 71, 112, 160
Esther, Book of, 209
Euphrates River, 73, 75
Eve, 138
exile, 12, 44, 139, 147, 159
Exiles, 153
prophet of, 12
Exodus, 141
Book of, 97, 100, 132, 143
Ezekiel, 12-15, 17, 26, 29, 40-41, 60, 105, 108, 230
Book of, 90, 103
Ezra ben Solomon, 119
Ferdinand, King, 152
Fiddler on the Roof, 202
Flagellants, 112
Flusser, David, 52
Fox, George, 192
Frank, Jacob, 182-183
Frankfurter, Naphtali, 160
Frankists, 182
Freud, Sigmund, 249
Gabriel, the angel, 22, 42-43, 141
Galatians (Book of), 55
Galilee, 51, 62-63, 153-155
Sea of, 63, 65, 71, 73, 75, 158, 173
Gamaliel, Rabbi Simeon ben, 61, 86, 100-101
Gamla, 63
Gamzo, the man of, 84, 85 (see also Nahum)

Gaon, 201
Gaza, 177; Nathan of (see Nathan)
Gehenna, 86
gematria, 97-98, 110, 121, 188, 220
Genesis (Book of), 21, 23, 58, 90, 104, 112, 131-132, 134-138, 141
Gentiles, 55
Gerushin, 248
Gevurah, 98, 105, 131
Glory, 115-116
Throne of, 21, 23, 57, 90, 108, 137, 230
gluons, 231, 233
Gnostics, 123
God, feminine aspect of, 147, 151
name of, 23-25, 48, 50, 88-90, 92, 110, 113, 121, 132, 158, 175, 192-193
Princes of, 46
secrets of, 32
sons of, 53, 186
throne of, 11-12, 41, 49, 230
Golem, 163-170, 190
Gospels, 52, 54-55, 184
gravitation, 231
gravitons, 231
Great Secret, The (*Raza' Rabbah*), 114
Guide for the Perplexed, 123
Hadrian, Emperor, 70, 72
Hamlet, 191
Hanina ben Dosa, Rabbi, 53, 60-62

Hanukkah, 215
Hasdai ibn Shaprut, 149
Hasidic, 20, 29, 50, 52, 93, 154, 201, 203-204, 206, 208-209, 212, 214, 217, 223
Hasidim, 52, 110-113, 201-204
of Ashkenaz, 111
Hawking, Stephen, 225-227, 234
heavens, seven, 56
Hebron, 69
Heikhalot, 57, 90-91, 114, 137
Herod, King, 73
Hesed, 93, 95, 99, 105, 131
"Hidden Commentary" (*Midrash ha-Ne'elam*), 124
Hillel, Rabbi, 74
Hiyya, Rabbi, 148
Hod, 96, 98
Holocaust, 169-170, 172, 208, 211, 214, 222
Hosea, the prophet, 176
Hubble, Edmund, 226, 235
Hurwitz, Isaiah, 160
Inquisition, 151-152
Isaac, 114, 140, 142
Isaac of Acre, 126
Isaac the Blind, 118
Isaac Rabbi, 119
Issac, Rabbi Jacob, 208
Isabella, Queen, 152
Isaiah, 26, 116
Ascension of, 55
Assumption of, 26

Book of, 115-116
Islam, 121, 180-181
Israel, Lost Tribes of, 120
State of, 170, 216
Israel ben Eliezer, 77-78, 192, 195-196
Jacob, 68-70, 140, 142, 173
James, the apostle, 37
Jehovah, 25
Jeremiah, Book of, 100
Rabbi, 78
Jerome, 25
Jerusalem, 7-8, 14, 18, 48, 55, 58, 64, 69-70, 73, 100, 116, 149, 156, 159, 176
Celestial, 56
Desert of, 44
Hebrew University of, 220
New, 45
Jesus of Nazareth, 8, 11, 49, 51-54, 58-60, 62, 110-111, 115, 177, 184, 186
John, the Baptist, 8, 59, 175, 177
John, Book of, 54-55, 62, 184
John, Saint of the Cross, 118, 149, 185
Jose, Abba, 82-83
Josephus, the historian, 51
Joshua, Rabbi, 78, 85-87
Jubilee, year of, 26
Jubilees, book of, 25-26, 124
Judah ha-Levi, 152
Judah the Pious, 108

Judah, Rabbi, 23, 76
Jude, Book of, 80
Judea, 12, 17, 19, 28, 50, 60, 62-64, 70-73, 153, 253
Judgment, 94
Jumpers, 192
Kanah ibn Gedor, 150-151
kavanah, 37, 195, 198, 248
Keter, 92, 93, 99, 104-105, 117, 131, 134, 137, 238, 240
Khokhmah, 93, 99, 104, 132, 134, 238, 240
Khoni, the Circle-Drawer, 50, 52-53, 193
Kiddush ha-Shem, 113
Kings (Book of), 40
Kittim, 43-45
Klee, Paul, 219, 221
Kohen, Rabbi Isaac, 119
Rabbi Jacob, 119
Lederman, Leon, 232
Leonardo da Vinci, 186
Lévinas, Emmanuel, 222
Leviticus, (Book of) 132, 145
Light of Wisdom, The 121
Life of Adam, 26-27
Lilith, 81, 119
Loew, Judah ben Bezalel, 162-164, 166-168, 190
Lore of Creation, The 58
Lot, 138
Lovingkindness, 93-95

Lubavitcher Hasidism, 203, 213
Lublin, Hasidic rabbis of, 209
the Seer of, 208-209
Lucretius, 229
Luke (Book of), 52, 54
Luria, Rabbi Isaac, 156-160, 175
Luzzatto, Moshe Chaim, 22
Ma-aseh, Beresheet, 75
Machon, 56
magic, black, 187-188
white, 188
Maimonides, Moses, 109, 123
Majesty, 96
Malkhut, 97, 99, 117
Manasseh ben Israel, 160
Manna, 144
Manual of Discipline, The 30-36, 42
Maon, 56
Mar, fourth century Sage, 100
Mark (Book of), 52
Marranos, 151
martyrdom, 51, 112
Masada, 9, 63-64, 253
Matthew (Book of), 52, 110
Mayim, 98
Medzibosh, town of, 199, 201
Menelaus, 18-19
Merkavah, 11, 14, 26-28, 31, 35, 40, 45, 49, 57-58, 75, 81, 90-91, 108, 215
Meron, 77
Messiah, 29, 43, 54,

63, 68-70, 85, 120, 153, 156-158, 172-173, 176-178, 180-181, 186, 191, 198-200, 203, 206, 209, 216-217
Above, 55, 58
Below, 55
Metatron, 23
Michael, the angel, 22, 27, 42-43, 56
Michelangelo, 186
Midrash, 114
mikveh, 164, 196
mimesis, 40
Mirandola, Pico della (see Pico della Mirandola)
Mishnah, 7-8
Mitnagdim, 201-203
Moses, 16, 23, 25, 65, 68, 80, 100, 141-142, 157, 232, 236
the Law of, 32, 158, 215
Tabernacle of, 145
Moses de Leon, 123-124, 126-129, 220
Mystical Torah, 118
Naaar, Isaac, 242
Nachman, Rabbi of Bratzlav , 205-208
Nachman, Moses ben, 126
Nahum, the man of Gamzo, 83-84
Nathan of Gaza, 176, 177, 181, 178
Naxos, Duke of, 154
Nebuchadnezzer, 23
Neoplatonism, Renaissance, 187
Nephilim, 21

Nero, 64
Netzakh, 95, 99
neutrinos, 237
New Testament, 30, 37, 45-46, 49, 52, 60-61, 80, 171, 184
Nicholas, Pope III, 121
Nile, River, 156
Noachide, 215
Noah, 21, 136
  sons of, 215
Numbers, Book of, 68, 132, 145
Occult Philosophy, 188-189
Ofanim, 105
Oldenburg, Heinrich, 242
On the Act of Creation, 125
Ottoman empire, 180
Pakhad, 94-95
Parthia, 71
Passover, 77, 113, 167
Patmos, island of, 59
Paul, the apostle, 49, 55-59, 111, 184
Pelimo and the beggar, 79-80
Pereira, Abraham, 242
Peter, the disciple, 110
Pfefferkorn, Johann, 187
Pico della Mirandola, 185-187, 189
Plato, 40
Power, 94, 105
Practical Kabbalah, 62, 66, 73, 75-76, 81, 83, 89, 190, 196, 208, 253
Prepared Table, The 155
Proverbs, Book of, 94, 114

Psalms, Book of, 94, 105, 143
Pseudepigrapha, 21, 25, 124-125
Pumbeditha, 73, 75
Quakers, 192
quark, 231, 237
quasars, 235
Qumran, 28, 39, 43-44, 63
Rachel, (wife of Akiva) 64
Rakia, 56
Raphael, the angel, 22, 42-43
Razei El ("Secrets of God"), 31
Relativity 224, 234
Renaissance, 187
  German, 186
  Italian, 186
Resh, 99
Reuchlin, Johannes, 186-187, 189
Revelation, Book of, 45, 59-60, 208
Revolt, Great, 64
Rome, 9, 63-64, 66, 70, 85-86, 151, 253
Rotterdam, Erasmus of, 188
smichah, 199
Sabbath 39, 150, 156, 158-159, 214
Safed, city of, 77, 154-155, 157-159
Sagan, Carl, 240
Sages, 17, 20-21, 50, 52, 53, 108, 127, 142, 147, 157, 160, 173, 184, 197-199, 205
Samael, the angel, 81, 140

Samuel he-Hasid, Rabbi, 108
Sandage, Allan, 228, 235
Sanhedrin, 65
Sarah, 176
Sariel, the angel, 42-43
Satan, 44, 79-81, 119, 197
Schneerson, Menachem Mendel, 203, 212, 213, 216-217, 240
  Rabbi Yosef Yitzhak, 212-213
Scholem, Gershom, 16, 128, 220-221
Seer of Lublin, 208-209
Sefer ha-Bahir, 114-117
Sefer Hakanah, 150-151
Sefer Yetzirah, 88, 98, 102, 114, 116, 118, 120, 133, 164
Sefirah, 101, 104-105, 134, 224, 233, 241
Sefirot, 57, 91-92, 97-104, 116-117, 119, 121, 131-132, 134, 137, 139, 142, 145-147, 238, 240
Seleucid dynasty, 19
Sepphoris, 69, 73
Seraphim, 105
Shabbateans, 183
Shaddai, El, 142-143
Shakers, 192
Shakespeare, William, 190
Shavout, 77
Shechakim, 56-57
Shechinah, 14, 74, 97, 116, 131, 141-142, 146-147, 197-198
Sheth, sons of, 68

Shimon ben Coseba, 69, 72

Sh'virat ha-kelim ("The Breaking of the Vessels"), 236

Sicarii, 63

Simeon ben Shetakh, 53

Simeon ben Yokhai, 76-77, 124, 126-128, 132, 144, 155, 157, 160, 220

Sinai, Mount, 16, 25, 100, 141

Smaller Book of Celestial Palaces, The (Heikhalot Zutartey), 68

Smyrna, 171, 174-175, 177, 179

Solomon, 12, 40
  Temple of, 14, 73, 149

Song of Soloman, 125

Song of Sabbath Sacrifices, The, 9, 11, 15, 39-40, 253

Soul of Wisdom, The (Ha-Nefesh ha-Hakhamah), 125

"sparks," 201

Spencer, Edmund, 190

Spheres, 139-140, 227, 240
  of Nothing, 92-93, 97-99
  Ten, 90

Spinoza, Baruch de, 179, 241-242

Sufi mystism, 149

Sura, 73

Tabernacles, 146-147

Talmud, 7-8, 50, 56-57, 67, 74-76, 78-79,

81-83, 85, 112, 118, 127 150, 156, 158, 163, 174, 194, 202

Teacher of Righteousness, 29, 32

tefillin, 29, 158, 214

Temple, 21, 23-24, 39-40, 53, 56, 58, 61, 64-65, 67, 74-75, 147, 153, 157
  Mount 70, 74

Ten Commandments, 16, 25, 98, 117, 144

Teresa, Saint of Avila, 188, 124

Tetragrammaton, 24-25, 99, 106, 121

Thomás de Torquemada, 152

throne, Chariot-, 11, 22, 29, 40, 198

Tiber River, 73

Tiberias, 73, 75

Tiferet, 95, 99, 131

Tigris River, 75

Tikkun Olam, 216

Titus, 63-64

Torah, 9, 18-19, 65-66, 69-70, 78, 89-90, 98, 132-133, 141, 144-145, 148, 157, 201, 213, 216, 219, 227

Treasury of the Hidden Eden, 121

Trinity, Holy, 185

Turin, Shroud of, 125-126

Turner, Michael, 236-238

Tz'dakah, 196

Tzadik, 37, 162-165, 167-168, 175, 203, 206, 208, 209

Tzimtzum, 226, 235

tziruf, 121

tzirufim, 164

UFO, 14

Understanding, 93, 104, 132, 240 (see also Binah)

Uriel, the angel, 22

Usha, town of, 65

Valladolid, 124, 126

Vermes, Geza, 52

Vespasian, General 63-64

Victory, 95

Vilon, 56

Vital, Moses, 160

Vital, Samuel, 160

Viverro, 124

Western Wall, 14

Warner, Nick , 234

Watchers, the, 21

Waterloo, 210

Weinberg, Stephen, 232

Wheeler, John Archibald, 232

Wisdom (Khokhmah), 93, 104, 115, 132, 134, 203, 238, 240

Wisdom of Solomon, 54

Wolf, Rabbi Laibl, 251

Works of Creation, The 75

X particle, 233-234, 237

Yakhini, Abraham, 176

Yalkut Shimeoni, 86

Yavne, 65, 73, 75

yeshiva, 155, 193

Yeshu, 52

Yeshua, 51-52

Yesod ("Foundation of the World"), 99

Yetzer ha-Ra ("Evil Inclination"), 197
YHVH, 137, 145-146, 158
Yiddish, 179
Yitzhak, Ha-elohi Rabbi, 155-156
Yodfat, 63
Yohanan ben Zakkai, 65
Yohanan the Withdrawn, 53

Yom Kippur, 24
Zacut, Moses, 242
Zalman, Rabbi Elijah ben Solomon, 201-203
Rabbi Schneur, 212
Zealots, 9, 28, 63, 71
Zebul, 56
Zechariah, the prophet, 80
Zion, 12, 73, 153
Mount, 7, 21, 70

Zionism, 220
Zohar, 22, 124-127, 130-148, 155, 157, 173-174, 185, 220, 226, 239-240
Z particle, 232
Zvi, Shabbetai, 174-183, 200, 242